Nature and Religious Imagination

Nature
and
Religious Imagination

From Edwards to Bushnell

CONRAD CHERRY

FORTRESS PRESS   PHILADELPHIA

Library of Congress Cataloging in Publication Data

Cherry, C   Conrad.
  Nature and religious imagination.

  Includes bibliographical references and index.
1. Nature (Theology)—History of doctrines.
2. Theology, Doctrinal—New England—History.
3. United States—Religion—To 1800.
4. United States—Religion—19th century. I. Title.
BT695.5.C47   230   79-7374
ISBN 0-8006-0550-0

7695E79   Printed in the United States of America   1-550

For
Cynthia

Contents

Preface

This book is an analysis of the role of physical nature in the American religious imagination during a period of about one hundred fifty years. That period, from the early eighteenth to the middle of the nineteenth century, witnessed the ascendancy of nature, as fact and as idea, in Western culture in general and American culture in particular. Countless excellent studies have examined the role of nature in American painting, literature, philosophy, science, and social policy. This book attempts to complement those studies by attending to the religious responses to nature, represented by major American theologians, against the broad background of intellectual and social changes in Europe and America.

I have focused my study on the religious mind of New England. I certainly would not want to suggest, thereby, the notion that all important American religious history arose in New England, nor would I want to imply that the religious meaning of nature was pertinent only to Anglo-Saxon life, much less only to New England thinking. Also, I am well aware that even within my focus I have ignored a host of influential thinkers. I am persuaded, however, that for the period of the study the question of the relation between nature and religious imagination in America was given its broadest and most intensive examination in New England. I am convinced, as well, that New Englanders' reflections on the question had an impact on other parts of the country and had implications for the larger American culture. Finally, I have chosen to deal with figures who, if their thinking did not exhaust the New England mind, were representative of the issues at stake within the subject I have traced.

Most historical studies spring in part from the contemporary concerns of the historian, and this study is no exception. Although I find the period and the subject of my book to be inherently interest-ing, I do believe that they cast considerable light on current prob-lems in American religion. A pattern of conflict between religious symbolism and religious moralism which evolved in the period has shaped later American attitudes. And contemporary American theologians who reflect upon nature's symbols stand to gain histor-ical perspective upon their enterprise if they join their reflections with the issues of their own heritage.

I owe much to many for assistance on this book. Research and reflection on the topic were started during the summer of 1973 at the Institute for Ecumenical and Cultural Research, Collegeville, Min-nesota. I am grateful to Father Kilian McDonnell, President, and to the Board of Directors of the Institute, for providing a peaceful retreat for study, and I recall with gratitude the stimulating dis-cussions with the other scholars in residence. Thomas Magner, Associate Dean for Research and Graduate Studies in Liberal Arts at the Pennsylvania State University, supported my research at sev-eral points with grants from the Central Fund for Research. Penn State's Institute for the Arts and Humanistic Studies, under the direction of Stanley Weintraub, gave valuable help in the form of a travel fellowship during the last year of my research. The dean of my college, Stanley Paulson, and the head of my department, Yoshio Fukuyama, were patient about a book seemingly forever in the making, and they provided encouragement by approving my application for sabbatical leave. Daniel Davis, Luther Harshbarger, Robert Hudspeth, and Harrison Meserole forced time from their busy schedules to give my entire manuscript a careful reading and to offer constructive suggestions and trenchant criticisms. Two of my former graduate students deserve special thanks: Robert Schneider, in his research on Horace Bushnell, and John Goodell, in his work on the Beecher family, ably taught their teacher. In the one person of Mrs. Dorothy Baumler I was blessed with an adroit typist and a keen proofreader. Everyone knows it, but it still needs to be said: none of these helpful persons can be held responsible for the shortcomings of this book.

Grateful acknowledgment is made to *The New England Quarterly* for permission to reprint in chapter 6 materials originally appearing in the December 1978 issue of that journal.

Nature and Religious Imagination

Introduction

Landmarks of a period of history are as discernible in its shib-boleths as in its institutional structures or social customs. Values, issues, and perspectives characteristic of a cultural epoch are re-flected in language. "The energies of social life are compressed into words," Rosenstock-Huessy has observed. "The circulation of ar-ticulated speech is the lifeblood of society. Through speech, society sustains its time and space axes."[1] Axial speech is constituted in great part by key words and expressions which are clear enough in meaning to act as authoritative touchstones of judgment but which are also ambiguous enough to invite further inquiry. Key words are the symbols of an age, calling up the principal issues for discussion, abbreviating into shorthand what is deemed valuable, and hinting at depths of meaning below their surface.

This study of American theology attends to the relation between two terms that became passwords for entrance into the literate culture of the West. In America "nature" and "imagination" reached their zenith as lively symbols during the first half of the nineteenth century, but the groundwork for their full flowering was prepared in the preceding century. Ralph Waldo Emerson has cor-rectly been taken as a representative of both the power of the two terms and their grand synthesis. Emerson sought to portray nature as a symbol for spirit and summoned the poet as redeemer who would, through his imagination, free men from conventionality and make translucid for them the divine aura in natural forms. A century earlier, however, Jonathan Edwards had turned his atten-tion to nature as a symbol of spirit and had delineated a mental activity which penetrates to the divine meaning of the natural world. Edwards was no Emerson in eighteenth-century dress.

1

Many of his religious presuppositions were radically different from Emerson's, and his reflections on the limits of nature and the role of the symbolic imagination led to different theological conclusions. Nonetheless, Perry Miller's generalization captures an essential truth: there was, from early Puritanism to Edwards to Emerson, a persistent effort in New England to confront images of God within the physical universe. So long as Miller's own warning is heeded that this is not to be construed as an argument for a direct line of intellectual descent, his observation points to the manner in which seventeenth- and eighteenth-century New England included an incessant drive, culminating in the nineteenth century, to correlate the natural world and the religious imagination.[2]

To take one's interpretive cues from the bywords of a period is by no means to suggest that all the theologians of the period used as their chief building blocks the concepts associated with those words. It is to propose, rather, that the theologians' constructive enterprises be viewed within the context of the axial language of their time and space. In arriving at his crucial theological judgments, Jonathan Edwards referred not to nature as his authority but to scriptural history and the supernatural work of the Holy Spirit, and he warned against relying upon an "imagination" which every person has "by nature." Edwards's judgments on such matters must be read carefully in the light of the different meanings attached to "nature" and "imagination" in the eighteenth and nineteenth centuries, but it is clear that he was not always captive of the spirit and shibboleths of his age. Emerson's contemporary, Horace Bushnell, devoted one of his longest and most complex books to demonstrating that nature not only lacked authority for the decisive dimensions of human existence but also was incomprehensible apart from its systematic correlation with supernature. Bushnell did acknowledge, however, that "nature" dominated religious discourse in his day and that the situation called for commentary from the theologian. In brief, some American theologians refused to take their culture's key words as norms, but that refusal may well be a mark of their creativity. As Lionel Trilling has written, a culture is a dynamic, dialectical struggle of forces rather than a smooth flow. The more a writer simultaneously reflects the terms of the struggle and yet manages to rise above them, the more notable he is as an "artist."[3] According to that criterion, theology from

Edwards to Bushnell yielded its share of artistic and inartistic thinkers.

Nature scarcely appeared overnight as a key word in the modern world. *Natura* and *phusis* had long pervaded philosophical discourse as words denoting such ideas as the original state of anything, the primordial stuff of the cosmos, the essence of a thing, the primary principle of motion and rest. And in theology, "nature" referred to man's state apart from saving grace, and to the counterpoint of "person" in trinitarian discussions. The authoritative uses to which the various ideas of nature were put are illustrated by Carl Becker:

> Aristotle justified slavery on the ground that it was in accord with nature. The stoic emperor, Marcus Aurelius, understood that "nothing is evil which is according to Nature." Roman jurists endeavored to reconcile positive law with the law of nature and right reason. Thomas Aquinas knew that the "participation of the eternal law in the rational creature is called the natural law." According to Calvin, "Natural equity . . . demands that princes be armed . . . to defend the subjects committed to their care whenever they are hostilely assailed."[4]

What emerged as the characteristic idea of nature in the eighteenth century was the world as empirically observable. Taking natural law to mean the observed harmonious behavior and relation of material objects, eighteenth-century intellectuals were inclined to understand nature less as an ideal image of creation deduced from the character of its creator and more as the actual (or as the ideal fully embodied in the actual) state of things. The actual state of things was what directly confronted human perception, or what the mathematical mind discovered when working on the basis of perception.[5] The emergence of this view of nature was owing largely to the impact of Newtonian science upon the eighteenth-century intellect. *A priori* theorizing about the cosmos was abandoned in favor of an empirical approach which assumed that material phenomena could be explained with mechanical laws inductively discovered.

As a consequence of this characteristic perspective, what particularly attracted eighteenth-century man to nature-language was its apparent clarity and stability. In searching out the background to the divinization of nature in nineteenth-century British literature, Basil Willey concluded that the origins of the apotheosis appeared in the preceding century: "Nature was the grand alternative to all that man had made of man; upon her solid ground therefore—upon the *tabula rasa* prepared by the true philosophy—must all the religion, the ethics, the politics, the law, and the art of the future be constructed."[6] Nature as the Great Machine was dependable, whereas human history was uncertain; it was tangible, whereas ideas about supernature were insubstantial; it promised secure knowledge, while human creeds and opinions issued in doubt and confusion. However much nineteenth-century romantics would protest the false securities and binding rigidities of the new scientific world view, they themselves were heirs of its axial language. Emerson would repudiate the scientific outlook in favor of "Reason" and poetic imagination, but his central word "nature" had already been baptized and sanctified by previous generations, and his counsel that one should take his personal bearings from the spirit in nature rather than from the opinions of history had the ring of eighteenth-century rhetoric. Coleridge would invoke the vital past in defiance of scientism's disdain for history, and he would defend the "supernatural acts of the will" against the encroachments of nature's mechanisms, but when he defined nature as the realm of cause and effect he borrowed from the eighteenth-century view of nature as the Great Machine. Despite the real divisions, there were also strong continuities of language and concept between eighteenth-century rationalism and nineteenth-century romanticism.

"Nature" possessed only surface clarity and only apparent stability, however, even for the eighteenth century. Like all other key words, it was subject to the disparate interpretations of thinking persons; it, as much as historic creeds and opinions, generated questions and confusion. Within the span of one hundred years, "nature" was defined as the cosmic system of interconnected parts, as everything reasonable in the world, as everything instinctual in the world, as the subhuman and the nonhuman and the impersonal, as the domain of causal determinism, as the actual state of things, as the potential state of things. Within that same span of time, David Hume challenged an assumption regarding nature's rational, stable orderliness with his argument that external order is based on belief, not on reason's logic, that the inference of nature's causes is not rational detection but "a species of instinct" in which the mind associates one object with another. And Immanuel Kant impugned the epistemology of a simpler view of nature with his intricate thesis that objects of sense experience are appearances rather than things in themselves. As the eighteenth century passed into the nineteenth, "nature" was in definitional disarray and its previously assumed stability under question. As a normative concept it was also leading individuals to draw totally opposite social and political conclusions:

> Rousseau, prophet of revolution, was afterwards appealed to by the reactionaries; the Revolution was made in the name of Nature, Burke attacked it in the name of Nature. . . . Wordsworth and Coleridge saw Nature symbolized first in revolutionary France, and then in reactionary England.[7]

"Nature" was a key word in the eighteenth and nineteenth centuries, but its superficial qualities of clarity and stability by no means guaranteed it uniformity of meaning or consistency of application. Its correlation with another key word, "imagination," could therefore evoke an almost infinite number of significations.

In the middle of the nineteenth century, the American theologian Horace Bushnell issued a plea for an imaginative Christianity that would replace the dogmatism that Christianity had come to be:

> The Gospel is no dogma. . . . The word dogma indicates . . . opinion offered to opinion as having a standard right; whereas the gospel is a revelation made up of fact and form and figure, and offered as a presentation to faith. . . . What is given to faith is put forth in some fact-form or symbol to be interpreted by imaginative insight, or the discerning power of faith. What is given to opinion is given to the notional understanding. One imports liberty, and the other a certain dictational right as respects thinking.[8]

In drawing these distinctions between dogma and gospel, opinion and symbol, notional understanding and imagination, Bushnell struck at what he believed to be the chief failure of theology in his day. In Bushnell's judgment, American theology had come to operate with the assumption that the Christian message is a set of dogmatic assertions addressed to the understanding. He would engage in the theological enterprise motivated by a different conviction: that the words of the Christian gospel—and the whole of nature and of history—are liberating symbols that may be appropriated only by the imagination. Most of Bushnell's theological contemporaries in America were unable or unwilling to share his basic conviction, but he had been preceded in his claims by others: notably by Samuel Taylor Coleridge, from whom he borrowed heavily, by Ralph Waldo Emerson, and—much earlier and through a different idiom—by Jonathan Edwards.

Like the word "nature," "imagination" (*imaginatio, phantasia*) has been subjected to widely divergent interpretations in the history of Western thought. In philosophical circles it has stood for detection of the outer skin of reality and for perception of the depths of reality, for the unification of human experience and for the disruption of the unified self, for the conjuring of untruths and for insight into Truth itself. In Christian theology, "image," "figure," "type," and the powers of "imaging," "figuring," and "typologizing" were the focus of considerable discussion and debate from Tertullian to Aquinas and beyond. To view the Old Testament as a type or image of the New was to raise the question of the relation between the literal and the figural meanings. To understand creation, and especially man, as an image of God was to force the issue of the relation between image and reality, and the role of imagination in the knowledge of God.[9] "Imagination" and "image" were crucial terms long before the modern mind made them words of enchantment, and many of the ideas associated with the long history of the terms have provided the points of reference for modern discussions.

In the English-speaking world, however, it was the nineteenth century, more than any other, that gave rise to "imagination" as a key word. And along with "imagination's" rise to prominence came the affirmation of the supreme value of "symbol." Essentially the claim was this: what is both constructed and discerned by the imagination is a symbol or an expression of truth which is inseparable from the truth expressed. Charles Feidelson has described the centrality of this conviction in nineteenth-century American literature. Emerson, Melville, Hawthorne, Poe, and Whitman made their chief literary contributions and anticipated contemporary literary theory through their attention to the mind's act of symboling. Their aims in their own imaginative construction were: in some way to become the reality of which they were writing (as in the "I" of Whitman's "Song of Myself") so that there was an interlocking of symbol, symbolist, and thing symbolized; to treat a work of art as creative in the sense that it might bring into existence its own meaning (the writing is not *about* something but presents a content through its form); to take words, rather than as arbitrary signs, as symbols intrinsic to the mind's growth, to its perception of itself, and to its understanding of its world.[10] Much nineteenth-century American literature embodied what Horace Bushnell pled for in theology: a vital symbolic imagination.

The single most important theory of the imagination available to Americans in the nineteenth century was that of Samuel Taylor Coleridge. Coleridge elevated "imagination" to the status of key word for literature and literary criticism, for philosophy, and for theology and biblical interpretation. At the heart of this theory was his distinction between imagination and fancy. The imagination's primary act is the power of perception as such and is similar to Immanuel Kant's "productive imagination" which unifies experience into a single, connected whole. The secondary act of the imagination is "an echo of the former" and "dissolves, diffuses, and dissipates, in order to re-create"; it is "essentially *vital*, even as all objects (*as* objects) are essentially fixed and dead." Imagination, then, is the mind's experience of itself in the act of thinking and is the power of creatively penetrating beyond the dead fixity of objects to their—and our own—symbolic meaning. Fancy is "a mode of Memory emancipated from the order of time and space"; like other modes of memory it "must receive all its materials ready made from the law of association."[11] Although imagination may be energized by fancy, the former is definitely distinct from and superior to the latter. Fancy merely combines and arranges given units of experience, whereas imagination penetrates and creatively modifies those units.[12] Coleridge's theory of the imagination had immense appeal to certain American thinkers who were eager to find a path between the barren mind of scientific objectivism and the equally infertile mind of unrestrained fancifulness.

Those Americans who adopted Coleridge's view of the imagination introduced significant innovations into their worlds of thought. Eighteenth-century American thinkers had been wont to understand "imagination" as Coleridge and his disciples understood "fancy"—as memory freed from the limits of time and space. And often they had believed those limits to be broken by bodily conditions and the wild improprieties of religious enthusiasm. John Locke's influence on eighteenth-century America was apparent here. Locke used "imagination" and "fancy" interchangeably to point to the human capacity for conjuring ideas which have no verification from sense experience and for inventing religious conceits which are not subject to the inspection of reason.[13] Jonathan Edwards, a careful reader of Locke's work, defined "imagination" as "that power of the mind, whereby it can have a conception, or idea of things of an external nature . . . when those things are not present, and be not perceived by the senses." Imaginings in themselves were for Edwards neither good nor bad—they were part of the human constitution—but they could easily become demonic when, as in enthusiasm, they were confused with divine revelation.[14]

In the light of this Lockean and Edwardean definition of "imagination," the imagination understood as the creative, symbol-producing, symbol-detecting power of the mind marked a major transition in the history of ideas in America. Yet the eighteenth century made its own contributions to the transition. Edwards, for example, employed the word "image" more positively than "imagination." An image or shadow was not a token of things absent in space and time; it was a representation of a visible object which opened up invisible truths within that object. And the mental power which could detect the deeper meaning within an image— what Edwards called the "sense of the heart" and "spiritual understanding"—had striking parallels with the "imagination" of the nineteenth century.

The following chapters of this book will investigate how representative American theologians used the terms "nature" and "imagination." But the thesis of the book presupposes minimal definitions of the two words. "Nature" means the physical universe, including the human body and the "brute creation." Within the scheme of the Great Chain of Being adopted by most of the theologians, nature stands for everything below man as spirit. "Imagination" means the human power of forming and grasping mental images not directly produced by sensation but believed to reflect, however accurately or inaccurately, the realities of the natural world. "Religious imagination" denotes the reading of images of the natural world as tokens of ultimate realities: of God, the final destiny of man, the overall purposes of nature and history.

In addition, the thesis of the book rests on a value judgment about how nature and imagination are best correlated: nature is best grasped by the religious imagination when the images of nature become symbols. This conviction accords, of course, with nineteenth-century predilections. It also presupposes a distinction which twentieth-century thinkers have drawn between "sign" and "symbol." According to Paul Tillich, a symbol, unlike a sign, participates in the reality to which it points. "Symbols, although they are not the same as that which they symbolize, participate in its meaning and power. The difference between symbol and sign is the participation in the symbolized reality which characterizes the symbols, and the nonparticipation in the 'pointed-to' reality which characterizes a sign."[15] Some words, for example, function as mere signs in that they point away from themselves to another reality. The word "desk" written on a piece of paper directs attention toward a reality quite distinct from the word itself. But some language, such as that of poetry and liturgy, conveys through itself the power and meaning of the reality that it points to. The word "cross," when employed by the devout Christian, does not simply point away to an object or event but calls up through itself the redemptive meaning of the Crucifixion. Paul Ricoeur aims at a similar distinction when he says that a symbol embodies a "double intentionality"—a literal or technical meaning and an analogical meaning. "Thus, contrary to perfectly transparent technical signs, which say only what they want to say in positing that which they signify, symbolic signs are opaque, because the first, literal, obvious meaning itself points analogically to a second meaning which is not given otherwise than in it."[16] The word "impure," for example, takes on symbolic meaning when, in religious discourse, it intends through its literal signification of the "physically unclean" the analogical meaning of "sacred defilement" or sin. Never to move beyond the literal or sign meaning of nature—simply to use nature's images as indicators of truth rather than as participants in or double intenders of that truth—is, according to the judgment underlying this book, to fail to realize the full potential of the religious imagination.

The thesis of the book is this: a symbolic-imaginative response to nature clearly appeared in the Puritan religion of Jonathan Edwards, declined in a period of American moralism, legalism, and rationalism, and was renewed in the religious romanticism of Horace Bushnell. For Edwards, nature was a collection of "images or shadows of divine things," a set of symbols calling for an awareness that detects the participation of those symbols in religious truth. Edwards's disciples and those American theologians influenced by Enlightenment philosophy saw nature less as an assemblage of symbols and more as a system of moral laws; for them, natural images were signs, didactic pointers to moral and religious truth, and not symbolic bearers of that truth. Horace Bushnell, principally because of his reading of Coleridge, understood nature as symbol and defined religious imagination as a grasping of religious meaning in and through nature's images. It should become clear in the chapters that follow, however, that this pattern of rise, decline, and renewal of the symbolic imagination was not formed by a series of radical historical ruptures. Nonsymbolic didactic moralism, which characterized New England theology between Edwards and Bushnell, was not lacking in Edwards's and Bushnell's religious interpretations of the natural world. And Edwards's religious vision was not totally squelched by his followers. A pattern of emphases did emerge in this period of American intellectual history, but in such a way that a tension between religious didacticism and religious symbolism endured in the theology of New England.

The terminal figure examined in the developing pattern is Horace Bushnell, rather than that other great nineteenth-century American symbolist, Ralph Waldo Emerson. Bushnell is chosen rather than Emerson, in part, because the latter's views of nature and symbol have already been explored in fine detail; the same cannot be said of Bushnell's views of those matters. But Bushnell is also selected because he is a better representative than Emerson of a religious romanticism with close ties to the theology of Jonathan Edwards. Unlike Emerson, Bushnell shared with Edwards a concern to safeguard in his theories of nature and symbol the basic tenets of the Augustinian-Calvinist theological tradition. And because he often did his thinking deliberately according to the terms associated with theological moralism, Bushnell reflects more clearly than Emerson the tension between symbolism and moralism in the New England mind.

The analyses of this book concentrate, then, upon American theologians. Although American literary artists occasionally are invoked for comparison with the theologians, they do not fall within the focus of the study. An enterprise that has not been previously undertaken—and a need which this book seeks to meet—is an analysis of ideas of nature and imagination in those American thinkers who chose to speak as Christian theologians, whose vocations were preaching and theological reflection rather than creative writing, and whose chief goal was to shape and reshape the religious beliefs and practices of Americans.

In another sense, however, the subject of this study is artistry. Jonathan Edwards, William Ellery Channing, Lyman Beecher, Horace Bushnell, and others who come under analysis were artists of the pulpit, and not a few of them achieved vivid metaphorical expression in their writings and sermons. Many would object to having the title "artist" applied to them: some out of modesty, and others because of their strong ties to a Puritanism which sought to avoid any rhetoric that called attention away from *what* was said to the style of speech. Nonetheless, they *were* artists. In their day preaching was a skill of learning and creative communication which reached more people than novels or poetry, and much of their written theology profited from the artistry of their preaching. This book, therefore, is as concerned with *how* the theologians employed natural imagery as with *what* their views of nature were; it attempts to deal with how imaginative they were, as well as with their theories of imagination.

The development traced in the book concludes roughly at the middle of the nineteenth century. During the last half of that century, American thinking on nature was radically transformed by Darwinism. Although Horace Bushnell's organic perspectives anticipated some features of Darwinian evolutionism, he remained adamantly opposed to Darwin's biology and left to later nineteenth-century American theologians the issues regarding nature and religion posed by the new science. Furthermore, after the Civil War "society" much more than "nature" would become the key word defining the milieu in which theologians must do their thinking. The religious imagination was more seriously challenged by problems associated with an industrialized society and the growth of cities than by the meaning of raw physical nature. Signs of the shift from one epoch to another are evident in the fact that the Darwinism which had most appeal to American theologians was a *social* Darwinism, and in the fact that the religion which sought to become the cutting edge of the new culture preached a *social* gospel.

The immense task of correlating nature and religious imagination, if not abandoned, was thrown into a new set of circumstances and faced with a new set of problems. In meeting the challenge of that correlation, however, American theologians from Edwards to Bushnell came to grips with issues that were to shape the American mind long after those theologians had passed from the scene. And the question of the relation between nature and the religious imagination remains for the contemporary thinker a problem of vast proportions.

NOTES

1. Eugen Rosenstock-Huessy, *Speech and Reality* (Norwich, Vt.: Argo Books, 1970), p. 16.

2. Perry Miller, "From Edwards to Emerson," *Errand into the Wilderness* (Cambridge: Belknap Press of Harvard University Press, 1956), pp. 184–85.

3. Lionel Trilling, *The Liberal Imagination* (New York: Doubleday Anchor Books, 1950), pp. 7 and 15.

4. Carl L. Becker, *The Heavenly City of the Eighteenth-Century Philosophers* (New Haven: Yale University Press, 1932), p. 53.

5. Ibid., pp. 54–57.

6. Basil Willey, *The Eighteenth-Century Background* (New York: Columbia University Press, 1940), p. 2.

7. Ibid., p. 205.

8. Horace Bushnell, "Our Gospel a Gift to the Imagination," *Building Eras in Religion* (New York: Charles Scribner's Sons, 1881), pp. 249–50.

9. See Erich Auerbach, "Figura," *Scenes from the Drama of European Literature* (New York: Meridian Books, 1959), pp. 11–76.

10. Charles Feidelson, Jr., *Symbolism and American Literature* (Chicago: University of Chicago Press, 1953), pp. 4, 18, 47–49, 75.

11. Samuel Taylor Coleridge, *Biographia Literaria* (London: George Bell & Sons, 1891), p. 144.

12. Owen Barfield, *What Coleridge Thought* (Middletown, Conn.: Wesleyan University Press, 1971), pp. 85–86.

13. John Locke, *An Essay Concerning Human Understanding*, ed. A. C. Fraser (New York: Dover Publications, 1959), 2: 332–33, 438–39.

14. Jonathan Edwards, *A Treatise Concerning Religious Affections*, ed. John E. Smith (New Haven: Yale University Press, 1959), pp. 113–14, 210–17.

15. Paul Tillich, *Theology of Culture* (London and New York: Oxford University Press, 1959), pp. 54–55.

16. Paul Ricoeur, *The Symbolism of Evil*, trans. E. Buchanan (Boston: Beacon Press, 1967), p. 15.

PART ONE

Nature's Images: Jonathan Edwards

As a boy, you built a booth
in a swamp for prayer;
lying on your back,
you saw the spiders fly,

basking at their ease,
swimming from tree to tree—
so high, they seemed tacked to the sky.
You knew they would die.

Robert Lowell
"Mr. Edwards and the Spider"

1

The Tradition of Typology

Friedrich Nietzsche once said that no idea could be true unless it was thought in the open air. Paul Tillich claimed that his own pivotal ideas were inspired by landscape and seascape. Jonathan Edwards (1703–58) described his early religious struggles and the emergence of his lasting religious perspectives as events that occurred in close league with the scenes of the natural world. Edwards, no less than Nietzsche and Tillich, was a man of books who spent the greater number of his waking hours at his desk. Yet, like them, he found in physical nature symbols which provoked his thought and fired his imagination.

At the outset of his ministry at Northampton, Edwards formed the habit of spending thirteen hours a day in his study, but the works composed during those long hours manifest his engagement with eighteenth-century American nature. His usual summer recreation was horseback riding, and as he rode the countryside he often would pin small pieces of paper on given spots of his coat as reminders of ideas that occurred to him. "From a ride of several days, he would usually bring home a considerable number of these remembrancers; and, on going to his study, would take them off, one by one, in regular order, and write down the train of thought, of which each was intended to remind him."[1] Judging by the frequent use of natural metaphor in his sermons and the numerous meditations on the symbolic qualities of nature in his private notebooks, not a few of those ideas triggered while riding must have been awakened by the sun, sky, and trees of New England.

In his youth Jonathan wrote a monograph on flying spiders of the North American forests, concentrating on the distance and times of their flights and on the construction of their webs. When he later engaged in revivalist preaching, he invoked images of the insect—of its functions, place in nature, and delicate web—as symbols of the predicament of the sinner before God. "A sensitive boy fixes instinctively upon his emblem, and is transfixed by it; the artist catches his glimpse, and is forever caught by it."[2] Edwards in his youthful wonder and in his adult artistry was captivated by the intricate operations of nature and their emblematic potential.

"Nature wears the colors of the spirit," and Jonathan Edwards was eminent proof of that Emersonian saw. Edwards's spirit was shaped by Calvinist theology and by Newtonian science. As a consequence, what he found symbolic about nature was not so much what immediately met the eye in static forms, but the laws and functions of the observed universe. He went to the displays of Deity in physical nature not in order to find alternatives to scriptural revelation but in order to discover epiphanies complementary, yet subordinate, to those of Scripture. Nature was beautiful, not in itself, but only to the extent that it reflected the harmony of the human mind and the glory of the Creator. Providing no peaceful place of escape from the chaos of history or the problems that beset the mind, nature betokened both the misery and the grandeur of man and was joined with struggles of the human spirit.

The broad contours of Edwards's approach to nature and its spiritual meaning emerge in his "Personal Narrative," an account which covers the turning points of his boyhood and young adulthood. He records there that when he was a boy he was very much concerned with the things of religion and underwent an "awakening" at the church of his minister-father in East Windsor, Connecticut. At that time he and some schoolmates built a booth in a swamp as a place for prayer. "And besides, I had particular secret places of my own in the woods, where I used to retire by myself; and was from time to time much affected." His affections proved to be passing ones, however, and he observes that he made the mistake of confusing such passing emotions sustained by his natural retreats with grace. Eventually "my convictions and affections wore off." Much later, after prolonged periods of "violent inward struggles," he experienced a "delightful conviction" of the sovereignty of God, a doctrine that had troubled him because of its apparent injustice and unreasonableness. The breakthrough came from Scripture, as the meaning of 1 Tim. 1:17 opened before him, "Now unto the King eternal, immortal, invisible, the only wise God, be honor and glory for ever and ever, Amen." On reading these words, he began to enjoy the glory of God, to have an "inward, sweet sense" of the "beauty and excellency" of Christ, and he felt himself "wrapt and swallowed up in God." There followed a new perception of nature. As he walked in his father's pasture, he read the majesty and grace of God in sky and clouds, and he heard the voice and beheld the presence of God in thunder and lightning, which formerly had sent him into a fright. The discovery of the existential meaning of God's sovereignty and the new sense of nature did not lay all of Edwards's problems to rest, for he continued to have "longings after God and Christ." But the new sense born of the discovery was lasting; now "the appearance of every thing was altered."³

Nature opened its hidden meanings only after a scriptural passage had given Edwards a changed perspective on the sovereignty of God. He continued his retreats to nature through solitary rides and walks in the open air, but there are no indications that nature in itself provided him religious solace: his boyhood experiences in the booth had doubtless demonstrated that deceptive affections could be sustained by nature. Nature took on a beautiful appearance because of an altered perspective, and its loveliness reflected the higher divine beauty. Nature was intimately associated with Edwards's religious experience, but it clearly was not an independent source of revelation.

To draw a line too quickly, even an indirect one, from Edwards to the Transcendentalists is to run the danger of overlooking these aspects of Edwards's religious response to nature. There are deeper continuities between Edwards and his Puritan predecessors than between Edwards and anything that nineteenth-century America produced. Puritan theology, poetry, and preaching established the patterns for Edwards's response to and reflections on the religious meaning of the natural world.

In comparison with a heterogeneous twentieth-century American culture, New England Puritanism possessed a remarkable amount of ideological and social unity. But Puritanism, in both its English and American phases, was nonetheless a many-sided movement. The multifaceted character of the Puritans was apparent in their postures toward the natural world. One side of Puritanism hungered after visible, tangible symbols of God in nature; another, iconoclastic side was skeptical of symbols, images, emblems as such. The same Puritanism that repudiated the sensual corporeality of the mass and roundly rejected ostentatious ceremonies, vestments, relics, and church architecture in favor of simplicity of form founded on scriptural precedent—this same Puritanism produced elaborate gravestone carvings, a poetry rich in imagery, and theories of the sacraments that sought a close correlation between the visible and the invisible. The Puritan Protestants who, in their desire to preserve the historical meaning of Scripture, criticized the allegorical speculations of medieval interpretation, nonetheless engaged in a typological exegesis that looked beyond the literal. And the Puritan theological heritage that esteemed logic as the highest of human enterprises also acknowledged aesthetics as a crucial part of human existence. Puritan Samuel Willard well knew the limits of human reason—it cannot know God's face, it knows only God's "backparts"—but he did assign reason an imperialist role over the other functions of the mind: "We know nothing of God but by putting some Logical Notion upon him. All things are conveyed to us in a Logical way, and bear some stamp of reason upon them, or else we should know nothing of them."[4] Puritan Cotton Mather scarcely fancied himself an unreasonable man, but he recognized that a logical mind devoid of an aesthetic sense was a poor mind indeed: "I cannot wish you a soul that shall be wholly unpoetical."[5]

Some of these contradictions within Puritanism are more apparent than real: they represent changing viewpoints over time, or they are dialectical yes's and no's within a single, consistent affirmation. Others, however, reflect deep tensions within Puritan life and thought. The tensions as well as the affirmations shaped the thinking of Jonathan Edwards.

Frequent note has been taken of how the Puritans were prone to discover the hand of God in every event, natural and historical, large and small. In the words of F. O. Matthiessen, seventeenth-century New England Puritans found "'remarkable providences' even in the smallest phenomena, tokens of divine displeasure in every capsized dory or runaway cow."[6] When the Pequot Indians undertook their bloody raids, fires raced through Boston, and the plague reached epidemic proportions, a synod was called to raise the questions, "What are the evils which have called the judgment of God upon us? What is to be done to reform these evils?" And when, in the midst of a synod, a snake behind the pulpit was killed by an elder, Bay leader John Winthrop drew the biblical, providential parallel: "This being so remarkable, and nothing falling out but by divine providence, it is out of doubt, the Lord discovered somewhat of his mind in it. The serpent is the devil; the synod, the representative of the churches of Christ in New England. The devil had formerly and lately attempted their disturbance and dissolution; but their faith in the seed of the woman overcame him and crushed his head."[7]

The Puritans' detection of divine action in the world about them was an extension of their typological interpretation of Scripture to the whole of nature and history. Typology, an exegetical method of the ancient church, was especially important to Calvin and the Puritans as an alternative to both an unimaginative literalism and a fanciful allegorizing. Typology aimed to take a text first of all for what it said, and then, without abandoning its plain meaning, move to its prefiguring of a later, historical meaning (the antitype). Above all, certain Old Testament passages were believed to adumbrate Christ. Such a method, the Protestant exegetes were quick to point out, was found in Scripture itself. St. Paul, for example, typologized in Rom. 5:14, "Nevertheless, death reigned from Adam to Moses, even over them that had not sinned after the similitude of Adam's transgression, who is the figure of him that was to come." And in Matt. 12:40, Jesus himself said, "For as Jonah was three days and three nights in the whale's belly; so shall the Son of man be three days and three nights in the heart of the earth." Unlike allegory, typology retains a certain factual concreteness; it is rooted in tangible realities rather than in abstract ideas. "The type exists in history and is factual. . . . By contrast, the allegory, the simile, and the metaphor have been made according to the fancy of men, and they mean whatever the brain of the begetter is pleased they should mean. In the type there is a rigorous correspondence, which is not a chance resemblance, between the representation and the antitype."[8] Conservative Puritan exegetes regarded as types only those events and figures of the Old Testament which were explicitly instituted by the New Testament. Others were willing to allow such images as Jacob's ladder to prefigure Christ's union of heaven and earth. The Puritan typologists who refused to bind themselves to

New Testament types sometimes reached the speculative heights of allegory, letting their imaginations run in such a way that they seemed to impose ideas on things, rather than letting things lead to ideas.[9] More commonly, however, New England typologists adhered to the concrete, and the most liberal of them rested their analogies on Christ as the consummate antitype, the historical fulfillment and interpretive paradigm of all types.

The Puritans extended their typological methods to their own history. Like most of the New England Puritan patriarchs who preceded him in Massachusetts, Cotton Mather looked upon the covenanted people in the American wilderness as a New Israel and upon the leaders of the New England churches as antitypes of Old Testament figures. His citation of a verse by Benjamin Woodbridge summarized his vision:

> Though Moses be, yet Joshua is not dead:
> I mean renowned [John] Norton; worthy he,
> Successor to our Moses [John Cotton], is to be.
> O happy Israel in America,
> In such a Moses, such a Joshua.[10]

The trials as well as the triumphs, the successes as well as the failures of Israel were types, shadows of historical events in Massachusetts. The lineaments of such an interpretation of history had long ago been drawn in the sixteenth century, when John Foxe's *Book of Martyrs* had led English Protestants to expect that their destiny in the world was to enact a new dispensation of God's truth revealed to the Israelites.[11]

American Puritans discovered types in their nature as well as in their history. Rom. 1:20 stated, "For the invisible things of him from the creation of the world are clearly seen, being understood by the things that are made, even his eternal power and Godhead," and the Bible was replete with analogies between religion and the creatures. There seemed ample scriptural warrant for Puritan poet Edward Taylor to see the whole world "slickt up in types." Puritan enthusiasm for making "heavenly use of earthly things" was especially stirred by seventeenth-century handbooks of devotional piety dedicated to "spiritualizing the creatures." In his *Navigation Spiritualized* and *Husbandry Spiritualized*, English Puritan John Flavel meditated upon the mariner's and the farmer's experiences with the elements of nature as spiritual types, and American Puritan Cotton Mather followed suit with his *Religious Husbandman* and monographs on the typological meanings of winter, thunder, and the rainbow. Seventeenth-century Puritan poets saw in their rustic, everyday world emblems of God and other "divine things." And the symbolizing of nature found its place in the popular art of gravestone carving among New Englanders. "After 1668 no Puritan family was ready to commit its loved ones to the cold earth without an appropriate cluster of symbols hovering protectively over the grave."[12] Vines, trees, suns, wings and birds, as well as grim skulls and skeletons, adorned the gravestones as tokens of death, eternal life, and resurrection. By the end of the seventeenth century, a typological method originally confined to Scripture had transcended the canon. "A biblical hermeneutic became a mode of interpreting the book of nature, and the expanded typology became an instrument of the piety of sensation."[13]

The Puritan piety of sensation directed toward nature could result in speculations bearing the marks of allegory. Thus Cotton Mather dealt with the detailed parts of an object as things with exact spiritual equivalents, an approach characteristically associated with allegorizing.[14] Generally, however, even when this extreme was reached, the plain, factual meaning of an object and its functions was the starting point for Puritan meditations on nature, and the factual led to the spiritual meaning. This is a feature characteristic of typologizing. It is also the chief feature of symboling according to Paul Ricoeur: "In the symbol, I cannot objectify the analogical relation that connects the second meaning with the first. It is by living in the first meaning that I am led by it beyond itself; the symbolic meaning is constituted in and by the literal meaning."[15] Even the devotional handbooks which were unrestrained in gleaning spiritual meanings from the everyday visible world preserved the concreteness of the world and were led to the spiritual by it. The method of a Flavel and a Mather, as Perry Miller observed, "was allegory turned inside out: instead of starting with abstract propositions and embodying them in figures" the Puritan method took some observable fact "and by analyzing it as though it were already the given allegory, extracted from it the abstraction."[16]

The Puritan was convinced that his natural typologies were rendered possible by one grand historical fact, the appearance of the Christ. The Christ was the antitype unifying and grounding all other antitypes and their shadows. What Karl Keller has said of Edward Taylor is true of the Puritan tradition of natural typologizing as a whole: "Taylor believed that reality has a symbolic structure in which nothing has meaning in itself but in which everything refers beyond itself . . . to Christ. It then follows that, if Christ were a cheat, there would be no meaning anywhere in all the Creation! To Taylor, although the Creation has a 'Naturall' existence, it is not 'spiritualized' unless it stands in some relationship to Christ."[17] What inspired the Puritans to probe for the spiritual meanings of the parts and functions of nature, what in their judgment founded analogies between the visible and the invisible, was God incarnate. An act of grace on the part of God had made the connection: the invisible had assumed the form of the visible. Henceforth the whole of creation could be illuminated according to its spiritual meaning by those who caught the light from the Light of the World. The Puritans were wary of confusing the visible with the invisible, of having all distinctions blurred by the blinding light of God's incarnation. Theologically, they took seriously the difference between the "two natures" of Christ. The confusing of the two in their opinion constituted the idolatry of Catholic and Anglican sensuality. But when cautions were properly observed, the visible creation could offer a host of images of the spiritual realm.

The imaginative, fairly cautious, approach to nature's spiritual meaning was the task inspiring much Puritan poetry. Reflecting the Puritan love of science, the American Puritan poet possessed a keen eye for his new land, often observing in fine detail such things as wind direction, topographical measurements, and Indian customs. Keenness of observation was part of his genuine fondness for the world and its pleasures.[18] "The key to Puritan aesthetics," Harrison Meserole says, "lies in their idea of proportion and utility. The notion of art for art's sake would have horrified them, if they had understood it. In their view nothing produced by man was for its own sake, but ultimately for God's."[19] The Puritan typically avoided two extremes which equally offended the glory of God: sensuous overindulgence, because it reduced man as the height of God's creation to the level of the brute; and aesthetic insensitivity, because it rejected the world as a gift of God. "He is the Richest, and most happy man,/Who is most moderate in his Desire," Richard Steere wrote; but the blessings of nature are given to be delighted in: "They do afford us various Delectations,/Beyond necessity to Satiate."[20]

The blessings of the created world which satisfied more than bodily cravings were types, "Free gifts to us giv'n by the hand/ Of God himself as Tokens sent from Heav'n."[21] Poetry, then, was a mirror held up to nature, which in turn reflected the Creator. But God's grace and excellency "Out vie both works of nature and of Art."[22] Because God surpasses both his world and the human creations which seek to mirror it, the poetic type can only capture imperfectly the divinity symbolized by nature. Ultimately all art must stand "amaz'd in Ambiguity."[23] The Puritan poet felt challenged to typologize nature as an image of divinity, but he knew that he was up against the well-nigh impossible task of expressing the inexpressible, that behind both nature and art lies the inexhaustible mystery of God.

The Puritan poet was not alone in his struggle with the links between nature and supernature. He had the company of Puritan sacramental theologians in Old and New England. John Calvin had referred to the Old Testament types as "sacraments" designed to lead men to Christ,[24] establishing an association that later Reformed theologians developed. Early English Puritans deliberately avoided the sense appeal of the sacraments and stressed their didactic function. Even at this early stage, however, Puritan theologians noted the corporeality of men which made necessary the sacraments as earthly signs of spiritual truths. By the third decade of the seventeenth century, English Puritans had proposed a wide spectrum of sacramental theories, and by the end of that century, they had produced pious handbooks that portrayed the sacraments as symbolic representations of God's truth. Much the same development occurred in New England. Originally New England theologians' introspective spirituality obstructed the sensible appeal of the sacramental signs, but by the early eighteenth century, sacramental devotion and theory were part of a new symbolic consciousness. Baptism became a visible spectacle for nourishing the spiritual life, and in the Supper, Christ was present according to his humanity in some mysterious way. The New England theologians continued to maintain, against both Rome and Martin Luther, that in the Supper *finitum non capax infiniti*. But they did adopt the spirit, if not always the letter, of John Calvin: the Holy Spirit mysteriously makes the whole Christ present in the sacrament.[25] New England Puritanism had moved from sign to symbol in its sacramental theory: from a notion of visible reality as a didactic pointer to divine truth, to a notion of visible reality as a participant in the truth to which it points.

The symbolic consciousness of the Puritans was Jonathan Edwards's deepest heritage. The Puritans' keen eye for detail and their penchant for detecting remarkable providences were legacies for Jonathan in the swamp, young Edwards in his father's pasture, and the Reverend Mr. Edwards in the pulpit. The Puritan extension of typology to nature, and the concreteness and Christocentrism of that process of drawing analogies, characterized Edwards's reflections on the natural world. There is no evidence that Edwards read the colonial American poetry of a Bradstreet, a Wigglesworth, or a Taylor; but he did pore over Homer, Milton, and Watts;[26] and his aesthetic sensibilities were those of the Puritan poets. In his controversy over the meaning of the sacraments, which eventually led to the loss of his pulpit at Northampton, Edwards proved his erudition in the history of Puritan sacramental theory, and his views of the relation between the visible and the invisible were similar to the symbolic perspectives of late seventeenth-century Puritan sacramentalism.

Above all, what Edwards shared with his Puritan forefathers was a cosmic theological viewpoint that unified all the mind's diverse exercises upon nature. It was the view that God is the free, sovereign Creator of the universe, that he continues to uphold that universe in its existence out of his overflowing love, and that the world is—and always will be—contingent and hence in need of the sustaining love of the Creator. The following words of Samuel Willard, a systematizer of colonial Puritan theology, may be taken as the essence of the faith informing Edwards's approach to nature:

> God is holy originally, the creatures are so by derivation. His Holiness is the prototype, theirs but the copy; his the substance, theirs but the image or shadows; his the fountain, theirs but some few drops, or small springs that issue from it. All the holiness that is in all the creatures is borrowed of him. He hath his in and of himself, and they have theirs of and from him.[27]

Edwards was no mere eighteenth-century repetition of his Puritan tradition. He made his own creative contributions to that tradition. His imaginative use of the natural image in his "awakening" sermons and even in his discursive treatises was unequalled by any American preacher or theologian who preceded him. His ideas on spiritual knowledge and his theories of being, virtue, and creation resulted in an epistemology and a metaphysic of far more sophistication than any produced by his theological harbingers. Still, his thinking was nourished by his theological heritage. He was Puritanism in its full flower.

NOTES

Notes for Chapters 1 through 3 use the following abbreviations:

> WD - *Works of President Edwards,* ed. Sereno E. Dwight, 10 vols. (New York: S. Converse, 1829–1830).
>
> WW - *Works of President Edwards,* 4 vols., reprint of the Worcester edition with additions (New York: Leavitt & Allen, 1856).
>
> WY - *Works of Jonathan Edwards,* the new critical Yale edition (New Haven: Yale University Press, 1957–).

1. "Life of Edwards," WD, 1:111.

2. Perry Miller, *Jonathan Edwards* (New York: Meridian Books, 1949), p. 146.

3. "Life of Edwards," WD, 1:59–62.

4. Samuel Willard, *A Compleat Body of Divinity* (Boston: B. Green & S. Kneeland, 1726), p. 44.

5. Quoted in Harrison T. Meserole, *Seventeenth-Century American Poetry* (New York: W. W. Norton, 1968), p. xxvii.

6. F. O. Matthiessen, *American Renaissance* (New York: Oxford University Press, 1941), p. 243.

7. John Winthrop, *The History of New England from 1630 to 1649* (Boston: Thomas B. Wait and Son, 1826), 2:330.

8. Perry Miller, "Introduction" to Jonathan Edwards, *Images or Shadows of Divine Things* (New Haven: Yale University Press, 1948), pp. 6–7.

9. See Mason I. Lowance, "Introduction" to Samuel Mather, *The Figures or Types of the Old Testament* (New York: Johnson Reprint Corp., 1969), p. xiii.

10. Cotton Mather, *Magnalia Christi Americana* (Hartford, Conn.: Silus Andrus and Son, 1855), 1:284.

11. See William Haller, *Foxe's Book of Martyrs and the Elect Nation* (London: Jonathan Cape, 1963).

12. Allan I. Ludwig, *Graven Images: New England Stonecarving and Its Symbols, 1650–1815* (Middletown, Conn.: Wesleyan University Press, 1966), p. 18. David Stannard has found evidence that before the end of the

seventeenth century New England Puritans had developed other elaborate trappings for death in their funeral ceremonies, a phenomenon that Stannard believes was occasioned by the Puritans' defensive, tribal response to social instability. David E. Stannard, *The Puritan Way of Death: A Study in Religion, Culture and Social Change* (New York: Oxford University Press, 1977), chap. 5.

13. E. Brooks Holifield, *The Covenant Sealed: The Development of Puritan Sacramental Theology in Old and New England, 1570–1720* (New Haven: Yale University Press, 1974), p. 137.

14. Mason I. Lowance, "Cotton Mather's *Magnalia* and the Metaphors of Biblical History," *Typology and Early American Literature*, ed. Sacvan Bercovitch (Amherst: University of Massachusetts Press, 1972), pp. 158, 160.

15. Paul Ricoeur, *The Symbolism of Evil*, trans. E. Buchanan (Boston: Beacon Press, 1967), pp. 15–16.

16. Perry Miller, *The New England Mind: From Colony to Province* (Boston: Beacon Press, 1953), p. 404.

17. Karl Keller, " 'The World Slickt Up in Types': Edward Taylor as a Version of Emerson," *Typology and Early American Literature*, p. 187.

18. Meserole, *Seventeenth-Century American Poetry,*, pp. xxi, xxv.

19. Ibid., pp. xxv–xxvi.

20. Richard Steere, "Earth Felicities, Heavens Allowances," ibid., pp. 256, 258.

21. Ibid., p. 258.

22. Edward Taylor, Meditation 2. 56, ibid., p. 136.

23. John Josselyn, "And the bitter storm augments; the wild winds rage," ibid., p. 404.

24. John Calvin, *Institutes of the Christian Religion*, ed. J. T. McNeill (Philadelphia: Westminster Press, 1960), 2:1296–97.

25. For a learned discussion of Puritan sacramental developments, see Holifield's *The Covenant Sealed*, which my paragraph summarized.

26. Thomas H. Johnson, "Jonathan Edwards's Background of Reading," *Publications of the Colonial Society of Massachusetts*, 28 (December 1931): 216–217.

27. Willard, *A Compleat Body of Divinity*, p. 73. For a full treatment of Willard's views of God and creation, see Ernest B. Lowrie, *The Shape of the Puritan Mind: The Thought of Samuel Willard* (New Haven: Yale University Press, 1974), chaps. 3, 4.

2

Images of Divine Things

Jonathan Edwards kept numerous notebooks in which he set down outlines of writing projects, quotations from books he was reading, and ideas as they occurred to him. One such notebook, containing 212 numbered entries which he made throughout his adult life, Edwards variously entitled "The Images of Divine Things," "The Shadows of Divine Things," "The Book of Nature and Common Providence," "The Language and Lessons of Nature." It was a collection of reflections on nature and its symbolic meanings, a series of ideas—some connected, many unconnected—on the emblematic qualities of nature. These private jottings contained no secret thoughts which Edwards was afraid to entrust to the public; they were, instead, notions in cursory form which he would explicate in his treatises and experiments in natural typologizing, many of which he would embody in his sermons.[1] There is something in the notebook, however, which one cannot find in the sermons and treatises—the *process* of a mind at work. The thinking on nature in the private workbook embraced three closely related mental activities: experimentation with natural imagery, reflection on the foundations of natural imagery, and meditation on what occurs when one adequately detects the spiritual meaning of nature.

Entry 168 summarizes the kinds of "common providences" which most occupy Edwards's attention:

> There are most representations of divine things in things that are most in view or that we are chiefly concerned in: as in the sun, his light and other influences and benefits; in the other heavenly bodies; in our own bodies; in our state, our families, and commonwealths; and in this business that mankind do principally follow, *viz.*, husbandry.[2]

It is the eventfulness of nature, especially the manner in which nature's events impinge upon human existence, that most attracts Edwards. He is not totally neglectful of the inherent qualities of nature as they directly impact the senses: the calm, temperate air of the visible heavens awakens images of the saints in glory; green fields, trees, and the rainbow symbolize the grace and love of God.[3] But the bulk of Edwards's imagery is devoted to nature's functions, its interacting parts, and its relation to human livelihood: roses growing upon briars are signs that "all temporal sweets are mixt with bitter"; spiders sucking flies and serpents charming birds into their mouths are "lively representations of the Devil's catching our souls by his temptations"; grass and vegetables being nourished by rain and sun are emblems of man's dependence on God's grace; rivers running to the ocean are symbols of all things tending to God; the foldings and turnings of the bowels are tokens of man's deceitfulness; the wilting heat of the summer sun is an analogy to the trials besetting the godly; the muddy days of early spring are a type of man's passage to a "summer" of higher glory.[4] Edwards's eye is that of the Puritan, trained upon the events of nature in his everyday world as "remarkable providences" of God.

Edwards sometimes makes the same feature of nature stand for widely different spiritual truths. The light of the sun is an image of both God's glory and human suffering. The color green (emerging out of winter's gray) represents God's grace and (as a fading color of fall) man's finitude. This aspect of Edwards's process of typologizing is doubtless owing in part to the fact that it occurs in a notebook where he makes no effort either to classify his images or to develop connections. But it is due to another reason as well: when nature is beheld principally in terms of its functions, rather than in terms of its static states, it is bound to take on many meanings. This is precisely the characteristic of typology in contrast to the allegory. Typology is led by the fact to the symbolic meaning, rather than establishing ahead of time strict, fixed equivalents between image and thing imaged.

Despite this fluidity of typologizing in the notebook, patterns do emerge. Some images dominate Edwards's occasional reflections; some of nature's events lead him rather consistently to specific spiritual truths.

The one image that dominates the entire notebook is light. The sun and its rays most frequently symbolize the Trinity, God's glory,

Christ, and resurrection. The variety of color in light attracts Edwards to the rainbow as an emblem of God's one Spirit in its variety of operations and attributes. Edwards's favorite color, excluding white, appears to be blue, the blue of a serene sky bathed in light as an image of spiritual purity.[5] Edwards is open about his preference for light imagery. For one thing, light, more than any other aspect of nature, conveys constancy and tenacity of act. "The beams of the sun can't be scattered, nor the constant stream of their light in the least interrupted or disturbed by the most violent winds here below, which is a lively image of what is true concerning heavenly light communicated from Christ, the sun of righteousness, to the soul."[6] Further, light is preferred as an image of spiritual truths because of its complex harmony. Beauty is the interpenetrating harmonies of God, soul, and cosmos, and "what an infinite number of such like beauties is there in that one thing, the light, and how complicated an harmony and proportion is it probable belongs to it." Fascinated by his reading of Isaac Newton's *Optics*, Edwards typologizes upon the supremacy of the imagery in light and its actions: "That mixture we call white is a proportionate mixture that is harmonious, as Sir Isaac Newton has shown, to each particular simple colour, and contains in it some harmony or other that is delightfull. And each sort of rays play a distinct tune to the soul, besides those lovely mixtures that are found in nature."[7]

Edwards was fully cognizant of the wide use of light imagery in Scripture, and his scriptural commentary in the notebook gravitates toward those texts where light metaphors prevail. But Edwards's preference for the symbol of light was bred by his own personal experience as well as by his reading of the Bible and Newton. According to his "Personal Narrative," his changed perspective on nature following his new sense of God's sovereignty was one that first of all forced his eyes up to the sky and clouds and then to a world fully illuminated. His earliest thoughts on the meaning of holiness led him to write that "the soul of a true Christian" is "like such a little white flower as we see in the spring of the year; low and humble on the ground, opening its bosom to receive the pleasant beams of the sun's glory."[8] And Edwards records that in 1725 when he lay ill for a quarter of a year, he noticed that those who attended him watched anxiously for the morning. This brought to his mind "those words of the Psalmist, and which my soul with delight made its own language, 'My soul waiteth for the Lord, more than they that watch for the morning; I say, more than they that watch for the morning;' and when the light of day came in at the window, it refreshed my soul, from one morning to another. It seemed to be some image of the light of God's glory."[9] Light, so dominant in his notebook on nature and so closely associated with his personal experience, would become a recurrent image of divine things in Edwards's sermons and treatises.

Water symbolism also frequently appears in the notebook, with the running water of rivers betokening the infinite flow and nourishment of God's goodness and the far reaches of the oceans his boundless power.[10] Deep, still waters usually call up sin and evil; in fact, depth itself is an image of human evil and damnation: the depth of water, caverns, valleys, the human body, wounds and sores.[11] And as Edwards's mind plays upon these and other images, he characteristically uses them in contrasts, a form of rhetoric he perfected in his revivalist sermons. The purity and sublimity of the sky are contrasted with dark and dire caverns, thunderclouds with a serene day, mountains with valleys, light with darkness, the vastness of the visible heavens with the smallness of the earth.[12] Regarding the last contrast, Edwards notes that the increase of scientific knowledge has pointed up "the greatness of the heavenly bodies and their height, and the smallness of the earth in comparison," and so he expresses his delight in and his appreciation for the invention of the telescope.[13]

Edwards attended to types in nature with the Puritan poet's conviction that God's gift of the creation is intended for more than the satisfaction of bodily needs: "Thus we have food not only to keep us from famishing and remove the pain of hunger, but to entertain and delight us; so we have not only clothes to cover our nakedness, but to adorn us, and so of other things. As God in the redemption of Christ does not only provide for our salvation from misery, but provides for us positive blessedness and glory."[14] Above all, the delightfulness of nature resides in its capacity to symbolize spiritual things.

Edwards often remarks in his notebook on nature that his own recurrent images are employed in Scripture, and although he does at times seem to quote Scripture to confirm an independent natural image,[15] more frequently he goes to nature to confirm a scriptural metaphor. His priorities are made clear when he says, "Wherever we are, and whatever we are about, we may see divine things excellently represented and held forth. And it will abundantly tend to confirm the Scriptures."[16] Yet Edwards does not contend that the priority of scriptural authority means that he must merely repeat the imagery of Scripture in its original form. Scripture establishes the grounds of Edwards's own typologizing by providing precedents and by revealing mysteries that invite natural typologizing.[17]

From the standpoint of the typological method itself, then, revelation in Scripture is the prius and authoritative sanction for revelation through nature. From a more cosmic point of view, the book of Scripture and the book of nature are linked by a harmony which God establishes between different kinds of language. The language of Scripture remains authoritative from this perspective, but the created world is a language of God.[18] The two languages are the one word of the one God, connected by a harmony of consent or agreement which is the principle of God's creative activity:

> There is a wonderfull resemblance in the effects which God produces, and consentaneity in His manner of working in one thing and another throughout all nature. It is very observable in the visible world; therefore, it is allowed that God does purposely make and order one thing to be in agreeableness and harmony with another. And if so, why should not we suppose that He makes the inferiour in imitation of the superiour, the material of the spiritual, on purpose to have a resemblance and shadow of them?[19]

The universe is a spiritual language which is arranged on a scale of ascent both ontologically and spatially. Nature's "words" about the human spirit grow fainter as one moves down the scale of being from brutes to plants to metals. Nature's language about God is clearer in the visible heavens than in mountains; it is more vocal about hell in the depths of the earth than in valleys.[20] The harmony of all the scales is Christ, God incarnated as master visible image toward whom all natural and historical images point and grand medium of all typological knowledge of God.[21] In his notes on the language, harmony, and scales of nature, Edwards hints at what he will develop in his treatises, *The Nature of True Virtue* and *The End for Which God Created the World*.

There is a considerable amount of didactic moralism in Edwards's notebook on "natural providences." He is reminiscent of those Puritans who believed that the visible world contained moral and religious "instructions" when he comments that the difficulty of climbing a hill is eased when we have a good prospect at the top, that young twigs readily bent warn of the malleability of youth, and that the clouds and darkness of affliction are necessary for holy humiliation.[22] Yet the notebook moves beyond this didactic approach in theory and in practice, toward that strain of Puritanism which drew a closer symbolic correlation between type and antitype. Edwards indicates his own dissatisfaction with didactic moralism and his aspiration for something higher when he writes that there is a difference between the world understood as "image" and the world taken as "signification." The latter is an illustration of meaning; the former is an evidence of the truth conveyed. "Christ often makes use of representations of spiritual things in the constitution of the [world] for argument, as thus: the tree is known by its fruit. These things are not merely mentioned as illustrations of his meaning, but as illustrations and evidences of the truth of what he says."[23] Edwards discovers in St. Paul the same encouragement to transcend mere illustration of meaning in typologizing: "The Apostle argues after such a manner from what is in the body of man to what should be in the mystical body of Christ or church of God [to] show that something further than meer illustration is intended: it shews that there is a real type or intended representation of the other."[24]

The aim of the true "type" or "image" is to re-present through itself a higher meaning, rather than simply to point toward that meaning. The intention of the image is to provide experiential participation in a truth, rather than moral enlightenment regarding that truth. Along with the didactic typologizing in his workbook on nature, Edwards experiments with this other form of shadowing. The very first image in the manuscript connotes something more than moral instruction:

> Death temporal is a shadow of eternal death. The agonies, the pains, the groans and gasps of death, the pale, horrid, ghastly appearance of the corps, its being laid in the dark and silent grave, there putrifying and rotting and becoming exceeding loathsome and being eaten with worms (Isa. 66:24), is an image of the misery of hell. And the body's continuing in the grave, and never rising more in this world, is to shadow forth the eternity of the misery of hell.[25]

In his published writings on spiritual perception Edwards delineated the mental activity which carries one beyond moral enlightenment into knowledge by participation. And in his most "affective" sermons he achieved what he toyed with—albeit in utmost seriousness—in his private notebook: an imagery designed to lead one into the beauties and the terrors, the comforts and the pains, of the natural, visible world in such a way that one partakes of the delights of heaven and the miseries of hell.

During the years 1734–35, the preaching of Jonathan Edwards was partly responsible for igniting the fires of a revival that spread through the Connecticut River Valley. Edwards had launched a career as a revivalist minister that would continue through the height of the Great Awakening of the 1740s. Edwards's private experiments with and meditations on images of divine things found a public forum in his awakening sermons. The sketches done in his study developed in his preaching into a full-blown art of sensational shadowing.

Edwards did not devote his preaching solely to the twin tasks of awakening sinners to their imminent eternal death and comforting them with promises of God's grace. Even during the Great Awakening years, when he urged people in all walks of life to do everything in their power to promote revivals, he preached a large number of sermons that were strictly instructional and ceremonial. He explained to his congregation the basic tenets of the Puritan faith, publicly examined the lives of his parishioners, and preached at funerals and at services of the sacraments. Furthermore, there is some evidence that after the waning of the excitement of the revivals of the Awakening, Edwards gave less attention to the composition of his sermons, and his preaching consequently suffered an increasing loss of artful imagery.[26] But during and immediately following those years of the revival that engulfed the whole of New England and touched every social class, Edwards perfected a style of hortatory discourse that sought both to win the intellect and to move the will.

Edwards shared with his Puritan forefathers a disdain for elaborate imagery, and he even distrusted concern for style itself. When he was sixteen years old, he drew up some rules on style for a projected work on natural science. They would be the rules for his preaching as well:

2. To give but few prefatorial admonitions about the style and method. It doth an author much hurt to show his concern in these things. . . .
4. Let much modesty be seen in the style. . . .
9. To be very moderate in the use of terms of art. Let it not look as if I was much *read*, or was conversant with books, or with the learned world.[27]

Modesty and plainness of style were adopted in order to avoid obstructing directness of contact between preacher and congregation, or between congregation and the grace of God which Edwards believed could operate through the words of the preacher. As Edwards said of his sermons which fired the revivals in Northampton in the 1730s, it was well for him to "neglect, forget, and despise such ornaments as politeness and modishness of style and method, when coming as a messenger from God to souls deeply impressed with a sense of their danger of God's everlasting wrath, to treat with them about their eternal salvation."[28] Whatever artful imagery he constructed, therefore, he hoped would not call attention to himself as an artist. It must briefly, plainly, and modestly direct the hearers to their impending doom and their hope for deliverance. With this in mind, Edwards carefully wrote out his revival sermons, following the conventional tripartite structure of clarification of the biblical text, delineation of the doctrine within the text, and application of text and doctrine to the experience of the auditors.

Edwards was critical of the wild, unintelligible outbursts of some of the revivalists in the Awakening. He maintained that not only should people's emotions be stirred, their understanding should be addressed as well. And his pulpit demeanor lacked the kind of personal fervor that marked the preaching of England's George Whitefield, whose junkets across the colonies were chiefly responsible for the earlier ripples of revivals turning into a flood in the early 1740s. One fellow minister described Edwards as "a preacher of a low and moderate voice, a natural way of delivery; and without any agitation of body, or anything else in the manner to excite attention; except his habitual and great solemnity, looking and speaking as in the presence of God, and with a weighty sense of the matter delivered."[29] Edwards's solemn presence and the weight of what he said had their effects, however—some of them unfortunate. According to Edwards's own testimony, toward the end of the revival period in his parish in 1735, a man "being in great spiritual trouble" was thrown into deep melancholy and unsuccessfully attempted suicide. Another, "an useful honorable person in the town"—this was Joseph Hawley, Edwards's uncle by marriage—was driven into despair over his spiritual state and took his own life by cutting his throat.[30] Events such as these were signs to Edwards that the Spirit of God had begun to withdraw from the revival and that Satan had been loosed. Yet he pointed to aspects of the revival which he felt its critics too quickly overlooked: young people reformed their ways; the Reformed doctrine of justification by faith was effectively affirmed over against the Arminian heresy; public praises of God were enlivened. The positive signs that the force moving in revival was the Spirit of God far outweighed the negative for Edwards. Furthermore, to insist that evangelical preaching was to be avoided because it leads to enthusiasm or because it reduces man to brute emotions was to misunderstand both the nature of man and the substance of the Christian religion. Man is not simply a reasonable creature; he is also will. The affections, man's "lively exercises of the will," are the springs of his existence. The fully developed human being, therefore, is not one who carefully suppresses his affections with his reason; he is, rather, one whose reason is affectionate and whose affections are intelligent. And it struck Edwards as patently obvious that at the heart of Christianity lay affections such as love and joy.[31]

Edwards had no reservations, then, about raising the affections of his hearers. If his sedate pulpit presence did not allow him to rant or even to lift his voice, it did not prevent him from appealing to the affections through other means—through his earnestness, through the sheer weight of his subject matter, and through the power of his imagery. So long as he was decorous, so long as he did not engage in emotional delivery simply for effect, Edwards could endorse in his own preaching a style pitched to the human emotions:

> An appearance of affection and earnestness in the manner of delivery, if it be very great indeed, yet if it be agreeable to the nature of the subject, and ben't beyond a proportion to its importance and worthiness of affection, and there be no appearance of its being feigned or forced, has so much the greater tendency to beget true ideas or apprehensions in the minds of the hearers, of the subject spoken of, and so to enlighten the understanding.[32]

Modesty and plainness of style, combined with earnest, affectionate delivery were the chief characteristics of Edwards's revivalist homiletics. No flowery imagery, no purple prose, no feigned emotions were to intervene to destroy the lean directness of the art form. The purpose of the sermon, after all, was not to entertain but to win the hearts of men to the truth of God. Edwards's father had stated the task in such a way that it must have impressed the son as a motto: "Let us labour in a very particular, convincing and awakening manner to dispense the Word of God; so to speak as tends to reach and pierce the Hearts and Consciences, and humble the Souls of them that hear us."[33] The son understood better than the father, however, that if elaborate, abstract imagery could not pierce the heart, pointed, concrete, sensational imagery could.

Edwards's preaching was "sensational" in a restricted meaning of that word. In its most artful form his preaching developed vivid images of the natural world as sense tokens of the spiritual. Edwards designed his images to renew for his hearers—and, indeed, for himself, as the pathos of his private notebooks makes clear—the sense experience of fire: the intense pain created in its contact with the body, the blinding brilliance of its flames, the roar of its consuming power. By imaginatively participating in the fires of experience, one could attain a proleptic, experiential understanding of the despairing agony of eternal death. And he sought to awaken his congregation to the wonders of the light of the sun: its startling illumination of a new world each day, its regenerating warmth during a cold New England winter, its dispensing of ominous shadows as clouds clear before the path of its rays. By imaginatively recalling the functions of the sun's light, one had an experiential base for comprehending Christ as the light of the world. What differentiated Edwards the revivalist preacher from so many extemporaneous exhorters of his day was his careful construction of sense images as avenues into the terrors of hell and the joys of heaven. And what clearly divided him from a later, nineteenth-century revivalism was his impatience with a moralism that simply urges men and women to "do good." He preferred to paint the Good in colors that invited a love of it. Edwards aimed at more than frightening men out of a hell of the future; he tried to give them in the present a foretaste of its frights. He intended to lure men to heaven not so much by pointing to its future rewards as by giving them a current vision of its excellency.

When Edwards bade farewell to his congregation after his dismissal from Northampton, he referred to his search for appropriate language and to his failure to move men adequately with that language:

> I have not only endeavoured to awaken you, that you might be moved with fear, but I have used my utmost endeavours to win you: I have sought out acceptable words, that if possible, I might prevail upon you to forsake sin, and turn to God, and accept of Christ as your Saviour and Lord. . . . But yet, with regard to you whom I am now speaking to, I have not been successful.[34]

Even during the gloriously successful years of the Awakening, Edwards knew—and his knowledge saved his farewell sermon to his contentious congregation from bitterness—that all of the sensational imagery at his disposal could not guarantee its successful penetration of men's hearts. The limitations of language, the nature of human intelligence, and the mystery of God's grace rendered trust in guarantees fatuous.

Edwards had learned from John Locke that "words have no natural connection with our ideas" and that "it is a difficult thing to find words to exhibit our own ideas."[35] Communication of one's ideas to the minds of others cannot be assured simply by sounding the words in an image. Communication inheres not in the power of the words themselves but in shared experiences. The limitations of language are especially apparent when one attempts to communicate what Locke called a "simple idea." In the Lockean scheme of things, the raw materials of thinking are supplied by observation of either sensible objects or the internal operations of our own minds. The materials so supplied are simple ideas (e.g. coldness, hardness, thinking, willing). Neither words nor wit, only sensation and internal reflection, can supply a simple idea. "He that thinks otherwise," Locke said, "let him try if any words can give him the taste of a pine apple, and make him have the true idea of the relish of that celebrated delicious fruit."[36] For Edwards faith was a simple idea. It was not a Lockean unit of experience derived from sense or internal reflection; it arose as a new perception from the Spirit of God residing in the human heart. But like Locke's simple idea, faith was firsthand, discrete, uncontrived knowledge, "as the sweet taste of honey is diverse from the ideas men get of honey by only looking on it, and feeling it."[37] Conveying to others images of a simple idea like faith could not provide them with the idea itself.

Edwards did move considerably beyond Locke's views of language and knowledge in his efforts to connect as closely as possible images and ideas and in his linking of the simple idea of faith with the human affections.[38] He decided to meet head-on the difficulty of finding words to exhibit ideas by dedicating himself to discovering images that "left naked"[39] the raw ideas of man's miserable state of sin and God's plan of deliverance. And he sought to safeguard the unity of the human subject by addressing his words to the affections as well as to the intellect. But such efforts could promise no real hearing of what he said. Edwards believed that ultimately only the power of God could give men ears to hear; only the mysterious, uncontrollable Spirit of God could soften human hearts to the impact of the images he used. If God refused to open men to the effects of Edwards's language, God had his own, concealed reasons; if He chose to make the language effective, that too was owing to his own reasons and not to the artistry of the preacher. "Grace is from God as immediately and directly as light is from the sun, and that notwithstanding the means that are improved, such as word, ordinances, etc.," Edwards wrote in one of his notebooks. "For though these [means] are made use of, yet they have no influence to produce grace either as causes or instruments . . . and yet they are concerned in the affair of the production of grace and are necessary in order to it."[40] Edwards engaged in his sensational shadowing with a set of assumptions that soon would be lost to American revivalists: that only God could convert men, that the art of rhetoric even at its best could prove fruitless, but that this was no cause for despair since God could, when he would, include the art in his plan of redemption. Without the slightest contradiction or pretension, therefore, Edwards could labor tirelessly to win his hearers to faith and still be genuinely surprised when a victory was won.

As Edwards told his congregation in his farewell address, his linguistic labors were bent toward awakening fear in them and winning them to better prospects. The dreadful pictures of the human condition and God's wrath which Edwards painted in his sermons borrowed heavily from the natural images of his private workbook. Pervading that famous sermon which Edwards preached so effectively at Enfield, Connecticut, and at other towns during the Awakening, "Sinners in the Hands of an Angry God," is the pull of the depths as a shadow of man's propensity to evil and destruction. Edwin Cady has estimated that, contrary to popular tradition, fire imagery in that sermon "amounts to little more than a quarter of the total figures." The fires of hell are at the periphery of the scene, not front and center. The focus is upon "the predicament of the sinner, how dreadfully he dangles *just before* he plunges to eternal agony."[41] The text for the sermon is Deut. 32:35, "Their foot shall slide in due time," a metaphor which would not escape New Englanders who must walk on icy paths. Edwards uses other emblems of suspension and heaviness: an insect suspended over a fire by a slender thread, men walking on a rotten covering stretched over a deep pit, dammed waters waiting to flood valleys. Figures of insect, gravity, and depth are merged in a most striking image:

> Your wickedness makes you as it were heavy as lead, and to tend downwards with great weight and pressure towards hell; and if God should let you go, you would immediately sink and swiftly descend and plunge into the bottomless gulf, and your healthy constitution, and your own care and prudence, and best contrivance, and all your righteousness, would have no more influence to uphold you and keep you out of hell, than a spider's web would have to stop a fallen rock.[42]

In many of Edwards's sermons, fire *is* the controlling image of man's imminent destruction. The following passage illustrates how Edwards could press the details of the consuming fires of an oven as experiential shadows of the fires of hell:

> But to help your conception, imagine yourself to be cast into a fiery oven, all of a glowing heat, or into the midst of a glowing brick kiln, or of a great furnace, where your pain would be as much greater than that occasioned by accidentally touching a coal of fire, as the heat is greater. Imagine also that your body were to lie there for a quarter of an hour, full of fire, as full within and without as a bright coal of fire, all the while full of quick sense; what horror would you feel at the entrance of such a furnace! And how long would that quarter of an hour seem to you! If it were to be measured by a glass, how long would that glass seem to be running! And after you had endured it for one minute, how overbearing would it be to you to think that you had it to endure the other fourteen! . . . O then, how would your heart sink, if you thought, if you knew, that you must bear it forever and ever![43]

The pattern of the horrible scene follows the track of typologizing: from beholding an oven and touching a hot coal (a common enough experience for eighteenth-century New Englanders) to eternal consumption by flame; from enduring intense pain a minute, then several minutes, to imagining the torment of constant, unrelieved pain. No pulpit antics could have possibly done justice to the sheer dread of these images. Edwards simply read his manuscript in deep earnestness and let the brutal power of the language find its mark, God willing.

The first entry in Edwards's notebook on nature is a treatment of "death temporal as a shadow of eternal death," and in his sermons, he often dwells on the deathbed scene. It is not the sentimental, moralistic spectacle of sinners repenting before they meet their Maker. Instead, Edwards recalls the details of bodily death that were all too familiar to men and women unprotected by modern medicine from frequent infant mortality and the unassuaged pains of dying or by modern hospitals from the dying patient himself. "The struggles, and groans, and gasps of the body when dying, its pale awful visage when dead" are for Edwards "faint shadows of the state of the soul under the second death." And the poisons of sin are to the spirit what the ravages of cancer are to the body: they "ripen" one for death. "We look upon persons far gone in a consumption, or with an incurable cancer, or some such malady, as in doleful circumstances. But that mortal disease, under whose power natural men are, makes their case a thousand times more doleful. That mortal disease of natural men, does, as it were, ripen them for damnation."[44]

Edwards preached some sermons directed strictly to the conscience of the sinner, casting shadows of man's sinful condition and impending doom unmatched by images of the state of salvation. Such sermons were explicitly "preparatory"; that is, they fell within the classical Puritan practice of softening human hearts through conviction, compunction, and humiliation before offering them the comforts of grace. Yet Edwards never understood his ministry simply as the task of terrifying human consciences. The chief responsibility of ministers, Edwards said in an ordination sermon, was "to be the instruments of leading souls to the God of all consolation . . . they are sent as Christ was . . . to preach good tidings to the meek, to bind up the broken hearted, to proclaim liberty to the captives . . . and to comfort all that mourn."[45] Edwards therefore usually followed his sermons of terror with sermons of comfort. He believed, further, that the highest form of humiliation before God sprang not from a state of terror but from having experienced the grace of God as rescue. "So that at the same time that God lifts up the soul with comfort, and joy, and inward sweetness, he casts it down with abasement. Evangelical and gracious humiliation and spiritual comfort are companions, which go one with the other, and keep company together."[46] In accord with this perspective, Edwards often linked images of the comforts of grace with shadows of the horrors of hell. The connection was made by way of contrast. Christ is a "stream of cool water" to those traveling in a parched world of sin; God is a "new light" breaking through clouds of despair, and his comfort is an overflowing fountain in comparison to the tiny streams of the world's enjoyments; salvation is a peaceful day that replaces the dark night of sin.[47]

Edwards's symbols of the joys of grace were conventional to the core; most he lifted directly out of Scripture. None was more conventional than his favorite, the image of light. Yet in his sustained metaphors of illumination, Edwards managed to empower what had become commonplace. His reading in Scripture and in Newton, together with his own sickbed experience of waiting for the morning, led him to find unusual imaginative potential in the light of the sun. He concluded, in fact, that the supremacy of light imagery was founded on a special analogical relation which God had established between two universes:

> There is an analogy between the divine constitution and disposition of things in the natural and in the spiritual world. The wise Creator has not left the natural world without light; but in this our solar system has set one great light, immensely exceeding all the rest, shining perpetually with a transcendent fulness and strength, to enlighten the whole; and he hath appointed other lesser, subordinate, or dependent lights, that shine with the communications and reflections of something of his brightness. So it is in the spiritual world; there God hath appointed Jesus Christ as a Sun of Righteousness: the church of God has not the sun to be her light by day; nor for brightness does the moon give light to her, but the Lord is her everlasting light, and her God her glory.[48]

Edwards would devote every effort to bringing into vivid expression the analogy between the two heliocentric universes. The illumination and warmth of the sun, the harmony of its colors and the play of its rays, were the major pathways through which he intended to lead his hearers into the light of the Sun of Righteousness. At the close of a particularly frightening imprecatory sermon, Edwards could hold out the promise of God as a light which opens the eyes of the blind, enlightens the whole soul, and illuminates a new world.[49] And in a sermon on the peace which Christ offers his followers, Edwards contemplated the tranquil, delicate light of day which is nonetheless brilliant and searching enough to lead one to see things as they really are. Such light can only torment those who prefer the darkness of evil:

> The peace that the people of Christ have, arises from their having their eyes open, and seeing things as they be. The more they consider, and the more they know of the truth and reality of things, the more they know what is true concerning themselves . . . the more they know of God. . . . The more their consciences are awakened and enlightened, and the brighter and the more searching the light is that they see things in, the more is their peace established: whereas, on the contrary, the peace that the men of the world have in their worldly enjoyments can subsist no otherwise than by their being kept in ignorance. . . . Their peace can live nowhere but in the dark. Light turns their ease into torment . . . whereas, the peace which Christ gives his true disciples, is the light of life, something of the tranquility of heaven, the peace of the celestial paradise, that has the glory of God to lighten it.[50]

The art of Jonathan Edwards's preaching was remarkably free of techniques. In fact, his only deliberately planned device for achieving the desired results of terrifying consciences and luring lost souls was the carefully wrought image, constructed to move men from the sense experience of nature to the spiritual knowledge of divine things. There was about his preaching none of the psychology of human engineering that would soon characterize American revivalism: no "anxious benches," pulpit performances, or advertising gimmicks. He even downgraded the artfulness of his art by insisting—and thoroughly believing—that his "means" of preaching had no power in itself to convert men to the sweet taste of God in Christ. How different an insistence was that of Charles G. Finney, who attributed the success of his nineteenth-century revivals solely to the "right use of the constituted means—as much so as any other effect produced by the application of means."[51] Edwards's use of sensational images in his preaching set him apart from another feature of later American revivalism: he sought not to bully human wills into submission but to set before persons symbols that captured their minds and thereby won them over. To be sure, he wanted to do more than store ideas or stimulate images. He desired to change wills and awaken affections. But his appeals to sinners took the route of the image leading through the thicket of inter-

mingled ideas, choices, and emotions. Nineteenth-century revivalists would take a more direct course: "Do, because you must."

Jonathan Edwards was more than an artful preacher. To say that
is not to denigrate what Edwards and his contemporaries considered the most noble and challenging of vocations. It is to suggest,
rather, that the mind of Edwards possessed a richer complexity than
his sensational sermons alone could embody. His revivalist preaching and work on his theological discourses were not hermetically
sealed compartments of his life; they flowed into and mutually
nourished each other. But he found that he had to turn to the
treatise, the essay, and the doctrinal sermon in order to gain the
precision of thought that lent substance to his imaginative preaching and that specified the grounds and meaning of the symbolic
imagination.

NOTES

1. This is not to say, of course, that Edwards published all of his private
reflections or even to deny what Stephen Stein has suggested: that in his
notebooks Edwards could engage in "a kind of theological play, for
amusement and relaxation." There is, however, no basis for Perry Miller's
claim that Edwards pursued in his notebook on nature something "deliberately veiled in the published works," *viz.* "a secret and sustained effort to
work out a new sense of the divinity of nature and the naturalness of
divinity." Stephen J. Stein, "Jonathan Edwards and the Rainbow: Biblical
Exegesis and Poetic Imagination," *The New England Quarterly*, 47, 3 (Sep-
tember 1974): 456. Perry Miller, "Introduction" to Edwards's *Images
or Shadows of Divine Things* (New Haven: Yale University Press, 1948),
pp. 2, 18.

2. *Images or Shadows of Divine Things*, p. 119.

3. Ibid., pp. 47, 49.

4. Ibid., pp. 43, 45, 75, 87, 94, 105.

5. See especially ibid., pp. 44, 45, 56, 58, 61–64, 87, 93.

6. Ibid., p. 88.

7. These observations on light and harmony are contained in another
unpublished item by Edwards, "The Beauty of the World," which Perry
Miller included in his edition of *Images or Shadows*, p. 136.

8. "Life of Edwards," WD, 1:61, 65.

9. Ibid., pp. 98–99.

10. See, for example, *Images or Shadows of Divine Things*, pp. 46, 75, 155.

11. Ibid., pp. 47, 49, 82–83, 85, 90, 93–94.

12. Ibid., pp. 47, 49, 57, 67, 70.

13. Ibid., pp. 97, 102.

14. Ibid., p. 127.

15. Ibid., pp. 48, 53–54. Perry Miller advanced the thesis in his "Introduction" to *Images or Shadows*, pp. 28–29, 36, that Edwards exalted nature to a level coequal with scriptural revelation and quoted Scripture to confirm an independent natural revelation. Mason Lowance follows closely on Miller when he insists that Edwards believed nature to have "equal value to scriptural revelation." Lowance, " 'Images or Shadows of Divine Things' in the Thought of Jonathan Edwards," *Typology and Early American Literature,* ed. Sacvan Bercovitch (Amherst: University of Massachusetts Press, 1972), pp. 222, 236. My argument is directed against these claims.

16. *Images or Shadows of Divine Things*, pp. 69–70.

17. Ibid., p. 109.

18. Ibid., p. 61.

19. Ibid., p. 44.

20. Ibid., pp. 84–85.

21. Ibid., pp. 77, 79. Cf. Edwards's "Miscellanies" (MS. in Yale Beinecke Library), entry 777.

22. *Images or Shadows of Divine Things,* pp. 43, 49, 50, 83.

23. Ibid., pp. 48–49.

24. Ibid., p. 98.

25. Ibid., p. 43.

26. Wilson H. Kimnach, "The Brazen Trumpet: Jonathan Edwards' Conception of the Sermon," *Jonathan Edwards: His Life and Influence,* ed. Charles Angoff (Rutherford, N.J.: Fairleigh Dickinson University Press, 1975), pp. 41, 43.

27. "Notes on Natural Science," WD, 1:702–3.

28. Preface to "Five Discourses on Important Subjects," WD, 5:349.

29. Cited by C. C. Goen in his "Introduction" to *The Great Awakening,* WY (1972), p. 72.

30. "A Faithful Narrative of the Surprising Work of God," ibid., pp. 205–7.

31. Edwards's first extensive effort to discern and test the spirits in revivalism was his "Distinguishing Marks of a Work of the Spirit of God," ibid., pp. 226–88. His mature effort, in the context of a discussion of the nature of man and Christianity, was his *Treatise Concerning Religious Affections,* WY (1959).

32. "Some Thoughts Concerning the Present Revival of Religion in New England," *The Great Awakening,* WY, p. 387.

33. Quoted by Wilson Kimnach, "The Brazen Trumpet," p. 33.

34. "Farewell Sermon," WD, 1:645.

35. John Locke, *An Essay Concerning Human Understanding,* ed. A. C. Fraser (New York: Dover Publications, 1959) 2:105. "Observations Concerning Faith," WW, 2:611.

36. Locke, *Human Understanding,* 1:121–24, 145; 2:37.

37. *Religious Affections,* WY, p. 206.

38. For a suggestive analysis of Edwards's dependence on and departures from Locke's sensational psychology, see Perry Miller, "The Rhetoric of Sensation," *Errand into the Wilderness* (Cambridge: Belknap Press of Harvard University Press, 1956), pp. 167–83.

39. "Notes on Natural Science," WD, 1:702.

40. "Miscellanies," (MS. in Yale Beinecke Library), entry 539.

41. Edwin H. Cady, "The Artistry of Jonathan Edwards," *The New England Quarterly*, 22 (1949):69.

42. "Sinners in the Hands of an Angry God," *Jonathan Edwards: Representative Selections*, ed. C. H. Faust & T. H. Johnson (New York: Hill & Wang, 1962), p. 162. Cf. "Natural Men in a Dreadful Condition," WD, 8:9–10, 24.

43. "The Future Punishment of the Wicked Unavoidable and Intolerable," *Representative Selections*, pp. 146–47, 151–52. Cf. "Sinners in Zion Tenderly Warned," WD, 6:449–50; "The Eternity of Hell Torments," WD, 6:107ff.; and an unpublished sermon on Luke 16:24 (MS. in Yale Beinecke Library).

44. "Natural Men in a Dreadful Condition," WD, 8:18, 21–22. Cf. "The Future Punishment of the Wicked," *Representative Selections*, p. 146.

45. "The True Excellency of a Gospel Minister," WD, 8:443.

46. "Hope and Comfort Usually Follow Genuine Humiliation and Repentance," WD, 8:96.

47. See "Hope and Comfort," WD, 8:89; "The Christian Pilgrim" and "The Peace Which Christ Gives His True Followers," *Representative Selections*, pp. 131, 137–38; sermon on John 15:5 (MS. in Yale Beinecke Library).

48. "True Excellency of a Minister," WD, 8:442.

49. "Natural Men in a Dreadful Condition," WD, 8:43.

50. "The Peace Which Christ Gives," *Representative Selections*, pp. 138–39.

51. Charles G. Finney, *Lectures on Revivals of Religion*, rev. ed. (Oberlin, Ohio: E. J. Goodrich, 1868), p. 12.

3

Being, Beauty,
and Spiritual Knowledge

Edwards employed the words "nature" and "natural" in different ways in different contexts. In his defense of the Augustinian-Calvinist view of justification by grace through faith and its complementary doctrine of original sin, nature referred to those human powers, principles, and states which every person inherits at birth: understanding, will, affections, conscience, self-love, alienation from God.[1] In his treatise on the meaning of the will, nature stood both for the identifying essence of a thing (as in "the nature of the will is the act of choosing") and for the extramoral factors which impinge upon human decisions (such as bodily illness and the law of gravity).[2] In his discussions of how faith and salvation are united, Edwards said that the union is "natural" rather than "moral"; that is, faith and salvation belong together because of their "agreeableness" with each other, not because faith earns or causes salvation.[3] And in his examination of true virtue, "natural" signified what in creation lacks the qualities of mind and heart as well as what is instinctual in man.[4]

These various meanings of "nature" and "natural" are collected into a single perspective in Edwards's view of the being and beauty of the cosmos. The world owes its origin and its continued existence to the communicative nature (essence) of God, and its capacity for imaging divine things springs from the design of the Creator. Man transcends nature as the realm of the instinctual and extramoral through his intellect and will; those same faculties install him at a superior level in the creation's shadowing of divine things. Human virtue is a form of beauty, but it is a beauty that man does not have naturally or as a birthright; it requires the infusion of divine grace.

45

In some youthful observations on the meaning of being, Edwards defended the priority of mind to matter: "The existence of the whole material Universe is absolutely dependent on Idea." It was inconceivable to Edwards that anything could have existence and not have a consciousness mindful of it. "Nothing has any existence anywhere else but in Consciousness, no certainly nowhere else but either in created or uncreated Consciousness." Neither the materiality of things in the world nor a human sense which renders them outward objects establishes the existence of things. Only ideas of things give them their status in being. Qualities such as color or shape, which we may out of habit attribute to things in themselves, are no more *in* the things than pain is in a needle; they are "strictly nowhere else but in the mind." Edwards concluded from all this that the ontological truism that there is something rather than nothing argues for the "Eternal Existence of an All-comprehending Mind." Furthermore, it is not only the case that beings possessed of consciousness are superior to those lacking it; they are the only beings of substance: "Those beings which have knowledge and Consciousness are the only proper and real and substantial beings, inasmuch as the being of other things is only by these. From hence we may see the gross mistake of those who think material things the most substantial beings and spirits more like a shadow, whereas spirits only are properly substance."[5] Edwards never pursued all of the ramifications of his fragmentary idealism, but a number of his youthful observations, most likely inspired by an early reading of Locke and Newton, shaped his mature view of the being of the world. According to that perspective, an understanding of the world requires movement beyond the dictates of common sense, every entity in Creation has its continuity from one moment to the next solely by virtue of the mind of God, and the physical universe both "is" and "means" only as it is imaged by minds.

Reason, despite its many limitations, can arrive at plausible, even demonstrable, truths regarding the cosmos. But in doing so, it must surpass the premises of common sense. Common sense, understood not as the common rules of reasoning (such as the laws of contradiction and agreement), of which Edwards was an avid defender, but as the common inclinations and assumptions of men based on sense perceptions, is a truncated version of human intelligence. Reliance on such common sense leads one to protest any claim that cannot be verified directly by sense experience. Edwards approvingly quotes Andrew Ramsay's *Philosophical Principles of Natural and Revealed Religion* on this point: "It is . . . a fundamental maxim in all true philosophy, that many things may be incomprehensible, and yet demonstrable; that though seeing clearly be a sufficient reason for affirming, yet, not seeing at all, can never be a reason for denying."[6] Even the clarity of an idea based on its strict adherence to a concrete object is not itself an ultimate test of reason's operations. Mathematics is proof of this to Edwards: " 'Tis not necessary that persons should have clear ideas of the things that are the subject of a proposition, in order to being rationally convinced of the truth of the proposition. There are many truths of which mathematicians are convinced by strict demonstration, concerning many kinds of quantities, as surd quantities and fluxions, concerning which they have no clear ideas."[7] Both limitations and advantages are inherent in demonstrating without seeing. Limitations are transparent in an intelligence which can "hold" a truth without "having" it as a clear idea: the truth is less than entirely one's own, though one may easily overlook that fact. The advantages are not to be denied, however. For one may demonstrate that an Eternal Mind is required for the existence of the world without "seeing" or "having" the Eternal Mind as such. One may demonstrate the truth of the proposition that the beauty of the physical universe is dependent on human beauty, though that demonstration is not a lesson of common sense. To put the intelligence to work on nature in order to determine the status of its images involves more than inferring directly off the senses; it entails penetrating to the laws and relations of the parts of nature. As Edwards said in his treatise on virtue, one may be pleased by the harmony in a tune "and yet know nothing of that proportion or adjustment of the notes which by the law of nature is the ground of the melody."[8] The human mind can probe for the law that is the ground of harmony's appeal to the senses.

Through such probing Edwards believed that he could show that the whole of creation would be a throng of disconnected and discontinuous moments apart from the agency of God who transcends in intelligence and power the being of the world: " 'Tis certain with me that the world exists anew every moment, that the existence of things every moment ceases and is every moment renewed."[9] According to common sense, an object—say, the moon—"is" now as it "was" a moment earlier, does not cease to be between the two moments, and seems to have its present being from its past. Reason leads us beyond these impressions, however, to the knowledge that "no cause can produce effects in a *time* and *place* in which itself is *not*. . . . The moon's past existence was neither *where* nor *when* its present existence is. In point of time, what is *past* entirely ceases, when *present* existence begins; otherwise it would not be *past*. . . . Nor could the past existence of the particles of this *moving body* produce effects in any *other place* than where it then was." These reflections move Edwards to conclude that all objects are maintained in existence from moment to moment by the creative power of God, and that this divine act is equivalent "to his creating those things out of nothing at *each moment* of their existence."[10] Edwards knew the shortcomings of his version of the proof for God from contingency: its evidence was not built upon a "simple idea" of God. Yet the demonstration could render reasonable what was hidden from common sense, what was proclaimed with clarity in Scripture, and what faith's "simple idea" could establish in the depths of the heart: God alone gives the world its existence from moment to moment.

Reason can discover another truth about God: his relation to the world is one of spirit. The greatness of God, his transcendence over and omnipotent acting upon the world, is analogous to man's "greatness of soul." It is an immensity of spirit:

> The greatness of a soul consists not in any extension, but its comprehensiveness of idea and extendedness of operation. So the infiniteness of God consists in His perfect comprehension of all things and the extendedness of His operation equally to all places. God is present nowhere any otherwise than the soul is in the body or brain; and He is present everywhere, as the soul is in the body. We ought to conceive of God as being omnipotence, perfect knowledge, and perfect love, and not extended any otherwise than as power, knowledge, and love are extended, and not as if it were a sort of unknown thing we call substance, that is extended.[11]

The infinite mind of God is the metaphysical foundation for nature's role as image. The whole of creation has its origin from a God who is "a communicating being,"[12] and the creation is the language of God as Spirit. "It is very fit and becoming of God, who is infinitely wise, so to order things that there should be a voice of

His in His works. . . . The works of God are but a kind of voice or language of God to instruct intelligent beings in things pertaining to Himself."[13] The Creator communicates himself through his world neither out of some inner compulsion nor because something outside of him requires it; rather, he freely and unconditionally determines to express himself in the language of creation.[14] In the terms of Edwards's posthumously published essay on the topic, *God's ultimate end in his creation of the world is himself.* Both reason and scriptural revelation establish God himself as the end of creation. Reason can affirm as God only the greatest and best of beings. But if such a being adopted a lesser end than himself in his creation, he would not make the best choice; he would choose something less than the highest good. Scripture proclaims the purpose of both creation and redemption to be the manifestation of God's "glory," which is none other than the weight, perfection, or greatness of God's own internal life.

The relation between God and his language is one of emanation and remanation. The world is an emanation of God's fulness *ad extra,* God's outward communication of himself. But the creation is a language that speaks back to God as well; it is a remanation back to him of his glory. "So that the whole is *of* God, and *in* God, and *to* God, and God is the beginning, middle and end in this affair."[15] Edwards uses a number of metaphors to express this relationship. Wheels of a machine working together for one purpose typify the parts of the cosmos serving the single end of God's glory. Waters in a stream drawing their existence from their source image the world as an emanation of God. A tree putting forth leaves and fruit is a shadow of God's external exhibition of his nature.[16] It is the imagery of light, however, that best serves Edwards here. In Edwards's judgment, it is no accident that Scripture so often compares God's glory to a refulgence of light, for light "is the external expression, exhibition and manifestation of the excellency of the luminary, of the sun for instance. . . . It is by this that the sun itself is seen, and his glory beheld, and all other things are discovered." The image of light best captures the manner in which the things of creation are beautiful solely by virtue of their Creator: "It is by a participation of this communication from the sun, that surrounding objects receive all their lustre, beauty and brightness." And light best signifies the creation's reflection of God's glory back to him: "The refulgence shines upon and into the creature, and is reflected back to the luminary. The beams of glory come from God, or are something of God, and are refunded back again to their original."[17]

All parts of the created world are by no means of equal status in the emanation/remanation scheme, however. Creatures of intellect and will occupy the top echelon on a scale of being; apart from their minds the remainder of creation neither exhibits nor reflects the divine fullness. Arthur O. Lovejoy has said that the eighteenth-century thinker, fascinated by the concept of a chain of being, typically held that each link in the chain had its own integrity and that the "lower creatures" did not exist solely for man. When connections along the chain were made, they were usually downward, stressing man's proclivity toward the lower creatures.[18] If this is the case, Edwards was atypical for his time. He adopted the more traditional claim that although man is an end inferior to God's own glory in the creation, he is nonetheless a created end for the remainder of created beings. Man's moral capacity, his ability to make rational decisions and act on them, is one factor that grants him this role:

> It is evident, from the constitution of the world itself, as well as from the word of God, that the moral part is the end of all the rest of the creation. The inanimate unintelligent part is made for the rational as much as a house is prepared for the inhabitant. . . . But it is further evident that whatsoever is the last end of that part of creation is the end of all the rest, and for which all the rest of the world was made, must be the last end of the whole.[19]

The idealism of Edwards's view of reality also figured into his elevation of the human on the scale of being: "If the world is not conscious of its being, it had as good not be as be." So the conscious portion of creation, which is the creation's consciousness of itself, becomes the means through which the mind of God bestows reality upon the world.[20]

The status of man's knowing and symboling God through nature can now be located within the total scope of being. First of all, all creaturely knowledge is itself an image of God; it is an emanation of God's own self-knowledge out of himself and a return of his knowledge to himself: "This knowledge in the creature, is but a conformity to God. It is the image of God's own knowledge of himself. It is a participation of the same . . . as the particular beams of the sun communicated, are the light and glory of the sun in part."[21] Second, man's knowledge of God is imaginative or symbolic in that he has no direct access to the interior being of God. He knows God only through the images of the world, only through the "words" of nature and history, which are words in the divine language: "Jesus Christ is admitted to know God immediately, but the knowledge of all other creatures in heaven and earth is by means or by manifestations or signs held forth."[22] Third, the physical universe is an image of an image, a reflection of the conscious creature's reflection of God. Those portions of creation lacking mind, or the twin faculties of intellect and will, gain their being and meaning from human consciousness, which is itself an image of the consciousness of God. Nature is subordinate to history; unintelligent creation exists in a relation of dependence to the intelligence which moves human affairs. Edwards did not intend to belittle the symbolic power of the physical world by "scaling it down"; he desired only to point to what was even more powerful as a symbol—the human mind. The majesty of outer space and its harmonies Edwards found quite overwhelming, but even more spectacular was the inner space of man which is shadowed by the outer:

> When we think of the sweet harmony of the parts of the corporeal world, it fills us with such astonishment that the soul is ready to break. Yet take all that infinite variety of sweet proportions, harmonious motions, and delightful correspondencies that are in this whole company of bodies, and they are all but shadows of excellency in comparison of those beauties and harmonies that may be in our finite spirits.[23]

Students of Edwards's ontology have remarked upon the Neoplatonic cast of his scheme of creation. The monism implied in a vision of created being as a flow out of God himself which then returns to the Godhead would seem to compromise if not directly contradict Edwards's professed Calvinism which maintains a qualitative gulf between the Creator and his creation.[24] It is clear that Edwards's thinking was influenced by the Platonism of the "Cambridge School," and his ontology is reminiscent of Plotinus's notions of the flow of the many out of the One.[25] It is also true that Edwards's essay on creation fails to unravel such puzzles as the relation between emanation and the Fall, or the difference between God as "Highest Being" and God as "Being in General."[26] At a number of points, however, Edwards enters caveats that indicate his desire to avoid all charges of pantheism.

First, Edwards draws a distinction between God's *being* and God's *glory* and submits that the latter, not the former, is the end of creation: "It is evident that God does not make his existence or being the end of the creation; nor can he be supposed to do so without great absurdity. His being and existence cannot be conceived of but as prior to any of God's acts or designs; they must be presupposed as the ground of them."[27] God himself flows out as the end of creation, but the flow is the interior character of God, not the being of God. The qualities of excellence which constitute God's glory—his knowledge, love, and power—are reflected in the world, but not his being, which is from itself alone. Furthermore, God *gains nothing* in being or in glory from the creation, any more than the sun gains anything from its reflected rays. God is perfect quite apart from his creation, and this establishes the difference between independent Creator and dependent creature: "The notion of God's creating the world in order to receive any thing properly from the creature, is not only contrary to the nature of God, but inconsistent with the notion of creation; which implies a being's receiving its existence, and all that belongs to its being, out of nothing. And this implies the most perfect, absolute, and universal derivation and dependence."[28] Finally, the conformity between God and intelligent beings is by way of participation, not by way of identity. The being and excellency of the creature do not merge into the being and excellency of God; rather, the intelligent creature "partakes" of God's glory, as a jewel partakes of the light of the sun. Or, as Edwards also puts it, the union is one of "interest": God and man become as one when man adopts God's end as his own, just as "the interest of a man's family is looked upon as the same with his own interest."[29] And although Edwards believes that it is God's intention to bring the creature's purposes into increasing conformity with his own, "there never will be any particular time, when it can be said already to have come to such a height."[30] Edwards left unsolved a number of problems in his metaphysic, but he clearly did not want to suggest that nature and history are essentially undifferentiated from the divine life.

Beauty, as well as being, is scaled in Edwards's perspective. The beauty of the natural world is an image of a higher beauty, human virtue. Edwards's *Nature of True Virtue,* the companion treatise to his treatment of creation, sets the question of human morality within a discussion of beauty, beauty representing the "first principle" or cardinal characteristic of being.[31] Moral beauty is the chief quality of essential human being, and cosmic beauty, a reflection of the former, is the chief quality of the being of the material world.

Beauty is harmony, the consent or fitness of things to one another. *Primary or moral beauty,* which is virtue, is *cordial consent,* a consent on the part of a being possessed of intellect and will to other beings possessed of intellect and will. *Secondary beauty,* which Edwards designates "natural," involves no union of mind with mind, heart with heart. Primary beauty "most essentially consists in benevolence to Being in general. Or perhaps to speak more accurately, it is that consent, propensity and union of heart to Being in general, that is immediately exercised in a general good will." But Being in general, the object of benevolence, is not all beings; it is *"intelligent* Being in general. Not inanimate things, or Beings that have no perception or will, which are not properly capable objects of benevolence."[32] Natural beauty is outward, secondary, and a mere shadow of cordial consent; it "is not peculiar to spiritual Beings, but is found even in inanimate things; which consists in a mutual consent and agreement of different things in form, manner, quantity, and visible end or design; called by the various names of regularity, order, uniformity, symmetry, proportion, harmony, etc." The agreement of the sides of a regular polygon, the harmony of a tune, and the order of a well-regulated, just society are illustrations of secondary beauty.[33]

As in his scale of being, in the scale of beauty Edwards intends no rejection of the imaginative value of the physical universe. It is beautiful indeed, possessing "sweet mutual consents, either within itself or with the supreme being,"[34] and its harmonies betoken the cordial consents of the finite and infinite minds. Yet apart from mind, there is no beauty in nature. In refusing to include nonintelligent beings as objects of primary beauty, Edwards does not relieve man of the responsibility of caring for the mindless world. The benevolent person "will seek the good of every *individual* Being unless it be conceived as not consistent with the highest good of Being in general," and he operates from a disposition of "general good will" toward the whole of being.[35] Yet primary beauty itself is cordial consent, the agreement of mind with mind, heart with heart, and its principal object is God. The physical world remains in Edwards's aesthetic, as in his metaphysic, an image of an image.

The world is beautiful to the extent that it reflects the beauty of human virtue, and human virtue is beautiful insofar as it reflects the benevolence of God. Such is the essential nature of things. Edwards never tired of saying, however, that human virtue is no simple possibility available to all men and that the essential nature of things has gone awry. The finite creature does not become virtuous by his own moral acts; virtue arises from the infusion of God's grace. Sin has added a loud discordant note to the inner harmony of man and the outer regularity of the universe. Men require more than reason, and more than imagination, to arrive at that state of being in which mirror reflects mirror, outer harmony reflects cordial consent. They require "spiritual knowledge" properly to discern images of divine things within themselves and in their world. That knowledge springs not from the light of nature, not from things as they are, but from the light of the Sun of Righteousness, from the light that restores things to what they should be. Edwards's view of virtue as harmonious beauty had many similarities with the Deist versions of morality in his day. But in contending that the light of nature is not light enough, he parted company with the Deists: "The light of nature teaches that religion which is necessary to continue in the favour of the God that made us: but it cannot teach us that religion which is necessary to our being restored to the favour of God after we have forfeited it."[36] Full religious understanding of nature's images requires God's converting light.

Conversion. Repentance. Ecstasy. How easily the words slide from the lips of those who have been overwhelmed by outpourings of religious revival. How difficult it is to tell whether they describe a deep, abiding transformation in the lives of their users or merely a passing emotion. And how readily the outer-directed experience to which the words attest turns into an inner-directed subjectivism, the "standing outside oneself" of ecstasy becoming a preoccupation with involutions of one's private experiences. Jonathan Edwards, vigorous apologist of revivalism though he was, had a nose for the counterfeits of religious enthusiasm and an abhorrence for sanctimonious absorption in private experiences. He knew from his own "struggles of spirit" that religious emotions could be so fleeting that they left the course of one's life unaltered, and conversions in his own parish proved that some lifechanges were at best "conditional."[37] He also found in his own life, and in Scripture, the distinction between "believing," which involves pitching one's life in trust and hope upon the grace of an all-powerful God, and "believing that you believe," which is a second order awareness that may not always accompany believing. One could be a believer and still doubt, and the assurance which relieved doubt was to be had more through action than through self-examination, more by "pressing toward the mark for the prize" than by scrupulous study of one's inner experiences.[38] So Edwards interjected into his analysis of religious experience a healthy dose of skepticism. In sermon after sermon, in treatise after treatise, he labored to produce tests which would help each person discover for himself whether his religious affections were genuine or fake, born of the Spirit of God or products of the "natural imagination." Edwards would not pretend to know another's heart: everyone must apply the tests to his own life. And he would not prescribe a series of fixed steps in which one must be converted—the work of the Spirit of God cannot be schematized. Yet Scripture demands that we "try the spirits whether they are of God," so analysis, as well as revivalist preaching, was a responsibility of the minister; and wonder, as well as profession of conversion, was a mandate to the believer.

Nonetheless, Edwards was a proponent of the necessity of conversion. He advanced his tests fully convinced that lives could cease to skate thoughtlessly across the surface of existence, that they could be turned around, redirected, and pulled beyond a posturing self-importance. Persons close to him had proved the authenticity of conversion to an abiding religious faith. His wife Sarah underwent a conversion during the Awakening that bred no wild emotions, private revelations, or suicidal melancholic states. Her life simply took on a new shape: a "sweet solace, rest and joy of soul," a "lively sense of the infinite beauty of Christ's person" together with an awesome "sense of the greatness and majesty of God," a steadfastness of faith when surrounded by pain and death, and "a particular dislike of placing religion much in dress."[39] Edwards found in David Brainerd (a missionary to the Indians who died in the arms of Edwards's daughter Jerusha) a person given to depression but still possessed of a religion deeper than his psychological states: "His religion was not like a blazing meteor, or like a flaming comet flying through the firmament with a bright train, and then quickly departing into perfect darkness; but more like the steady lights of heaven, constant principles of light, though sometimes hid with clouds."[40] And, of course, Edwards recorded in his "Narrative" that after much struggle he himself arrived at a "new sense" that did not exclude doubts but did reach abidingly into the center of his being and transform the appearance of everything.

A new seeing was the consequence of authentic conversion; new perspectives emerged from alterations of the heart. Henceforth the physical universe could be more than a sign; it could be a symbol. It could become more than a means of knowing *about* God; it could be a means of *knowing* him, of participating in him. The new knowledge was not produced by reason itself, not even by the kind which escapes the myopia of common sense. It was a knowledge given only to the spiritual perceptions of faith. Such knowledge, in fact, was for Edwards a crucial test of the authenticity of religious conversion.

In 1734, long before the Great Awakening had swept through the whole of New England, Edwards explained to his Northampton congregation that the spiritual knowledge of faith is a kind of illumination altogether different from the light of the "natural imagination." Spiritual knowledge "is no impression upon the mind, as though one saw any thing with the bodily eyes," Edwards said in his sermon *A Divine and Supernatural Light*. "It is no imagination or idea of an outward light or glory, or any beauty of form or countenance, or a visible lustre or brightness of any object." Although the spiritual light may, as an accidental consequence, awaken such imaginings, its proper work is something else. It is an illumination provided by the Spirit of God who "acts in the mind of a saint as an indwelling vital principle"; it is not an external light which produces objects absent in space and time. It is an inward light which attaches itself as a new principle to the human faculties of intellect and will; it is not itself a new faculty. It "gives a due apprehension of those things that are taught in the word of God"; it is not a source of new, private revelations.[41]

The distinction between natural imagination and spiritual illumination reappeared in Edwards's *Treatise Concerning Religious Affections*, his major attempt to "try the spirits" of the revivals of the 1740s. There he held that a product of the imagination, a mental image "of some external thing in the mind, when that thing is not present in reality," originates in man's animal or bodily spirits. It is also the means through which the power of evil can work as effectively as the power of God. Above all, imagination leaves man's sinful nature unchanged. Spiritual illumination, on the other hand, is "supernatural": its origin is God, whose operation is "altogether of a different kind from anything that men find within themselves by nature, or only in the exercise of natural principles."[42]

The obstacle to spiritual knowledge, the factor which divides natural imagination from spiritual illumination, is sin. "Sin," quite as much as "conversion," becomes hackneyed in its usage in revivalist religion, pointing more toward acts of wrongdoing than to a desperate human condition. It was such a usage that Edwards detected among an Arminianism growing by leaps and bounds in England and New England. In defending the power of man to make some contribution to his own salvation, Arminianism undermines the power of original sin. But sin, Edwards said in his treatise attacking John Taylor's Arminian interpretation of the doctrine, is more than a series of immoral acts and more than a slight blemish of character; it is a state of life that makes men incapable of achieving true virtue. Every person's fallenness causes his spiritual seeing to be founded on the principle of self-interest rather than on the principle of non-self-seeking benevolence. The consequence of the Fall, a consequence that extends from Adam to all his heirs because of the continuity of identity which God maintains between moments of the creation, is the loss of the superior, supernatural principle of benevolence and the retention of the natural principle of self-love.[43] Now the human faculties of intellect and will, though not destroyed by the Fall, function without benefit of truly virtuous intentions. In short, the whole of man's being is pervaded by the power of sin: "The *understanding* is under the reigning power of this enmity against God, so that it is entirely darkened and blinded with regard to the glory and excellency of God. The *will* is wholly under the reigning power of it," so that unconverted man can choose only the idols of self or creation as his highest good.[44]

The Fall has affected the entire system of creation, turning it from an harmonious structure that gains divine symbolic meaning from man's intellect and will, into a chaotic swarm of idols arising from man's self-love.[45] Sin misdirects the human eye from superior to inferior beauty. Essential manhood would keep the priorities straight:

> Now the rectitude of human nature and of rational beings most certainly is that they should be most highly affected with the highest excellencies. . . . that the things that are most beautiful and amiable, as soon as ever they are seen, should most delight the eye, and those things which are less beautiful should less please the sight.

As a consequence of the Fall, however, the aesthetic priorities are reversed:

> We are the highest species with the lowest excellencies. We have the easiest and greatest delight in things that in themselves are least delightful. Things that are less beautiful and amiable in themselves strike much quicker and deeper with the sense and proportion and constitution of the mind than things that have in themselves the highest excellence, most charming beauty, and exquisite sweetness.[46]

Fallen perceptions do have their fortunate side, however: the miserable relish of the wrong things can provide a contrast to faith's taste of true excellency. "Man's sin and misery is made an occasion of his greater happiness, as he has now a greater relish of happiness, by reason of his knowledge of both. In order to happiness there must be two things, *viz.* union to a proper object—and a relish of the object. Man's misery is made an occasion of increasing both these by the work of redemption."[47] The tragedy of the Fall, seen from the vantage point of redemption, is a movement out of naive innocence into a state that provides the necessary bitter contrasts for appreciating the exquisite sweetness experienced in faith. Only grace, however, only the undeserved, unearned power of God's redemption can restore to man the supernatural principle of benevolence and redirect him to the primary beauty of the world.

The new sense that arises from grace is *new* both in *how* it knows and in *what* it knows. Spiritual perception is new in its manner of knowing because it is a wisdom of the heart. The illumination provided by God's Spirit strikes to the center of the human self and supplies a new foundation of knowing. No new faculties are implanted in the self, but now the intellect is employed in a new way, it functions on a different base: "The Spirit of God is given to the true saints to dwell in them, as his proper lasting abode; and to influence their hearts, as a principle of new nature, or as a divine supernatural spring of life and action . . . so united to the faculties of the soul, that he becomes there a principle or spring of new nature and life."[48] Now one does not simply know *about* God; he knows God firsthand: "He does not merely rationally believe that God is glorious, but he has a sense of the gloriousness of God in his heart. . . . There is not only a speculatively judging that God is gracious, but a sense how amiable God is upon that account, or a sense of the beauty of this divine attribute."[49] The manner of knowing in spiritual knowledge is the direct apprehension of a "simple idea" and a commitment of will to the truth of that idea.[50]

Edwards does not suggest, however, that this manner of perception excludes or replaces other rational activities. Although the sense of the heart differs from speculative understanding, it can aid the latter in two ways: "As the prejudices that are in the heart, against the truth of divine things, are hereby removed" by spiritual illumination, "the mind becomes susceptive of the due force of rational arguments for their truth." And spiritual knowledge "makes even the speculative notions the more lively" by engaging "the attention of the mind, with the more fixedness and intenseness to that kind of objects."[51] In a sermon on Christian knowledge, Edwards urged his hearers not to let their piety lead to the abandonment of the acquisition of knowledge: "The faculty by which we are chiefly distinguished from the brutes, is the faculty of understanding. It follows then, that we should make it our chief business to improve this faculty. . . . But we cannot make a business of the improvement of our intellectual faculty, any otherwise than by making a business of improving ourselves in actual knowledge."[52] And over against the extremists of the revivals who reduced religion to emotions devoid of intellectual substance, Edwards took the position that *religion is knowledge.* Although true religion is not the holding of complex notions, is not speculative understanding, it is an act of the intellect which grasps the truth of a simple idea. The converted man is a knower; the heat of his affections is intimately joined with the light of his knowledge.[53]

The chief *content* of spiritual knowledge is the beauty of God's holiness. "The beauty of holiness is that thing in spiritual and divine things, which is perceived by this spiritual sense, that is so diverse from all that natural men perceive in them: this kind of beauty is the quality that is the immediate object of this spiritual sense: this is the sweetness that is the proper object of this spiritual taste."[54] In everything that the spiritual knower beholds, the holiness of God may appear. That holiness is none other than God's "purity and beauty as a moral agent, comprehending all his moral perfections, his righteousness, faithfulness and goodness."[55] God's holiness can be known because he abides in the knower as *holy* Spirit. Like knows like, "for nothing can be more agreeable to any nature than itself; holy nature must be above all things agreeable to holy nature; and so the holy nature of God and Christ, and the Word of God, and other divine things, must be above all other things, agreeable to the holy nature that is in the saints."[56] Knowledge of holiness springing from the holy principle within the self is, however, less than perfect knowledge. The human agent is not divested of his finite creaturehood, nor are the full effects of sin completely destroyed. The knower is not "Godded with God" or "Christed with Christ"; instead, he is a "partaker of God's fulness ... according to the measure and capacity of a creature."[57] The limitations of finitude and the remaining propensity to sin in the spiritual knower mean that he "sees the glory of God but by a reflected light."[58]

Despite the imperfections of spiritual knowledge, it is the one alternative to the misperceptions of the natural imagination. Both the manner and the content of the new knowing transform one's world. Knowledge of God through his images becomes participatory knowledge: it is a participation in the holy beauty of God's light which shines into the self and through natural and historical symbols. Participation differentiates the spiritual from the natural interpretation of types in Scripture:

> 'Tis possible that a man might know how to interpret all the types, parables, enigmas, and allegories in the Bible, and not have one beam of spiritual light in his mind; because he mayn't have the least degree of that spiritual sense of the holy beauty of divine things ... and may see nothing of this kind of glory in anything contained in any of these mysteries, or any other part of the Scripture.[59]

And participation in the holy beauty of God provides insights into physical nature that are unavailable to the unredeemed imagination:

When the true beauty and amiableness of the holiness or true moral good that is in divine things, is discovered to the soul, it as it were opens a new world to its view. . . . This shows the glory of all God's works, both of creation and providence: for 'tis the special glory of them, that God's holiness, righteousness, faithfulness and goodness are so manifested in them.[60]

The relish of God's holiness in spiritual knowledge rediscovers the real beauty of the universe. It detects and adores the glory of God as the end of creation and thereby returns entities on the scale of being below essential manhood to their status of secondary images of divine things. As William Clebsch has succinctly described Edwards's sense of beauty, "Holiness made one's life a work of art."[61] And for Edwards that work of art restored the harmony of the spheres.

Since the nineteenth century, Jonathan Edwards's personality has been subjected to the probings of numerous psychological tools: the old "hysteria" thesis, Freudian categories, Eriksonian developmental theory. None of them has gained more than a peek into the immensely private life of this very public figure, and none has begun to unravel the complexities of his mind. On occasion Edwards did drop hints about the make-up of his personality, however, and how it was related to his thought. The following notebook entry on the "Pleasantness of Religion" is particularly revealing:

It is no argument against true pleasantness of religion that it has no tendency to raise laughter, and rather to discourage [it], for that pleasure which is raised by laughter [is] never great. . . . The greater part of true pleasure don't raise laughter, as the joy of the light and enjoyment of most dear friends sincerely, but only raises a smile and not shaking laughter, which always rises from a mixture of pleasure and sorrow, and never from pure pleasure. . . . The pleasure of religion raises one clear above laughter, and rather tends to make the face to shine than to screw into a grimace; though, when it is at its height, it begets a sweet, inexpressible joyful sense and we have only smiles, as so often by the great pleasure of a dear friend's society. The reason why the pleasures of religion be not always attended with such a smile is because we have so many sins and have so much offended God; and almost all our religious thoughts are unavoidably attended with repentance and a sense of our own misery. . . . The reason why religious thoughts will cause one to sigh sometimes is not from the melancholiness of religion, but because religious thoughts are of such an high moral and spiritual nature as very much abstracts the soul from the body, and so the operations of the body are deadened.[62]

Edwards's religion, if sedate, was not altogether somber. His associations with his world produced no belly laughs, but they were often joyful ones which led him beyond the grimace. There was about Edwards's life and thought no knowing smile produced by an ironic transcendence over human foibles. The transcendence which he managed to attain lifted him above even the ironic perspective. And his tragic sense of the oppressive weight of sin made even the pleasant smile difficult to achieve.

Edwards's transcendent vision—clear enough to his intellect but terribly difficult, he was the first to admit, to incorporate fully into his life—is the vision of a whole self in a whole world. The balanced self in a harmonious world is, in fact, a test of "truly gracious affections." The life of the person of faith should reflect the "symmetry and beauty in God's workmanship"; his affections are meant to exist in "beautiful symmetry and proportion."[63] Edwards was quick to remark that symmetry in this life is never perfect, and he confessed that his own personality lacked the proportion which he desired.[64] He devoted himself to its realization, however, and he achieved a remarkable balance in his thinking and preaching on nature and imagination. He complemented his didacticism with a sensational shadowing that went beyond moral dictates to direct participation in spiritual truths. He supplemented his pleas for "actual learning" with invitations to a type of knowing in which intellect and affections join in concert. His view of creation linked all levels of the scale of being into a harmonious praise of God's glory, and his theory of virtue brought into symbiotic relation the beauty of the cosmos, the beauty of human morality, and the beauty of divine benevolence.

Most American theologians and preachers who immediately succeeded Edwards lost the vision of this balance. His disciples defended and developed his categories, but they were more attracted to his didacticism than to his participatory knowledge. Those who "corrected" his Calvinism on behalf of human freedom ended with a universe more closed and less free than anything Edwards conceived. Those who "improved" his revivalist technique appealed to sentiments rather than to affections, and their sentimentalism ignored the indirect path of his symbolic imagination. Those who candidly repudiated Edwards's theology and preaching substituted sweet reasonableness for the sense of the heart, and gentle persuasion for sensational shadowing. Men of morals, men of sentiment, and men of reason lost sight of the whole self in a whole world and hence severely restricted the human response to physical nature.

NOTES

1. See *Religious Affections,* WY (1959), pp. 197–208; *Original Sin,* WY (1970), pp. 380ff.
2. *Freedom of the Will,* WY (1957), pp. 137ff, 156ff.
3. "Justification by Faith Alone," WD, 5:365–69.
4. "The Nature of True Virtue," WW, 2:273.
5. "Of Being" and "Notes on the Mind," *Jonathan Edwards: Representative Selections,* ed. C. H. Faust and T. H. Johnson (New York: Hill & Wang, 1962), pp. 18–23, 27–29.
6. "Observations Concerning the Mysteries of Scripture," WD, 7:315.
7. Miscellany 1100, *The Philosophy of Jonathan Edwards from His Private Notebooks,* ed. Harvey G. Townsend (Eugene: University of Oregon Press, 1955), p. 213.
8. "The Nature of True Virtue," WW, 2:273–74.
9. Miscellany 125, *Philosophy of Edwards,* p. 76.
10. *Original Sin,* WY, pp. 400–1.
11. Miscellany 194, *Philosophy of Edwards,* pp. 183–84.
12. Miscellany 332, ibid., p. 130.
13. *Images or Shadows of Divine Things,* (New Haven: Yale University Press, 1948), p. 61.
14. "Dissertation Concerning the End for Which God Created the World," WW, 2:196–97, 206–7.
15. Ibid., p. 255.
16. Ibid., pp. 202, 208–9, 255.
17. Ibid., pp. 254–55.
18. Arthur O. Lovejoy, *The Great Chain of Being* (Cambridge: Harvard University Press, 1936), chap. 6.
19. "End of Creation," WW, 2:223–24.
20. Miscellany 1, *Philosophy of Edwards,* pp. 195–96. This is an argument for immortality on the basis of the causal connection between consciousness and being.
21. "End of Creation," WW, 2:210.
22. "Miscellanies," (MS. in Yale Beinecke Library), entry 777.
23. Miscellany 42, *Philosophy of Edwards,* p. 238.
24. See, for example, Frederic I. Carpenter, "The Radicalism of Jonathan Edwards," *The New England Quarterly,* 4 (April, 1931): 634–35; Clyde A. Holbrook, *The Ethics of Jonathan Edwards* (Ann Arbor: University of Michigan Press, 1973), pp. 138ff.
25. Edwards approvingly cited such Cambridge Platonists as John Smith and Ralph Cudworth, and both Locke and Newton, whose ideas triggered Edwards's idealist speculations, were closely associated with the Cambridge school of Platonists. As Gerald Cragg has pointed out, the Cambridge Platonists "quoted Plotinus even more freely than Plato" since to them the Plotinian metaphysic "had carried Plato's thought forward."

Gerald R. Cragg, *The Cambridge Platonists* (New York: Oxford University Press, 1968), p. 15.

26. See Thomas A. Schafer, "The Concept of Being in the Thought of Jonathan Edwards" (Ph.D. diss., Duke University, 1951), pp. 260–61.

27. "End of Creation," WW, 2:223.

28. Ibid., p. 200.

29. Ibid., pp. 210–11.

30. Ibid., p. 256.

31. This is the thesis pursued by Roland Delattre in his treatment of Edwards's ethics, *Beauty and Sensibility in the Thought of Jonathan Edwards* (New Haven: Yale University Press, 1968).

32. "The Nature of True Virtue," WW, 2:262–63.

33. Ibid., pp. 272–73, 275.

34. "The Beauty of the World," *Images or Shadows of Divine Things,* p. 135.

35. "The Nature of True Virtue," WW, 2:264–65.

36. "Miscellaneous Observations," WD, 7:298. Cf. ibid., p. 275.

37. Letter to James Robe, *The Great Awakening,* WY, p. 537.

38. *Religious Affections,* WY, pp. 195–96.

39. "Thoughts Concerning the Revival," *The Great Awakening,* WY, pp. 331–41.

40. "Memoirs of David Brainerd," WD, 10:421.

41. "A Divine and Supernatural Light," *Representative Selections,* pp. 103–5.

42. *Religious Affections,* WY, pp. 205, 211, 288–89.

43. *Original Sin,* WY, p. 381.

44. "Men Naturally God's Enemies," WD, 7:37.

45. *Original Sin,* WY, pp. 125–26.

46. Miscellany 34, *Philosophy of Edwards,* p. 241.

47. "Wisdom Displayed in Salvation," WD, 7:97.

48. *Religious Affections,* WY, p. 200.

49. "A Divine and Supernatural Light," *Representative Selections,* p. 106.

50. Ibid., pp. 107, 109.

51. Ibid., pp. 107–8.

52. "Christian Knowledge," WD, 6:272.

53. *Religious Affections,* WY, p. 120.

54. Ibid., p. 260.

55. Ibid., p. 255.

56. Ibid., p. 261.

57. Ibid., p. 203.

58. "Praise, One of the Chief Employments of Heaven," WD, 8:308.

59. *Religious Affections,* WY, p. 278.

60. Ibid., p. 273.

61. William A. Clebsch, *American Religious Thought: A History* (Chicago: University of Chicago Press, 1973), p. 58. Cf. *Religious Affections,* WY, p. 258.

62. Miscellany X, *Philosophy of Edwards,* p. 236.

63. *Religious Affections,* WY, p. 365.

64. See Edwards's "Letter to the Trustees of the College of New Jersey," *Representative Selections,* p. 410.

PART TWO

Nature's Moral Teachings

We are sent into this world in the midst of a blind, confused jangle of natural laws, which we cannot by any possibility understand, and which cut their way through and over and around us. They tell us nothing; they have no sympathy; they hear no prayer; they spare neither vice nor virtue. And if we have no friend above to guide us through the labyrinth, if there is no Father's heart, no helping hand, of what use is life?

Harry in Harriet Beecher Stowe's
Oldtown Folks

4

The New Divinity

Jonathan Edwards's religious vision was pervaded by images of relationship and open interchange among the parts of the universe. Although he judged holiness under the law of God to be the chief sign of a converted heart, Edwards remained convinced that the Christian religion was essentially a love and knowledge of divine truth that transcended obligation to mandates. Obedience to regulations was a manifestation of, not the substance of, this essential quality of the religious life. And although his mind was captivated by the laws of the physical creation, Edwards held that nature's lawful regularity was a symbol of something higher: the agreement of mind with mind, heart with heart. Physical nature had its didactic functions; it offered moral lessons, instructions in daily living. But, when beheld with a sense of the heart, nature did more than instruct: it carried the beholder into a participation in "divine things." Then the truths of God were not simply illustrated by the events of nature; they were vividly present in and through natural events.

Religious thought in New England from the middle of the eighteenth to the middle of the nineteenth century shifted its focus to the legal obligations of the religious life. Priority was given to rules of government as touchstones of religious truth. And nature became less an awesome set of images of divine things than a magnificent display of divine precepts. The change of emphasis was a subtle one at first, starting with Edwards's own disciples who had every intention of preserving both the spirit and the principles of the master's thought. By the turn to the nineteenth century, however, the shift was explicit. In the words of Joseph Haroutunian, moralism had replaced piety.[1]

In 1820, the father of American Unitarianism, William Ellery Channing, taunted his orthodox Calvinist contemporaries for ceasing to be Calvinists. Channing charged that they had softened their rigid theology by inadvertently adopting the spirit of a new age, a spirit that Unitarians proudly and eagerly heralded:

> A large number, perhaps a majority, of those who surname themselves with the name of Calvin, have little more title to it than ourselves. They keep the name, and drop the principles which it signifies. They adhere to the system as a whole, but shrink from all its parts and distinguishing points. . . .
>
> Calvinism, we are persuaded, is giving place to better views. It has passed its meridian, and is sinking to rise no more. It has to contend with foes more formidable than theologians . . . —we mean with the progress of the human mind, and with the progress of the spirit of the gospel.[2]

Channing knew well enough that the progressive mollification of Calvinism scarcely spelled the end of acrimonious theological dispute in his day. During the first half of the nineteenth century, Calvinist was arrayed against Unitarian, Calvinist against Calvinist, Transcendentalist against Calvinist and Unitarian, and most all churchly theologians against Deists. Not fewer but more theories of the principal doctrines of Christianity were raised for debate. Yet Channing was correct in pointing to a spirit growing with the age, a spirit that proposed common terms of argument for most of the disputants. Attention in the debates was increasingly drawn to what was *just, fair, legal,* and *responsible* in the universe. The actions of God, the purposes of history, the ultimate destiny of man, the meaning of physical nature, the intent of Scripture—all these were worried over according to the criterion of what was legal. Which view of God best preserves the lawful harmony of his universe? What notion of the human will safeguards man's obligations under the law? What doctrine of Christ's atonement renders God just and law-abiding, and the sinner responsible? How does nature serve God's government of the cosmos? These were the fundamental questions occupying religious thinkers after Edwards. Commonality of question, of course, assured no sameness of answer. Channing and his fellow Unitarians, for example, rejected the view of religion as something constituted by a strict code of laws, and they called for a friendlier, warmer relation between Creator and creature than that which they detected in other branches of American Protestantism. When suggesting what might be believed about their approachable Father-God, however, Unitarians measured him by a set of laws thought to be germane to the entire universe: God could not perform actions which offended the rules of fair play.

The Calvinism which Channing twitted ceased to be Calvinism precisely in its own subjection of God to a system of law. To be sure, traditional Calvinism had long followed the medieval practice of describing God's relation to his creation in legal terms. The description figured as a sizable part of "natural theology," an intellectual enterprise given over to truths available to all rational creatures by the light of nature. Such truths included God as Moral Governor of the universe and man's inherent obligation to live according to moral law. But traditional Calvinism also followed the medieval practice of engaging in another form of theology, the truths of which were available only to faithful reason and through the saving Word of God contained in the Bible. Such truths included the mysteries of the Trinity and the regeneration of the sinner, and they surpassed in meaning the categories of law and morality. The modified Calvinism of which Channing spoke moved the truths of revealed theology into the framework of natural theology, particularly into the categories of moral law and moral government. In the process, some of the distinctive pronouncements of an older Calvinism were muted. The sovereignty of God in his acts of creation and redemption, previously thought to be a mystery inexplicable according to human principles of justice, was now defended within a scheme of morality and law equally applicable to Creator and creature. The heartfelt responses of conversion and faith became obligations, dutiful acts directed to a Lawgiver and his precepts. Physical nature, so "slicked up in types" by the Puritans and Edwards, was now clothed in a mantle studded with moral dictates.

Much of the theological preoccupation with law was a consequence of the self-confident democratic feelings spreading in the New Republic. Whatever else national life under a constitution might mean for American religious thinkers—and it came to mean many things—it signified for a growing majority that political sovereignty belonged to the people and that all authority, be it political or religious, could no longer rest securely on the shoulders of a privileged class or an established institution. "The American self-consciousness authoritatively affirmed to each man his freedom. So fundamental a doctrine called sharply into question any social system that intermingled legal coercion with religion. At the same time, very few questioned the dependence of government upon the moral quality of its citizens or the significance of religion as the nursing mother of morals."[3] In fact, as the last traces of medieval regulatory institutions passed away—king, nobility, established church, entailed estates—it seemed all the more important to Americans, especially to American religious leaders, that freedom be assured by a common, voluntary, inwardly sensed morality. One thing was certain: the national morality must honor the rights of free individuals. The functions of government, church, and family must be measured by a morality that takes as its highest value "the free-contracts of autonomous persons" and their "conscious and dutiful reciprocity."[4]

American colleges, quite as much as the lower schools, were pressed into the service of a common morality. The senior college course in moral philosophy, frequently taught by the clergyman college president and eventually based on textbooks written by American moral philosophers, became a queen of the sciences. The course was designed to pull together within a moral framework the learnings offered by the entire curriculum and to ground America's future leaders on a solid ethical foundation suitable to the purposes of the new nation. Moral philosophy in the colleges was, according to D. H. Meyer, a determined effort to shape an American public ethic.[5] Those charged specifically with the training of the clergy, both in the parish setting and in the theological school, were no less concerned to develop a public ethic. Theology supportive of the morality of the new nation would grant man enough free will to pay homage to him as a responsible moral agent; it would make God accountable in his dealings with the human agent; and it would insist that the universe is governed by laws devoid of favoritism.

Nature and nature's laws proved to be prime considerations for the moral theologians. Nature was the cosmos of Newton—the observed harmonious behavior of material objects. Nature's God was the governor who bent every omnipotent act to preserve the harmony of his creation. Jonathan Edwards, himself an admirer of Newton's universe, would not have quarreled with this description of nature. But Edwards found in the laws and harmonies of nature symbols of other beauties that invited metaphysical probing. A long line of his successors found in nature and nature's laws clear, factual signs of moral truths. New Calvinist, Deist, and Unitarian were agreed on this much: the proper study of God is neither symbolic contemplation nor metaphysical speculation; it is, rather, an inductive examination of God's orderly disclosures of himself. "It is the perfection of God's works," Newton had said, "that they are all done with the greatest simplicity. He is the God of order and not of confusion."[6] It followed for the new American theology, as well as for Newton, that both the scientific and the moral interpretations of the universe should be simple, straightforward, and empirical. It followed, also, that there was an obvious analogy—one that needed no metaphysical analysis—between the physical and the moral aspects of the world.

The first step down the path to making theology legal in emphasis and nature didactic in import was not taken by thinkers who were infatuated with the new spirit of the age. It was taken, instead, by Jonathan Edwards's immediate intellectual offspring, theologians of the "New Divinity." To their own minds, at least, they took up the theological task not in order to make Christianity agreeable with the times but in order to make the Calvinism of Edwards consistent. Theirs was a theology systematic rather than apologetic in design. Whether they intended it or not, however, they were early spokesmen for the new spirit of the times.

The New Divinity party was composed of those clergymen, mostly graduates of Yale and mostly settled in Connecticut and the Connecticut River Valley, who claimed Jonathan Edwards and the revivalist tradition of the Great Awakening as their heritage. Their theology was deemed "new" by their opponents because it allegedly introduced unseemly innovations into orthodox Calvinism. Their chief spokesmen were Joseph Bellamy (1719–90), Samuel Hopkins (1721–1803), Stephen West (1735–1819), Jonathan Edwards, Jr. (1745–1801), and Nathaniel Emmons (1745–1840). They were a close-knit group. Bellamy and Hopkins were students under Edwards. Edwards wrote a laudatory preface to Bellamy's first work, *True Religion Delineated,* and during his years at Stockbridge was closely associated with Hopkins. West succeeded Edwards at Stockbridge and edited the autobiographical notes of Hopkins. Jonathan Edwards, Jr. studied under Hopkins and at his New

Haven parish insisted that the senior Edwards's stringent standards of church membership be followed, to the point of dividing his congregation. Emmons studied with John Smalley of New Britain who was a student of Bellamy. The closeness of the group, however, by no means resulted in a clique devoid of wider influence. Although some of the New Divinity men were unpopular preachers with a talent for alienating their parishioners, others received the profound and undivided affection of their congregations. Their books were widely distributed and read, and a long train of ministerial candidates passed through their instruction. Late in his life, Hopkins—a man, as we shall see, not given to boasting—took considerable comfort in the fact that more than a hundred ministers in the United States espoused "Hopkinsian" sentiments. And some Americans who found such sentiments abhorrent were forced to acknowledge the strength of New Divinity thought and the boldness of its defense of moral causes.[7]

Although they were not intellectual replicas of one another, the New Divinity men entered the theological scene agreed on certain fundamental ideas, and they drew considerable criticism from their contemporaries for the forthright proclamation of jarring doctrines. A claim that struck sensitive souls as particularly repugnant was Hopkins's announcement, repeated by other New Divinity spokesmen, that inasmuch as authentic virtue consists in disinterested benevolence, the truly virtuous person should be willing to be damned for the glory of God. Equally notorious was Bellamy's doctrine, only slightly altered by Hopkins, that sin is the necessary means God employs to achieve the greatest good in the universe. Sin is the means that God as Moral Governor uses to accomplish a higher end, salvation. Christ's atoning act on the cross also serves governmental ends: it meets the law's demand of punishment. "The atonement is *useful* on men's account, and in order to furnish new motives to holiness, but it is *necessary* on God's account, and in order to *enable* him, as a consistent Ruler, to pardon any, even the smallest sin, and therefore to bestow on sinners any, even the smallest favor."[8]

In that governmental theory of the atonement resides the key to the New Divinity's entire theological perspective. The at-one-ment achieved between the Creator and the fallen creature is part of a vast scheme of moral government that extends to all parts of the universe. It is this governmental view of things that determines how the disciples of Edwards interpret the religious meaning of physical nature, the content of spiritual knowledge, the beauty and being of the cosmos, and the role of the human agent within the divine plan of creation and redemption. It is a view that accentuates moral meanings detectable in nature and minimizes nature's symbols.

In a series of miscellaneous observations and occasional writings, Jonathan Edwards had proposed the rudiments of a moral theory of the atonement and God's overarching moral government, his ideas apparently prompted by a reading of Hugo Grotius and Joseph Butler. Edwards's theological heirs took those rudimentary reflections to their logical conclusions and added emphases all their own. "Epigoni," as William Hutchison has remarked, "do tend to internalize the master's principles and spirit—so much so that they scarcely realize how misleading it may be for them constantly to invoke his name."[9] In the case before us, Edwards's students so internalized and expanded some of the ideas of their teacher that they developed a perspective quite different from his larger outlook.

Samuel Hopkins was the first and most rigorous systematizer of the New Divinity; "Hopkinsianism" became another name for the school of thought. To him, therefore, one may turn for ideas basic to the New Divinity men's overall perspective and to their view of nature. There are additional reasons for looking at Hopkins. Of all the New Divinity figures, he seems to have been in closest touch with Edwards. A fast friend of the Edwards family, Hopkins was instrumental in securing the position for Edwards at Stockbridge, a settlement within only a few miles of Hopkins's parish at Great Barrington. The two men were in frequent conversation about the subjects of Edwards's late treatises on creation and virtue, Hopkins editing and bringing to publication those treatises after Edwards's death. William Ellery Channing even suggested that Edwards borrowed many of his late ideas from Hopkins.[10] However that may be, Edwards and Hopkins were intimate intellectual companions. To examine Hopkins, therefore, is to investigate a thinker who, for all of his departures from Edwards, intended to remain true to the spirit and principles of his teacher. It is to see the New Divinity aborning.

Throughout his life, Hopkins was plagued by loneliness, a deep sense of abstraction from people and things. His religious conversion only increased his alienation, and his tasks as a minister were felt as burdens which demanded but did not provide close contact with the world around him. His real joy in life, ecstatic at times, was found in forms of meditation, study, and prayer that were undisturbed by the outside world. He was happiest and making what he considered his only contribution to his world when lost in his thoughts. In a set of brutally self-critical autobiographical notes, Hopkins brought his personal inclinations under scrutiny:

> My strongest religious exercises, and highest enjoyments have taken place in my retirement and secret devotions; and in my public performances, praying and preaching have generally been very low; which I have sometimes suspected was an argument that my religion is not genuine. I know it is an argument against me, that I am very sinfully defective in my social and public religion! . . . I have loved retirement, and have never been comfortable when deprived of it; and have taken more pleasure alone, than in any company: And have often chosen to ride alone, when on a journey, rather than in the best company.[11]

Hopkins surpassed Edwards in his study regimen, devoting fourteen to eighteen hours a day to his reading, writing, and reflection.[12] He was not without contact with intimate friends, and his personal letters manifest genuine warmth, but, as he admits, he preferred to be alone, and that preference produced massive feelings of guilt.

Hopkins's religious conversion only temporarily opened new worlds to him; its cumulative effect was to increase his guilt, his withdrawal, and his sense of failure as a minister. As a student at Yale, Hopkins heard the revivalist messages of Tennent and Edwards, but it was a fellow classmate, David Brainerd, who convinced him of his lack of heartfelt Christian conviction. After severe inward struggles, Hopkins attained what he thought for a while might be an authentic conversion:

> At length as I was in my closet one evening, while I was meditating, and in my devotions, a new and wonderful scene opened to my view. I had a sense of the being and presence of God, as I never had before; it being more of a reality, and more affecting and glorious, than I had ever before perceived. And the character of Jesus Christ the mediator came into view, and appeared such a reality, and so glorious; and the way of salvation by him so wise, important and desirable, that I was astonished at myself that I had never seen these things before, which were so plain, pleasing and wonderful.[13]

Finding no one in the adjoining room to tell of his experience, Hopkins returned to his quarters where he read Watts's version of the Psalms, "the language of my heart to God." What began in the privacy of meditation ended the same way. In fact, he decided to tell no one of the experience for a long while, "still hoping and looking for something greater and better, and of quite a different kind."[14]

Employing Jonathan Edwards's distinction between "imagination" and "spiritual knowledge," one is led to suspect that Hopkins's experience was "imaginary." He saw visions of things absent in space and time rather than beholding given realities from a new perspective. And unlike Edwards's conversion, events of nature did not take on a new appearance. Symbols did not emerge. The words of Scripture which appealed to him were expressions of his feelings rather than symbols which connected him with "divine things." Perhaps such considerations bothered Hopkins and made him yearn for "something greater and better." At any rate, the experience became for him in time a source of frustration. After leaving Yale, while studying at Northampton, Hopkins confessed to Mrs. Edwards his despair over not being persuaded of his conversion. His hopes were raised for a while at Northampton, but he said later in life that his doubts more often than not had the upper hand over his hopes.[15] Edwards's own conversion experience, of course, did not cancel doubts, and he insisted always that faith and assurance of faith are not synonymous, but his experience, unlike Hopkins's, issued in an enduring, changed perspective on a world outside the self. Ecstasy was but a moment in Hopkins's religious vision; in time it only increased his awareness of his desperate loneliness. And it yielded no symbols to mediate between his yearning and the religious object of his desire.

Hopkins's lonely inwardness was intensified as he failed to move his parishioners to a heartfelt religion. Stephen West offered a defense of his friend's failure in the pulpit: "To estimate the character and fidelity of a gospel preacher by the number of conversions, which are effected under his immediate ministrations, would go near to reproach the great Saviour himself. But few, comparatively, were brought to the love of the truth under the ministrations of Christ on earth."[16] Hopkins found little comfort in such thoughts, if they ever occurred to him:

> My preaching has always appeared to me as poor, low and misera-
> ble. . . . And I have never wondered that my preaching has been
> attended with so little apparent good effect, since it has been so
> deficient every way. But few persons have appeared to have been
> awakened and converted by means of my preaching. The most appar-
> ent good it has ever been the means of doing is the instruction,
> quickening and comfort of Christians. . . . It has often given me
> pleasure to look forward to the millennium and consider what excel-
> lent preaching will then take place.[17]

Hopkins assumed that effective preaching was the kind which, as
during the height of the Great Awakening, led persons to radically
changed perspectives. So he could not avoid comparing his own
performance, to the point of utter frustration, with the greatest of
the Awakening preachers. "Heard Mr. Edwards preach all day," he
recorded in his diary. "I have been very dull and senseless; much
discouraged about preaching. Hearing Mr. Edwards makes me
ashamed of myself."[18]

Hopkins's failure as a preacher doubtless owed much to the
figure he cut and to the mood he created in the pulpit. He was over
six feet in height and over two hundred pounds in weight, aloof,
"drawling and monotonous," and making "but few gestures, and
those were awkward."[19] But Hopkins had a more serious flaw: his
preaching lacked potent symbols. "He selected his words clum-
sily," his biographer reports; he preferred the blunt statement and
the direct mandate to the lively image. His language reflected his
personal spirit: "He was at home in meditating on abstract truth,
and he seldom wandered among the beautiful illustrations of it. . . .
Meditative and grave, he seemed to live above the world."[20] Toward the close of his life, Hopkins bemoaned the fact that he had
given insufficient attention to the uses and meaning of language.[21]
Hopkins's sermons were based on no notebook on shadows of
divine things, no reflection on the possible links between God's
language of creation and the preacher's language in the pulpit, no
deliberate effort to fashion an imagery that would simultaneously
store heads and win hearts, no pursuit of the distinction between
illustrating a truth and making that truth linguistically present.

Hopkins's life and work, however, were not totally devoid of
lifting sublimities. He found his delights in theological abstractions
that were consonant with a purposeful, moral existence. Both na-

ture and Scripture triggered in his mind reflections on the moral and legal truths that a sovereign God had clearly revealed in his creation. His systematic development of those reflections, especially in *The System of Doctrines,* Hopkins considered his "greatest public service."[22] His theological labors overcame, at least indirectly, what he called his deficiencies in "public religion." Joy of his lonely life, systematic reflection on God's moral truths also launched him on a crusade against the public sin of slavery.

For all of Hopkins's inward loneliness and sense of failure, he was capable of rising to a vantage point quite characteristic of his New England theological heritage. From that perspective the majestic glory of God makes human experiences, religious or otherwise, seem trifling by comparison. After suffering a paralyzing stroke, Hopkins gave voice to a conviction that was the driving force of Jonathan Edwards's life and thought as well as Hopkins's own:

> My person and whole interest in time and to eternity is, compared with the grand whole, the glory of God, and the best interest of his kingdom, so small and inconsiderable, that when I have the latter in a sensible view, the former sinks into a mere speck or nothing, and is almost wholly overlooked and forgotten, and the language of my heart is, "Let God be glorified by all, and the best interest of his kingdom be secured and promoted, let what will become of me and my interest."[23]

There is no hint here of self-pity, only the God-intoxicated passion of an Edwards, a seventeenth-century Puritan, or an Augustine. The first thing to be observed about Hopkins's systematic theology is that its chief purpose is to pay obeisance to the transcendent God. The end of creation, including the creature who engages in the theological enterprise, is the glory of God.

Hopkins's creation is arranged hierarchically in the same manner as Edwards's. Creatures of intellect and will are an end of the remainder of creation, with God as the ultimate end of the whole.[24] Since every thing and act in the universe is a display, directly or indirectly, of God's glory, sin must also serve this ultimate end. Sin opens the possibility of redemption, or the new creation: "We cannot reconcile it to the wisdom of God that he should suffer a greater evil for the sake of a less good."[25] And every event of the universe, including the salvation of men, proceeds according to the election of the sovereign God: "The elect are not chosen to salvation, rather than others, because of any moral excellence in them.

. . . The difference between them and others, in this respect, whenever it takes place, is the fruit and consequence of their election, and not the ground and reason of it."[26]

The greatest beauty of the creation is Edwardean true virtue: the agreement of mind with mind, the essence of which is benevolence.[27] So the highest happiness of man is the love of God:

> [God's] whole character is superlatively beautiful, bright, and excellent; and it is impossible it should be properly discerned and understood, without giving the most noble and highest kind of enjoyment. And perfect discerning and love of this infinitely excellent and glorious being, accompanied with an assurance of his love and favor, must be the most perfect and highest kind of happiness of which we are capable or can have any conception.[28]

It follows that the essence of sin and misery is self-love or "selfish affections and exercises."[29] There is no reason to conclude, as has one interpreter,[30] that Hopkins has here abandoned Edwards's principles by measuring the value of religion with how much it promotes human happiness, thereby turning love of benevolence into love of complacence (the latter based on the degree of pleasure that love gives one). For Hopkins as for Edwards, the highest form of human happiness is a love of God which surpasses the interests of the self, and the first object of such benevolence is the beauty and brightness of God's own holiness. Subjective enjoyment of that love of holiness is a consequence of what is primary.

Hopkins also defines faith or spiritual knowledge in the language of Edwards. One knows the truth of God in faith when illuminated by the Spirit of God. Such illumination supplies no new faculties and no new truths; rather, the Spirit aids the natural faculties in their discernment of God's revelation in nature and Scripture.[31] Faith is an exercise of the heart, a tasting and relishing of divine truth. It is the harmonious interpenetration of intellect, will, and affections, "not an act of the intellect merely; but of the whole soul, in the exercise of a right taste and temper of mind, which is holiness, or the new creature."[32]

Formally, therefore, and in a number of crucial features, Hopkins's universe is that of Edwards. It is a world which bespeaks in all of its parts the glory of its sovereign Creator. Physical nature serves both the glory of God and the ends of human intellect and will. The highest beauty is true virtue, and virtuous access to the Creator is to be gained through spiritual knowledge or faith, a relishing of the truths of God. Hopkins's theological system embodies his proclamation, "Let God be glorified by all."

The specific contents which Hopkins painted into this very Edwardean picture of things resulted at a number of telling points, however, in a very different canvas. The glory of God becomes the glory essentially of a lawmaker and governor. And the highest form of human response to the revelation of God becomes obedience—heartfelt obedience, to be sure, but obedience nonetheless. Edwards's world of mirrors, each reflecting the glory of the outpouring of God's love or mirroring other reflections of that dynamic divine act, is replaced by a well-regulated system of moral government, each part tied to the whole by a set of precepts. Hopkins moralizes Edwards's symbolic universe.

One sign of the changed picture is apparent, as Joseph Haroutunian discovered, in Hopkins's refusal to invoke Edwards's ontology when sketching the end of creation and man's virtuous response to it.[33] Hopkins shows no interest in the ontological structures of being in general; his attention is focused on the law of God and the demands for obedience that define the relations within being in general. In fact, the being of God *is* his legislating activity, and the human response of love to God is obedience: "Love to Being in general is obedience to the law of God, commanding us to love God and our fellow creatures; for these are being in general and comprehend the whole of being."[34] In defining the relations among the beings of the cosmos, Hopkins follows Edwards by subordinating the natural to the historical, the physical to the mental, and he even insists that the laws of physical nature are emblems of intellectual reality:

> We may hence expect to find that in [nature] which bears a conspicuous analogy to holiness, the perfection and glory of the intellectual system. And this must be the general law of attraction, the common bond of union in our material system, by which all bodies are mutually attracted, and tend to one centre; every part, while it attracts, being also attracted by the whole, is fixed in its station and extends its influence to all; so that each particle has, in a sense, a regard to the whole, and contributes to the general good. This is the source of the order and beauty so obvious in our world . . . —a most clear, striking resemblance of universal benevolence in the moral world, in which all its union and glory consist.[35]

Such emblems, however, are never grounded by Hopkins in a theory of being which would account for the analogical relationship. Instead of spelling out a scheme of emanation and remanation which would elucidate the analogy by specifying nature's participation in intellectual truths, Hopkins is content to state the analogy as obvious and move to the lessons which nature teaches. In addition to instructing in the law of attraction, nature points directly to such higher truths as the Creator's providential care for his world and the deep crime of sin's disruption of the beautiful harmonies of the universe.[36]

Physical nature is, in other words, a set of instructions about God as Moral Governor. Nature's laws of government are signs of a superior form of government, that which regulates the destiny of man. The clearest and most direct revelation of moral government is found in the Bible, which is a "system of truth, and of duty," a "system of doctrines and commands, which man's wisdom does not teach, and never can; but which the Holy Ghost alone teacheth."[37] The Bible, in both its Old and New Testaments, contains a system of truths as harmonious, consistent, and connected as the facts of the natural world.[38] Within that system, sin, although "undesirable" and "contrary to divine holiness," is a crucial part of God's plan of moral government; considered from the governmental point of view, sin is both necessary and desirable as a step in making "the system in the highest degree perfect, happy, and glorious."[39] And the work of Christ as redeemer is chiefly his act of making possible the maintenance of the law of this system:

> The work of the Redeemer . . . has a primary respect to the law of God, to maintain and honor that, so that sinners may be pardoned and saved consistent with that, without setting that aside . . . and especially that the threatening [of the law] might be properly and completely executed, without which God could not be true or just in pardoning and saving the sinner.[40]

Faith is obedience to the Moral Governor and his laws. It is a form of spiritual knowledge, but its object is a lawgiver and his commands, and its posture is legal. Faith is "obedience to all special or positive directions and commands" of God, a "conformity of heart and life, to the doctrines and precepts contained in the scripture."[41] When Hopkins confronts the question whether the obedience of faith is freely willed by man or determined by the decrees of God, he insists that both things are true, "however unable we may be to reconcile them." Our feelings tell us that we are "perfectly free and accountable" as moral agents; but we know from the teachings of

Scripture that our saving faith is a gift of the sovereign God.[42] Just as Hopkins refuses to follow Edwards in delineating an ontology of natural symbols, so he does not adopt his teacher's approach of offering a psychology of motive, will, and act that would account for the relation between divine decree and human choice. Hopkins prefers to stick to the "facts" of experience and Scripture, however contradictory they may appear to be. Given his governmental views of creation, Scripture, redemption, and faith, it is hardly surprising that Hopkins defines preaching as a declaration of "the system of truth and duty." The means of conversion, the chief method for reaching desperate sinners, is to make persons experience the laws of the Moral Governor as duties to be obeyed. The task of the preacher is to instruct and command.[43]

The whole of Samuel Hopkins's theology is cast, therefore, within the framework of a system of moral government. God remains sovereign in the system, and government in both its natural and moral dimensions testifies to God's glory. But God, man, and the world are understood in decidedly legalistic terms. For all of Hopkins's love of abstract systematic reflection, he recoils from both psychological and ontological abstraction. He systematically considers moral laws derivable from the facts of nature, Scripture, and experience, but he refuses to account either for the acts of the human psyche or for the ground of symbols. Nature, like Scripture, instructs in the laws of moral government, and the appropriate human response to that instruction is obedience. Spiritual knowledge becomes a kind of practical wisdom, a sense of thankfulness for the goodness and beauty of God's scheme of creation and redemption that will issue in obedient behavior. As Hopkins speculated about the coming millennium (which he thought would commence by the end of the twentieth century), he assured himself that a great portion of the human happiness in that blissful period would consist of major advances in the practical knowledge of husbandry and the mechanical arts.[44] Man's highest form of response to physical nature itself, it would seem, is a practical knowledge capable of defeating nature's obstacles to human enterprise, just as the supreme response to God's moral laws revealed in nature is an obedient triumph over the sinful obstacles to the human will.

"I hate goodies," Ralph Waldo Emerson once snarled in a journal entry. "I hate goodness that preaches. Goodness that preaches undoes itself. . . . Goodies make us very bad. . . . We will almost sin to spite them. Better indulge yourself, feed fat, drink liquors, than go straitlaced for such cattle as these."[45] The potential for a hortatory, self-defeating, sanctimonious do-goodism inheres in the moralistic perspective of Samuel Hopkins. Indeed, shrill tones of self-righteousness emanated from the reform movements inspired by the moral vision of New Englanders like Hopkins. Voluntary benevolence societies formed by these theologians and preachers, societies dedicated to bringing American society into conformity with the moral government of God, were legion, and they were as unyielding in their moral demands as they were inclusive in their social outreach. Hopkins and his students were leaders in societies dedicated to temperance, missions, preservation of the Sabbath, and the elimination of curb swearing. Yet, if a considerable amount of evangelical do-goodism lay within these activities, so did a high degree of prophetic criticism of the social order. That is particularly true of Hopkins's response to the social evil of slavery.

Upon leaving Great Barrington to become minister of First Church in Newport, Rhode Island, Hopkins found himself at the very center of the slave trade. Many members of his congregation were slaveholders or otherwise financially involved with the trade. In this setting, he became one of the first Congregational ministers to denounce slavery, was a participant in abolitionist causes, and raised money to free slaves in his neighborhood. In his *Dialogue Concerning the Slavery of the Africans* (1776), Hopkins made quite clear the social implications of his theology of moral government. Assuming that the evangelical duty of man is benevolence to being in general, he branded slavery as the most wicked of public sins and insisted that self-love, or dedication of one's life to one's own narrow (in this case, business) interests, was at the root of the evil. His understanding of revelation as the unveiling of moral truths allowed him to cut through the literalistic interpretations of Scripture and see biblical justifications of slavery for what they were— thinly disguised rationalizations for treating the Negro as less than fully human. And however contradictory his view of the freedom of the will, Hopkins said quite straightforwardly that to deny a man his liberty is to deny him the essence of his humanity and that in the eyes of the Moral Governor of the universe there is an unjustifiable inconsistency between Negro slavery and the colonists' protesting their own enslavement by the Mother Country.[46]

As a vision of social evil, Hopkins's theological perspective put Edwards's to shame. It would stretch logic to the breaking point to conclude that only in becoming legalistic does religion adequately address social issues, but it is not too much to conclude that Edwards's ideas on the virtue of benevolence gained social impact in America only as they were baptized into Hopkins's scheme of moral government which required socially benevolent exertions of the will. Hopkins's achievement, however, was attained at a high price. For all of its social relevance, his theology lost the symbolic power of Edwards's religious viewpoint. Hopkins transformed Edwards's universe of natural images into a world of moral facts, his symbolic understanding of faith into discrete acts of obedience, the dynamism of being in general into the fixed structures of moral government. As American theologians became "enlightened" from abroad, they would surpass even the New Divinity in moralizing nature and religious imagination.

NOTES

1. Joseph Haroutunian, *Piety Versus Moralism: The Passing of the New England Theology* (New York: Harper Torchbooks, 1960).

2. William Ellery Channing, "The Moral Argument Against Calvinism," *The Works of William E. Channing* (Boston: American Unitarian Association, 1900), p. 468.

3. Elwyn A. Smith, "The Voluntary Establishment of Religion," *The Religion of the Republic*, ed. E. A. Smith (Philadelphia: Fortress Press, 1971), p. 155.

4. Haroutunian, *Piety Versus Moralism*, pp. xxiv–xxv.

5. D. H. Meyer, *The Instructed Conscience: The Shaping of the American National Ethic* (Philadelphia: University of Pennsylvania Press, 1972). See also Wilson Smith, *Professors and Public Ethics* (Ithaca: Cornell University Press, 1956); Daniel W. Howe, *The Unitarian Conscience: Harvard Moral Philosophy, 1805–1861* (Cambridge: Harvard University Press, 1970); Stow Persons, *American Minds: A History of Ideas* (New York: Holt, Rinehart and Winston, 1958), chap. 10.

6. Cited in Frank E. Manuel, *The Religion of Isaac Newton* (Oxford: Clarendon Press, 1974), p. 49.

7. A more detailed survey of the lives and ideas of the New Divinity men, a survey which my paragraph summarizes, is found in Sydney E. Ahlstrom, *A Religious History of the American People* (New Haven: Yale University Press, 1972), pp. 404–12. On the size and influence of the New

Divinity, see Richard D. Birdsall, "Ezra Stiles Versus the New Divinity Men," *American Quarterly*, 17, 2 (Summer 1965): 250–51; and *Sketches of the Life of the Late Rev. Samuel Hopkins*, ed. Stephen West (Hartford: Hudson & Goodwin, 1805), pp. 102–3.

8. This is Edwards A. Park's succinct statement of the "Edwardean theory of the Atonement" in his "Introductory Essay" to *The Atonement: Discourses and Treatises* (Boston: Congregational Board of Publication, 1859), p. xi. Cf. Frank H. Foster, *A Genetic History of the New England Theology* (New York: Russell & Russell, 1963; first published 1907), pp. 107–61.

9. William R. Hutchison, commenting on the relation between Horace Bushnell and his successors, *The Modernist Impulse in American Protestantism* (Cambridge: Harvard University Press, 1976), p. 43.

10. From a Channing letter of 1840, cited in Edwards A. Park, "Memoir of Samuel Hopkins," *The Works of Samuel Hopkins* (Boston: Doctrinal Tract and Book Society, 1852), 1:219. This edition of Hopkins's works is hereafter abbreviated WP.

11. *Sketches of Hopkins*, pp. 85–86.

12. Ibid., p. 84.

13. Ibid., pp. 35–36.

14. Ibid., pp. 36–37.

15. Ibid., pp. 40–43, 85.

16. Ibid., West's "Introduction," p. xi.

17. Ibid., pp. 88–89.

18. Cited in Park's "Memoir," WP, 1:49.

19. Ibid., p. 28.

20. Ibid., p. 30.

21. *Sketches of Hopkins*, pp. 91–92.

22. Ibid., p. 101.

23. Ibid., p. 108.

24. *System of Doctrines*, WP, 1:158f.

25. Ibid., p. 99; "Sin, Through Divine Interposition, An Advantage to the Universe," WP, 2:503-4.

26. *System of Doctrines* (Boston: Thomas & Andrews, 1793), 2:174. This edition of Hopkins's works is hereafter abbreviated WT.

27. *System of Doctrines*, WP, 1:49–50.

28. Ibid., p. 58.

29. Ibid., pp. 237–38.

30. Haroutunian, *Piety Versus Moralism*, p. 40.

31. *System of Doctrines*, WP, 1:410ff.

32. *System of Doctrines*, WT, 2:41.

33. Haroutunian, *Piety Versus Moralism*, pp. 81–84.

34. "An Inquiry into the Nature of True Holiness," WP, 3:69.

35. Ibid., p. 33.

36. *System of Doctrines*, WP, 1:162–63.

37. *System of Doctrines*, WT, 2:470, 475.

38. Ibid., pp. 9, 465.

39. *System of Doctrines*, WP, 1:99.

40. Ibid., p. 323.

41. Ibid., p. 178; *System of Doctrines,* WT, 2:29ff., 477.

42. *System of Doctrines,* WP, 1:76–77, 83–84.

43. *System of Doctrines,* WT, 2:109, 123–24.

44. "A Treatise on the Millennium," WT, 2:71–72.

45. Entry for June 23, 1838; *Selections from Ralph Waldo Emerson,* ed. Stephen E. Whicher (Boston: Houghton Mifflin, 1957), p. 91.

46. *A Dialogue Concerning the Slavery of the Africans* (New York: Arno Press, 1969), especially pp. 11, 14–16, 28–29, 41, 46, 56, 58.

5

American Theology Enlightened

In proclaiming that the American colonists were entitled to a separate and equal status among the peoples of the world by the "Laws of Nature and of Nature's God," the Declaration of Independence invoked magic words of Enlightenment philosophy. Nature, nature's laws, and nature's God signified stable realities within a Newtonian universe readily discernible to human reason. Thomas Jefferson joined numerous other eighteenth-century thinkers in setting his social credo within the larger context of a modern, or postmedieval, view of nature. Theologians, moral philosophers, and scientists who found themselves at the opposite end of the American political and religious spectrum from Jefferson employed the same language and developed their ideas within the same conceptual framework which that language implied. Few American intellectuals of the late eighteenth and early nineteenth centuries would have rejected the sentiment, despite some reservations about the tone, of Alexander Pope's exultation:

> Nature and Nature's laws lay hid in night:
> God said, *Let Newton be!* and all was light!

Americans' fascination with, indeed their devotion to, Newton's scientific perspective did not spring up suddenly during the American Revolution. Puritan theologians Cotton Mather and Jonathan Edwards were students of Newtonian science. By the middle of the eighteenth century, colonial college curricula were saturated with the ideas and methods of the new science, and American scientists were sending reports of their experiments, theories, and observations to the Royal Society.[1] Yet the full philosophical impact of the Newtonian outlook was not felt until after mid-century. From that point on, American theologians began increasingly to throw off what they took to be the medieval assumptions of Edwards's and Hopkins's approach to nature and to opt for a philosophical alternative more in keeping with the new science.

Acknowledging that the contrast between the medieval and the modern world views is often overdrawn, Frederick Copleston has nonetheless argued convincingly that an important shift was occasioned in Enlightenment philosophy by Renaissance natural science:

> Whereas a thirteenth-century theologian such as St. Bonaventure was interested principally in the material world considered as a shadow or remote revelation of its divine original, the Renaissance scientist, while not denying that Nature has a divine original, is interested primarily in the quantitatively determinable immanent structure of the world and its dynamic process.

For Galileo, for example, God remained creator and sustainer of the universe, but nature itself was for him a dynamic, mechanistic system of bodies in motion which could be understood mathematically without any immediate appeal to the Creator. Francis Bacon proposed an empirical, inductive approach to this enclosed, dynamic process of nature, and Isaac Newton's method combined the inductive discovery of mechanical laws with the deductive explanation of phenomena in the light of those laws. As philosophers became committed to the accuracy of the new science and its methods, they raised old questions in a new way and with a renewed sense of urgency. With the human being set so firmly within such a mechanistic universe, to what extent and in what manner, for example, could the exercise of his will be deemed free?[2] American theologians influenced by the new scientific world view reflected upon the same question as well as upon the correlative issues of God's role in the system of nature, the degree to which the mechanical universe bespoke a creator, and whether a theologian might be as empirical and inductive in his understanding of the world as any natural scientist.

Isaac Newton defined religion as obedience to the commands of God the Pantocrator. God's chief role was "his universal irresistible monarchical power to teach us obedience."[3] A host of New England theologians came to share Newton's religious outlook, but they did not learn it directly from him. They learned it instead from British

philosophers whose writings were aimed at showing that the Newtonian approach to nature was a boon to the theological enterprise
and that the new science need not issue in skepticism or Deism.
American theologians were taught this, above all, by the works of
Joseph Butler, William Paley, and the Scottish Common Sense
philosophers. In Butler's *Analogy of Religion,* they found an able
defense of the mysteries of scriptural revelation against the attacks
of the Deists; they discovered in that book also a well-constructed
bridge linking the moral and the material worlds. In the works of
William Paley, they encountered the same links between value and
fact as well as a lucid argument for God's existence from the design
in nature, an argument that sought to preserve the method and
outlook of the Newtonian scientist. In the Scottish philosophers,
they had ready to hand thinkers who showed them how to differentiate and relate human nature and material nature, develop a
science of the human mind, and save orthodox Christianity from
skepticism. In all three sources, American theologians found
further support for construing nature as a teacher of grand moral
truths.

Links Between Fact and Value:
Joseph Butler

Joseph Butler (1692–1752), Bishop of Bristol, then of Durham, first
established his reputation as a moral philosopher with the publication of his *Fifteen Sermons* in 1726, but it was his *Analogy of Religion*
of 1736 that secured him a high place among the ranks of apologetic
theologians. Standing within the empirical tradition of Newton
and Locke, Butler undertook in the *Analogy* to consider religion as a
matter of fact when answering the Deist claim that scriptural revelation is, in contrast to natural revelation, inherently unreasonable.
Around 1870, when spokesmen for the theory of evolution brought
Butler's argument under devastating attack, Butler's works rapidly
lost their appeal. But prior to that, his writings were standard texts
in British universities, and his *Analogy* enjoyed a solid reputation
among British thinkers of different stripes. John Henry Newman
spoke of Butler as "the greatest name in the Anglican Church."
David Hume deemed Butler one of the few modern theologians
worthy of refutation and classified him as among "some late

philosophers in England who have begun to put the science of man on a new footing." Butler deeply influenced the Scottish Common Sense philosophers who sought to overturn Humean skepticism.[4]

Butler's popularity on the American scene equalled his reputation in Britain. Edwards and his followers had been sympathetic readers of the *Analogy,* but by the turn of the nineteenth century, that book became standard reading in American colleges and seminaries. Francis Wayland, moral philosopher and president of Brown University, acknowledged Butler as "the author to whom I am under the greatest obligation." At Harvard, President James Walker told his students that Butler's *Analogy of Religion* was "the most original and profound work extant in any language on the philosophy of religion." While a student at Harvard, Ralph Waldo Emerson read the *Analogy* and in a senior essay saluted Butler as one of the modern moralists who had significantly advanced the discipline of ethics beyond primitive assumptions. William Ellery Channing looked upon Butler, "notwithstanding the alleged obscurities of his style," as one of the few Anglican moralists "worthy to be enrolled among the master-spirits of the human race." At Yale, where the *Analogy* was used as a text for decades, Butler shaped the thought of Lyman Beecher and Nathaniel Taylor, spokesmen for the "New Haven Theology." As president of Lane Seminary, Beecher began his courses with lectures on Butler's *Analogy.* Nathaniel Taylor's son-in-law, Noah Porter, observed that Taylor was most indebted to two writers, Jonathan Edwards and Joseph Butler, with the latter suggesting "the principles and the course of argument concerning the benevolence and equity of God's government, which were matured by him into a more exact system, and carried only to their legitimate conclusions." Even Horace Bushnell, who abandoned so many of the assumptions of his Yale training, in his mature work appealed to Butler's *Analogy* as a treatise that was essentially sound.[5]

The purpose of Butler's *Analogy of Religion* was to rebut a claim gaining credence among eighteenth-century rationalists: the claim that religious truth is available through the senses and reason trained upon the natural world, but not through faith in the implausible mysteries of scriptural revelation. In Butler's own words, such Deists (and he seems to have meant, above all, Matthew Tindal) "entertain prejudices against the whole notion of a revelation, and miraculous interpositions. They find things in Scripture, whether in incidental passages, or in the general scheme of it, which appear to them unreasonable. They take for granted, that if Christianity were true, the light of it must have been more general, and the evidence of it more satisfactory, or rather overbearing."[6] In reply, Butler takes the position that in its quest for truth, human reason operates under the law of probability. According to that law, natural revelation is plagued by as many perplexities as Christianity's special, scriptural revelation. "Probability is the very guide of life," and probable evidence is the best that creatures of finite intelligence may hope for. To be sure, there are degrees of certainty, but even high degrees of certainty still rest on probable evidence, and "low presumption often repeated, will amount even to moral certainty."[7] Only probability springing from our repeated experience of objects, for example, allows us to presume that "any one substance now existing will continue to exist a moment longer."[8] Butler therefore quotes Origen against those Deists who believe in a God of nature but find overwhelming difficulties in the God revealed in Scripture: "Origen has with singular sagacity observed, that 'he who believes the Scripture to have proceeded from him who is the Author of Nature, may well expect to find the same sort of difficulties in it as are found in the constitution of Nature.'"[9]

More positively, Butler's commitment to the law of probability leads him to view the facts of nature as the ground for inferring the truths of both natural and revealed religion. Natural facts do not, for instance, certainly falsify a belief in immortality; they even suggest the probable analogy for the continuance of life beyond the grave: "For we see by experience, that men may lose their limbs, their organs of sense, and even the greatest part of these bodies, and yet remain the same living agents."[10] The beliefs of Christianity arise from such natural analogies as this and from "a dispensation of things" superadded to natural reason. God's special providence in sending his Son and Spirit to deliver man from a state of ruin, particular obligations of duty to God and man—these dispensations are new revelations over and above those inferred from nature, and they have their own "particular evidences" in scriptural miracles and prophecies.[11] Butler is eager to preserve what he considers Christianity's distinctiveness, its special revelation with its special evidence. Christianity's God of redemption acts according to a plan "quite beyond our comprehension" and does not always conform to human expectations; God's is a "mysterious economy."[12] Yet Christianity's special revelation is not, for all of that, unreasonable. "Reason can, and it ought to judge, not only the meaning, but also of the morality and the evidence of revelation."[13] The ultimate reasons for God's action may be hidden from us, but in his special revelation He has provided analogies and probable evidence which *are* open to the inspection of reason. Thus, for example, God's acts of redemption in Son and Spirit, though they have their mysterious and inexplicable side, are specific dispensations that have analogies in general, natural providence: God "gave his Son in the same way of goodness to the world, as he affords particular persons the friendly assistance of their fellow-creatures . . . though in a transcendent and infinitely higher degree."[14]

To Harvard Unitarians, quite as much as to Yale evangelicals, Butler's argument proved to be an effective weapon against the debunkers of traditional Christianity. It was a clever *tu quoque* to the Deist rationalists: your natural religion is no less riddled with uncertainties than Christianity. Furthermore, Butler convinced American theologians breathing the air of the new science that by substituting inference from fact for arcane metaphysical speculation, they could engage in a reasonable task based on concrete probabilities. Above all, however, American theologians were drawn to Butler because of the links which his book constantly maintained between governments natural and moral.

The entire framework for Butler's discussion of natural analogy is the moral government of God, and his defense of Christianity's reasonableness is an attempt to show how that religion deepens our understanding of government. God's moral government is first of all apparent in the facts of nature and in human experience:

> As the manifold appearances of design and of final causes, in the constitution of the world, prove it to be the work of an intelligent Mind; so the particular final causes of pleasure and pain distributed amongst his creatures prove that they are under his government; what may be called his natural government of creatures endued with sense and reason. This, however, implies somewhat more than seems usually attended to, when we speak of God's natural government of the world. It implies government of the very same kind with that which a master exercises over his servants, or a civil magistrate over his subjects.[15]

Pleasure and pain are the consequences of creaturely actions and bespeak an author of nature who governs according to a system of rewards and punishments. Christianity's teachings also concern this government. Even Christ's vicarious sacrifice, which may appear to contradict a just scheme of reward and punishment, is, according to the longer view of things, really a service performed on behalf of God's system of government:

> The world's being under the righteous government of God does indeed imply, that finally and upon the whole, every one shall receive according to his personal deserts; and the general doctrine of the whole Scripture is, that this shall be the completion of the divine government. But during the progress, and, for aught we know, even in order to the completion of this moral scheme, vicarious punishments may be fit, and absolutely necessary.[16]

It follows that the whole of religion in both its natural and revealed branches is obedience to God the Moral Governor. Christian revelation adds to the precepts of nature.

Butler insists that God's moral government of the world is "beyond our comprehension" in that we cannot fathom all of the relations between the various parts of its immense system, but this does not deter him from claiming that it is reasonable to infer from nature and human experience that the moral and the natural governments are closely linked:

> Indeed the natural and moral constitution and government of the world are so connected, as to make up together but one scheme; and it is highly probable that the first is formed and carried on merely in subserviency to the latter, as the vegetable world is for the animal, and organized bodies for minds.[17]

With the world of fact and the world of value connected in one system of government, it is possible to read natural facts as moral lessons. In his own moral reading of nature, Butler adumbrated most of the themes which American theologians would develop in detail: government is just when rewards and punishments are in exact proportion to personal merits and demerits; man's probationary status within the scheme of moral government entails living under sanctions; common sense and the facts of human experience indicate that moral government presupposes man's freedom to respond to dictates; "habits of virtue . . . acquired by discipline are improvement in virtue" and, in turn, "improvement in virtue must be advancement in happiness, if the government of the universe be moral"; Scripture contains instructions in the laws of moral government which are added to the moral lessons of nature.[18]

Butler concluded his *Analogy* with a warning: the book was not meant to be a systematic, doctrinal exposition of the Christian faith. Rather, it was an effort to meet the Deists on their own grounds. For the sake of this apologetic task, Butler had been forced to focus on some ideas and neglect those which "I think true, and of the utmost importance."[19] Butler's caveat was ignored by American theologians who adopted and extended the arguments of his book. They used the dominant theme of the treatise, that of moral government, as the guiding principle of their systematic, doctrinal theology. They thereby collapsed Christian doctrine into apologetics, revealed theology into natural theology. That was an intellectual move which led American theology to surpass Hopkins in reducing the religious meaning of nature to the moral truths discoverable in the facts of a harmonious universe.

The Design in the Machine:
William Paley

William Paley (1743–1805) proved to be as influential as Butler in shaping American theology during the first half of the nineteenth century. A graduate of Cambridge, where he earned a distinguished record in mathematics, Paley stayed on at Christ's College for over a decade as a fellow and lecturer in ethics and theology. As a clergyman, and eventually as Archdeacon of Carlisle, Paley composed hundreds of sermons which became the basis of his published treatises. His best known works were *The Principles of Moral and Political Philosophy* (1785), an enlargement of his lectures at Cambridge, and *A View of the Evidences of Christianity* (1794) and *Natural Theology* (1802), his defenses of the reasonableness of Christianity and natural religion. These writings were the textbooks for several generations of British students, the *Principles* being required reading at Cambridge as early as 1786 and constituting part of the examinations into the nineteenth century, and the *Evidences* remaining on the Cambridge exam list as late as 1920.[20] Before the defeat of his natural theology at the hands of Romanticism and Darwinism, Paley's work had inspired the "Bridgewater

Treatises," a series of eight widely discussed essays published in the years 1833–36, written by mostly famous authors summarizing scientific knowledge that attested to "the Power, Wisdom, and Goodness of God as Manifest in Creation." The popularity of Paley is apparent from the fact that Samuel Taylor Coleridge thought it necessary to single out Paley's ethics and natural theology for a prolonged, bitter attack. And Charles Darwin, even as his *Origin of Species* began to replace Paley's mechanical view of nature with an organic perspective, said that he "hardly ever admired a book more than Paley's 'Natural Theology.'"[21]

Americans did not lag behind the British in their rush to make use of Paley's ideas. As one student of higher education has said, "The books on moral philosophy and natural theology by William Paley were once as well known in American colleges as were the readers and spellers of William McGuffey or Noah Webster in the elementary schools."[22] At Yale, Harvard, Brown, and other eastern colleges, as well as at the western college outposts of American culture during the first half of the nineteenth century, Paley's works were the textbooks in moral philosophy and natural theology.[23] What Ralph Henry Gabriel has said of Paley at Yale applies to most American colleges of the period: "In the history of Yale College no textbook ever approached the record of use for more than half a century established by the work of the Archdeacon of Carlisle."[24] Paley's ideas were not simply the means of introducing generations of college students to the disciplines of ethics and natural theology; they also became the inspiration for American theologians' own constructive efforts.

Even as American moralists and theologians used Paley's *Principles of Moral and Political Philosophy*, the book struck many of them as too brazenly utilitarian. Paley defined moral virtue as "the doing good to mankind, in obedience to the will of God, and for the sake of everlasting happiness."[25] The chief motive to virtue was not the glorification of God but human happiness itself. Paley described happiness as the condition "in which the amount or aggregate of pleasure exceeds that of pain" and held that happiness thus described consists of four parts: the "exercise of social affections," especially benevolence; the pursuit of some engaging goal in life; the prudent regulation of habits; and good health.[26] Since the motive to virtue was happiness—everlasting happiness—the basic rule of ethics was expediency: "Whatever is expedient, is right. It is the utility of any moral rule alone, which constitutes the moral obligation of it."[27] As D. L. LeMahieu has pointed out, Paley did not propose expediency as a moral substitute for justice; rather, "use" included "right" or "just" in the sense of "fit, proper, or suitable to the circumstances of the case."[28] And his rule of expediency, aimed at the production of happiness, sprang from his conviction that any unbiased observation of the creation would lead to the conclusion that its Creator wills the happiness of his creatures. Paley's version of utilitarianism presupposed, in other words, an essential feature of his natural theology:

> This rule [of expediency] proceeds upon the assumption, that God Almighty wills and wishes the happiness of his creatures. . . . No anatomist ever discovered a system of organization calculated to produce pain and disease; or, in explaining the parts of the human body, ever said; This is to irritate, this is to inflame; this duct is to convey the gravel to the kidneys; this gland to secrete the humour which forms the gout; if by chance he come at a part of which he knows not the use, the most that he can say is, that it is useless: no one ever suspects that it is put there to incommode, to annoy, or to torment. . . . God hath called forth his consummate wisdom to contrive and provide for our happiness.[29]

Although Paley's statement of his ethic seemed to many American theologians to be too utilitarian, when modified it did preserve the desired connections between the natural, the moral, and the practical. Francis Bowen of Harvard proposed that the statement, "Whatever is useful, is right," ought to be inverted to, "Whatever is right, is useful." And Timothy Dwight of Yale said that though to the finite mind unaware of all of the consequences of moral action, utility cannot be the measure of virtue, "to the eye of God it is the real rule."[30] Most American theologians at least approved of the intent of Paley's ethic: morality must be set within the framework of a natural and moral government that conspires for the practical promotion of human happiness.

These same American theologians, even "liberal" Unitarians in the early stages of their development, thought that Paley's *Evidences of Christianity*, an extended reply to David Hume's treatment of miracles, stood in little or no need of modification. In an argument embodying Butler's principles of analogy and probability, Paley advanced the thesis that belief in miracles is not at all unreasonable.

The force of experience as an objection to miracles, is founded in the presumption, either that the course of nature is invariable, or that, if it be ever varied, variations will be frequent and general. Has the necessity of this alternative been demonstrated? Permit us to call the course of nature the agency of an intelligent Being; and is there any good reason for judging this state of the case to be probable? Ought we not rather to expect that such a Being, on occasions of peculiar importance, may interrupt the order which he had appointed; yet, that such occasions should return seldom.[31]

Just as Paley made the order of nature the basis for claiming that the God *of* that order has disposal over it to the point of occasionally performing miracles, so he made the consistency of the scriptural witnesses, to the extent of their suffering persecution and martyrdom, the reasonable historical evidence for belief in miracles: "These men could not be deceivers—By only not bearing testimony, they might have avoided all these sufferings, and have lived quietly. Would men in such circumstances pretend to have seen what they never saw; assert facts which they had no knowledge of?"[32]

Supporting both his defense of the literal truth of miracles and his utilitarian ethics was Paley's view of the order of creation, a view spelled out in his *Natural Theology, or Evidences of the Existence and Attributes of the Deity Collected from the Appearances of Nature*. This book was the "centerpiece of his entire philosophic system."[33] Neither an original nor a brilliant work, its appeal lay in its nontechnical language and in its easily understood examples. It set out a lucid, popular argument for a designer of nature from the mechanical universe of the new science.

The opening sentences of the *Natural Theology* introduce the now-famous metaphor of the watch:

In crossing a heath, suppose I pitched my foot against a *stone,* and were asked how the stone came to be there: I might possibly answer, that for any thing I knew to the contrary, it had lain there for ever. . . . But suppose I had found a *watch* upon the ground, and it should be inquired how the watch happened to be in that place; I should hardly think of the answer which I had before given, that for any thing I knew, the watch might have always been there. Yet why should not this answer serve for the watch as well as for the stone? . . . For this reason, and for no other, *viz.* that when we come to inspect the watch, we perceive (what we could not discover in the stone) that its several parts are framed and put together for a purpose, *e.g.* that they are so formed and adjusted as to produce motion, and that motion so regulated as to point out the hour of the day; . . . This mechanism being observed, . . .

the inference, we think, is inevitable, that the watch must have had a maker; that there must have existed, at some time, and at some place or other, an artificer or artificers, who formed it for the purpose which we find it actually to answer.[34]

By analogy, the intricately designed universe with its material parts serving given ends implies a Designer. The argument for God from design is, of course, an ancient one, and even Paley's metaphor of the watch is unoriginal. Yet Paley's version of the argument has distinctive features. The watch is not simply one analogy among others in the *Natural Theology*; it is the controlling motif for the treatise. And the mechanistic view of nature bound up with the analogy leads Paley to stress those aspects of nature which buttress the view and to neglect or slight those which do not fit his model.[35] Chemistry, for example, cannot "afford the same species of argument as that which mechanism affords." And astronomy, though it reveals the magnificence of God's operations, "is not the best medium through which to prove the agency of an intelligent Creator." This is not to say that for Paley intelligent design is absent from those parts of creation, only that design has not yet been fully displayed in the scientific disciplines appropriate to those dimensions of nature.[36] So Paley concentrates his proof on the anatomy of animals and humans; there, he is convinced, resides the clearest evidence for intelligent design in a mechanical world.

Design not intentionally produced by organisms themselves is apparent in internal organic structures (the functioning of bones, muscles, organs of the body), in the structural adaptations of organisms to the environment (webbed feet for water fowl, protected eyes for the mole), and in "compensating contrivances" (a food-trapping web for the spider which cannot fly; a long, flexible proboscis for the elephant with unbending neck). Paley believes such evidence for a Designer to be overwhelming, and he devotes the greater part of his *Natural Theology* to displaying his evidence. Yet he insists that one telling sign—one watch on the ground—should be enough to convince the open-minded inquirer of an intelligent Designer of the material world: "Were there no example in the world, of contrivance, except that of the *eye*, it would be alone sufficient to support the conclusion which we draw from it, as to the necessity of an intelligent Creator. . . . If there were but one watch in the world, it would not be less certain that it had a maker."[37]

From Paley's angle of vision not only the existence but certain attributes of the Creator are discernible in the design of nature. The unity of God and his singleness of plan are to be observed in the overall unity of the natural system of interconnected parts.[38] And the Designer of the world must be personal. The coordinate functioning of heart and lungs, the unwitting adaptation of organisms to their environments, the supply of the mother's milk to the infant at the appropriate time—all bear witness to the design of a person with consciousness: "They require that which can perceive an end or purpose; as well as the power of providing means, and of directing them to their end. They require a centre in which perceptions unite, and from which volitions flow; which is mind . . . and in whatever a mind resides, is a person."[39]

Nature also testifies to the goodness of its Creator. Paley believes that nature's lessons about this attribute of God are reducible to two propositions: that the design of the world is, on the whole, beneficial; and that there is a surplus of pleasure in animal sensation. Regarding the first proposition, Paley says, "It is a happy world after all. The air, the earth, the water, teem with delighted existence." The bee flitting among the flowers, the young animal exercising its limbs, the old man dozing in his chair—these are evidences of a benevolent Creator. If it be objected that Paley has beheld the world between blinders, he has an answer at the ready: his instances "comprise large provinces of sensitive existence," with "every case which we have described, the case of millions." If we refuse to grant this, it can only be because of our insensitivity to the extensiveness of God's bounty, that insensitivity springing from our prizing "but little what we share only in common with the rest, or with the generality of our species."[40] It is only man's obstinate resistance to being driven down the scale of being that accounts for his unwillingness to acknowledge God's goodness in the whole of the creation. As to the second proposition—that there exists in nature an experience of pleasure quite beyond the satisfaction of the necessities of life—Paley says a single example will prove his case: "Why add pleasure to the act of eating; sweetness and relish to food? . . . This is a constitution which, so far as appears to me, can be resolved into nothing but the pure benevolence of the Creator."[41]

Jonathan Edwards and his Puritan predecessors also sang praises to the God who affords us "various delectations, beyond necessity to satiate." But both of Paley's propositions, advanced without sufficient qualification, would have appeared to them as naive shortsightedness. To the Puritan way of thinking, the beauties and bounty of nature certainly did attest to a benevolent Creator, but nature was also filled with tokens of human misery and divine wrath. To the person not illuminated by God's grace, the beauties of the world were tempting idols offering themselves as objects of desire alternative to their Creator. And God's provision of pleasure beyond the necessities of life, though emblematic of God's overflowing love, was also the occasion for man's sinful pursuit of his own enjoyment as an end in itself. The truth of the matter is that Paley's Anglican Latitudinarian vision, unlike the Puritan's, could at best allow evil, as the disruption of God's ordered universe, only a quick glance.

Paley insists that if it is properly understood, evil is not disruption at all. It is, rather, a relatively small and quite temporary adjustment that the good makes to given circumstances; seen from a larger perspective, evil is beneficent. Bodily pain, for example, "is a salutary provision; inasmuch as it teaches vigilance and caution; both gives notice of danger, and excites those endeavors which may be necessary to preservation." Furthermore, bodily pain "is not without its *alleviations*. It may be violent and frequent; but it is seldom both violent and long-continued: and its pauses and intermissions become positive pleasures." Paley also takes considerable comfort from another quantitative judgment—that "few diseases are fatal," citing data from a neighborhood hospital to the effect that of 6420 patients admitted, 5476 were cured and only 234 died.[42] As D. L. LeMahieu has remarked, it is important to note that the optimism of these observations did not arise from armchair abstraction, since Paley wrote them while suffering the intense pains of intestinal cancer; yet they "must have been cold comfort to the less hardy souls."[43] They were observations, moreover, which shed no light on what Paley dismissed as "of much less magnitude" than bodily pain:[44] social evil, or man's capacity for the physical and psychological destruction of his fellows, himself, and his environment. The instructions of Paley's altogether beneficent nature simply could not illuminate the evils of human history.

Like other *a posteriori* "proofs" for the existence of God, the teleological argument of Paley's *Natural Theology* was less convincing to the nonbeliever than to the Christian eager to found his faith on natural evidence. In fact, Paley directed his treatise to the believer rather than to the nonbeliever. He felt that his meditations on intelligent design in nature could expand the believer's awareness of God's awesome presence, so that "whereas formerly God was seldom in our thoughts, we can now scarcely look upon any thing without perceiving its relation to him."[45] For all of the mechanistic concepts of the treatise and the dominance of the watch analogy, Paley's God was no absent watchmaker who withdrew from his handiwork after its completion. The facts of nature spoke of the continuing presence of a benevolent Deity. Generations of college students and theologians in America nurtured their thoughts on nature with Paley's pious facts, finding persuasive both his anatomical evidence and his sentiment that in a well-regulated natural system all things work together for the good of the whole.

Adherence to Natural and Moral Law: Scottish Common Sense Philosophy

In his prize-winning undergraduate essay in moral philosophy at Harvard, Ralph Waldo Emerson wrote, "The first true advance which is made [in the science of ethics] must go on in the school in which Reid and Stewart have labored."[46] One twentiety-century scholar has suggested that the young Emerson's fascination with the ideas of the Scottish philosophers Thomas Reid and Dugald Stewart, especially their notions of the "moral sense" and the intuitive principles of reason, set the course of the later Emerson's movement into Romanticism and Transcendentalism.[47] What is altogether clear is that Emerson and his fellow Harvard students, as well as undergraduates at most American colleges of the time, were exposed in depth to the Scottish Philosophy of Common Sense.

By the late eighteenth century, books by Scottish philosophers appeared in enormous volume in American libraries and among American booksellers. At the College of New Jersey, President John Witherspoon, a graduate of the University of Edinburgh, modeled the college curriculum after the Scottish universities and drew upon Scottish Enlightenment thought in his lectures on moral philosophy. Similar patterns of Scottish influence appeared in Presbyterian colleges across the land and at the College of William and Mary, the College of Philadelphia, Harvard, Yale, and Brown. Thomas Jefferson met Dugald Stewart in Paris in 1789 and for the remainder of his life looked upon Stewart as the greatest of philosophers. In his correspondence with Jefferson, John Adams referred to Stewart as a profound genius. Among American theologians, the Scottish Philosophy of Common Sense became, in the words of Sydney Ahlstrom, "the handmaiden of both Unitarianism and Orthodoxy." Theologians as diverse as David Tappan and James Walker of Harvard, Timothy Dwight and Nathaniel Taylor of Yale, Edwards Amasa Park of Andover, and Charles Hodge of Princeton took their philosophical bearings from this school of thought. In the middle of the nineteenth century, James Walker summed up the influence of the Scots in his newly annotated abridgment of Thomas Reid's *Essays on the Intellectual Powers of Man*. The philosophy "generally taught in England and in this country for the last fifty years has been that of the Scotch School of which Dr. Reid is the acknowledged head. . . . The name of Reid therefore historically considered is second to none among the British psychologists and metaphysicians, with perhaps the single exception of Locke."[48]

The Philosophy of Common Sense arose as a vital part of the cultural renaissance in Scotland that put the Scottish universities at the forefront of European learning. Supported by the moderate wing of the Scottish Kirk, the Scottish philosophers, most of them professors of moral philosophy, formed the vanguard of the Scottish Enlightenment.[49] The principal spokesmen for the school of thought were Thomas Reid (1710–96) who taught first at King's College, Aberdeen and then at Glasgow as the successor to Adam Smith; James Beattie (1735–1803), professor at Marischal College, Aberdeen; and Dugald Stewart (1753–1828) of the University of Edinburgh. Although these three did not always agree on every philosophical point—Stewart and Reid were, for example, friendly critics of each other's works—Beattie and Stewart understood their philosophies to be extensions of Reid's ideas. Other Scottish philosophers more independent of Reid's thinking but still, on certain fundamental issues, in agreement with this core group were James Oswald (1715–69), George Campbell (1719–96), and Thomas Brown (1778–1820).

The type of thinking represented by these philosophers was

dubbed "common sense" because of Reid's book of 1764, *An Inquiry into the Human Mind on the Principles of Common Sense.* Directed against David Hume's "system of scepticism, which leaves no ground to believe any one thing rather than its contrary," Reid offered his book as an analysis of the objective reality of human perceptions in order to "justify the common sense and reason of mankind."[50] Reid insisted that behind Humean skepticism, which calls into question the rational assertion of a correlation between the human mind and realities external to the mind, lies a mode of thought that has pervaded the whole history of philosophy, but especially philosophy in its modern phase. It is the philosophical position which Reid calls the "theory of ideas." According to this theory, the only immediate objects of the mind are ideas or representations of things outside the mind; these mental constructs mediate between the mind and things external to the mind. Upon this theory, Reid says, our world dissolves and radical skepticism ensues, "for ideas being the only objects of thought, and having no existence but when we are conscious of them, it necessarily follows, that there is no object of our thought which can have a continued and permanent existence. Body and spirit, cause and effect, time and space, to which we were wont to ascribe an existence independent of our thought, are all turned out of existence."[51]

To counteract this idealist tradition (misrepresented, oversimplified, even invented, according to Reid's critics), Reid calls for an examination of those elementary data of human consciousness which indicate that we have direct contact not with ideas but with an external world. The mental operations in sense perception reveal that we both apprehend external realities and make judgments about the truth of those realities. In perceiving a tree, for example, I know that there is involved an object which is perceived and a mental act by which it is seen. But I know, further, that I both perceive the form of the tree and judge that it exists as an object in the present. "I know, moreover, that this belief is not the effect of argumentation and reasoning; it is the immediate effect of my constitution."[52] Such basic apprehensions and judgments constitute the common sense of mankind. They are self-evident premises on the basis of which we think. Reid classifies the truths of common sense as those which are necessary or logically axiomatic (e.g. that there is a cause for every effect) and those which are contingent or appropriate to concrete existence (e.g. that we have freedom over the determinations of our wills).

In the *Inquiry*, Reid implied a possible opposition between common sense and reason, an opposition which James Beattie magnified.[53] But in his later work, Reid made his meaning clear: reason has two functions, one intuitive and the other deductive. The intuitive function of reason is "common sense," an apprehension of self-evident truths, from which deductive reason then draws conclusions that are not self-evident.[54] Ultimately, then, Reid is convinced that human thought is based on intuition, that all reasoning rests on self-evident truths regarding the external world. Sir James Macintosh once remarked to Thomas Brown that Thomas Reid and David Hume "differed more in words than in opinion," to which Brown replied, "Yes, Reid bawled out, We must believe an outward world; but added in a whisper, We can give no reason for our belief. Hume cries out, We can give no reason for such a notion; and whispers, I own we cannot get rid of it."[55]

The point of that story would have been lost on most American theologians, as would have Immanuel Kant's remark that the Scottish Common Sense philosophers assumed what Hume questioned and proved what he never disputed. For few American intellectuals before the late nineteenth century showed any interest in Hume's *Inquiry Concerning Human Understanding*, the work which Reid's book sought to answer. Widely respected in America as a historian, Hume as a philosopher was known by Americans through his critics.[56] Quite apart from the accuracy or inaccuracy of their attacks on Hume, Hume's Common Sense countrymen demonstrated to the satisfaction of American theologians of great diversity that every man's judgments about the reality of the world around him were sound judgments and that there was every reason to safeguard in both theology and philosophy the common-sense truths of "the people" in a democratic republic. By the same token, there was no good reason to found theology either on the psychological fancies of philosophical skeptics or on the speculative meanderings of medieval thinkers.

The philosophical approach of the Scots thus had as much appeal to American theologians as any one of their philosophical arguments. It was an approach which sought to render reflection upon the things of human consciousness as scientific as the study of the things of physical nature. Moral philosophy, touching on most everything not embraced by natural philosophy (or natural science)—pneumatology, ethics, natural theology, economics, politics, aesthetics—could attain respectability only by learning from the success of natural science. What accounted for that success was the natural scientist's careful attention to facts and to laws gleaned from those facts. The Scottish Common Sense philosophers conveyed to their university students and to their readers a sense of urgency about the scientific task and a conviction that Scottish moral philosophy formed the cutting edge of an important new movement. Dugald Stewart told his students that although natural and moral philosophy were never to be confused, moral philosophy would never earn the high reputation achieved by the natural sciences until the scientific approach became universal. "As all our knowledge of the material world rests ultimately on facts ascertained by observation, so all our knowledge of the human mind rests ultimately on facts for which we have the evidence of our consciousness." Such knowledge of the mind by definition excludes the old-style "metaphysics," a kind of reflection which embarks from hypotheses.[57] In urging his own students to avoid metaphysical, hypothetical conjecture, Thomas Reid drew a moral from a well-known story:

> Mr. Locke was acquainted with an Indian who being asked what he thought supported the earth, said that it was supported upon the back of a huge elephant. And being asked what the elephant stood upon, he said upon the back of a huge tortoise. Such are the conclusions of all hypotheses which have no other source except in man's brain. . . . Let us therefore in our enquiry into the operations of the human mind give no attention to hypotheses but follow upon sure notions and not upon conjectures and man's fancy . . . and build upon sure evidence; although we may proceed slowly, yet we will proceed surely.[58]

The heroes of this inductive approach were Francis Bacon, who "first taught mankind to distinguish the fictions of human fancy from the oracles of nature," and, despite his occasional lapses into metaphysical dreaming, Isaac Newton. The Scottish philosophers were persuaded that they were doing for moral philosophy what Newton had done for natural philosophy.[59]

The conviction of the Scottish philosophers that all branches of inquiry could adopt the method of the new science bred a similar

belief among American theologians. The facts of human consciousness, of nature, and of Scripture, all of which yielded laws rather
than metaphysical fancies, were to provide the grounds of argument among evangelical Protestants, liberal Unitarians, and
literalistic orthodox Calvinists. The Scottish philosophers seemed
to point to an interpretation of reality which was even closer to the
modern scientific spirit than either Butler or Paley. And beyond the
techniques of philosophical approach, the Scots assisted American
theologians in coming to grips with the consequences of the difference between mind and matter, with the moral meanings of government, and with the respective roles of reason and imagination.

Although the mind, like material nature, functions according to
law, the laws of the mind are not the laws of physical nature. The
error of all psychological determinism is ignorance of the difference
between mind and matter. "It is no less unphilosophical," Stewart
said," to attempt an explanation of perception, or of the association
of ideas, upon mechanical principles; than it would be . . . to
explain the chemical phenomena of elective attractions, by supposing the substances among which they are observed, to be endowed
with thought and volition."[60] James Beattie was willing to entertain
the possibility that in perception the human mind and its laws are
hindered rather than aided by the organs of sense.[61] Even when the
Scottish philosophers did not move to that extreme, however, they
maintained that the mind has its own principles quite independent
of those of the material world. The mental principles that go a long
way toward explaining the difference between mind and matter
are those definitive of personal identity and those constitutive of
the will.

My identity is my mind—not the operations or contents of my
mind, but my mind itself. According to Reid, "I am not thought, I
am not action, I am not feeling; I am something that thinks, acts,
and suffers. My thoughts, and actions, and feelings, change every
moment . . . but that *self* or *I*, to which they belong, is permanent."[62] Mind or self can only be specified as a law of identity given
with the separate operations of the mind. Beyond that, Reid finds it
impossible to say *what* the self is. Personal identity thus defined is
the necessary presupposition of moral responsibility, for only a
human being permanent over time, rather than his changing ideas
and impressions, can stand morally responsible.[63] Moral responsi-

bility also presupposes a free will, a power over the determinations of the will, in addition to the mere ability to act as we choose.

As one commentator has said, Thomas Reid "will allow no exceptions to the principle of causation," even in the operations of the will.[64] The dictate of common sense that every effect must have a cause is as true of the human mind as it is of material nature; in fact, it is a law springing directly from human consciousness. And that law lays it down that our personal identity, our selfhood itself, and not the "motives of the will," is the efficient cause of our choices:

> The influence of motives is of a very different nature from that of efficient causes. They are neither causes nor agents. They suppose an efficient cause, and can do nothing without it. We cannot, without absurdity, suppose a motive either to act, or to be acted upon; it is equally incapable of action and of passion; because it is not a thing that exists, but a thing that is conceived. . . . Motives, therefore, may *influence* to action, but they do not act . . . motives suppose liberty in the agent, otherwise they have no influence at all.[65]

Reid carries this claim a step farther. Causation in the sense of originating cause applies only to the realm of mind, not to the realm of matter. The human mind possesses an "active power" or the ability to act without being acted upon; matter acts only when it is acted upon.[66] Originating cause, self-determination, is then a basic principle of moral government which, unlike the mechanical government of the material world, involves accountability, merit, and blame.[67]

The theme of moral government was a central consideration in the natural theology of the Scottish Common Sense philosophers. They drew heavily on Butler in their development of the theme, and in order to demonstrate the existence of God as Supreme Governor they advanced a teleological argument very much like Paley's. For the Scots, however, natural theology was more directly related to the facts of human consciousness than it was for either Butler or Paley. In Scottish Common Sense Philosophy, the moral attributes of God are derived from human moral perceptions. According to Stewart, "the distinction between Right and Wrong" is apprehended by our moral consciousness "to be eternal and immutable, no less than the distinction between mathematical Truth and Falsehood." This moral sense, more than any other human characteristic, elevates man above the brutes, so it must certainly extend as well to the Moral Governor of the universe. "To act in conformity to our sense of rectitude is plainly the highest excellence which our nature is capable of attaining; nor can we avoid extending the same rule of estimation to all intelligent beings whatever." Reflection on the moral truths of human consciousness leads also to the discovery of man's duties within a system of moral government: gratitude toward the Deity, promotion of the happiness of the whole of creation, resignation to the will of God as Governor. These duties follow upon a recognition that the Moral Governor of the universe must possess an infinite degree of the virtuous promptings of our own finite moral sense.[68] The existence of the Creator-Governor of the world may be discerned in the laws of physical nature, but his attributes and our obligations to him are to be discovered in the moral principles of the human mind.

Those same moral principles teach us that duty and self-interest coincide. Although the Scottish philosophers repudiated outright utilitarianism (and so American university teachers supplemented Paley's ethics with that of the Scots),[69] they did hold that a sense of duty within the system of moral government does not rule out a prudent interest in one's own happiness. In Reid's words:

> It is true, that a regard to our own good cannot, of itself, produce any benevolent affection. But, if such affections be a part of our constitution, and if the exercise of them make a capital part of our happiness, a regard to our own good ought to lead us to cultivate and exercise them, as every benevolent affection makes the good of others to be our own.[70]

According to Stewart, the duty of moral virtue is not to be confused with prudence since in all languages words the equivalent of "duty" and "interest" designate two different moral postures. Yet we may rest assured that happiness is the end result of duty; in fact, duty to the laws of God more than any other virtue ultimately meets the human interest in happiness. "The man who is successful in the pursuit of happiness is he whose ruling principle is a sense of duty, not whose end is immediate enjoyment."[71]

All judgments of reason, whether directed to material nature or to moral standards, are objective. They refer to truths independent of the human subject's inner feelings and ideas. Just as sense perceptions are more than a bundle of mediating ideas, so moral judgments are more than a collection of feelings. Conscience, or the "moral sense," is thus analogous to the five senses:

In its dignity [the moral sense] is, without doubt, far superior to every other power of the mind; but there is this analogy between it and the external senses, That, as by them we have not only the original conceptions of the various qualities of bodies, but the original judgment that this body has such a quality, that such another; so by our moral faculty, we have both the original conceptions of right and wrong in conduct, of merit and demerit, and the original judgments that this conduct is right, that is wrong. [72]

There is this further analogy between the moral and the sense judgments: the truths of right and wrong intuitively apprehended through the conscience are the basis of ethical reasoning, just as the intuition of elementary truths about physical nature are the ground of discursive reasoning about the material universe. Moral reason as conscience first of all gives us access to objective first principles (for example, that we should avoid doing to another what we think wrong if done to us in similar circumstances); only then can we reason *about* ethical actions (for example, that certain social acts are necessary for the promotion of justice). [73] The mental operations turned to both nature and morals are thus objective, uniform, and universal at the elementary level of the discovery of first principles. "There is good reason to believe," as Reid put it, "that the operations of the human mind about moral objects are no less uniform than about natural objects; and that men agree as much in what they call moral approbation and disapprobation, ought and ought not, as in what they call light and darkness." [74]

In their discussions of beauty, aesthetic taste, and imagination, the Scottish Common Sense philosophers were also eager to safeguard reasonable objectivity and uniformity of judgment. Reid, in fact, believed that he had first placed aesthetics on an objective, rational foundation. Plato and his admirers might be credited with having properly elevated intellectual beauty to a superior status on the aesthetic scale and for having united goodness and beauty. But they had handled "the subject of beauty rather with the enthusiasm of poets or lovers, than with the cool temper of philosophers." So Reid is "proud to think that I first, in clear and explicit terms, and in the cool blood of a philosopher, maintained that all the beauty and sublimity of objects of sense is derived from the expression they exhibit of things intellectual, which alone have original beauty." Reid is willing to season his immodest claim about his work with a small amount of doubt: "But in this I may deceive myself, and cannot claim to be held an impartial judge."[75]

Although Reid thinks it is impossible to single out one quality which renders any object beautiful, he does think it evident that anything beautiful elicits two actions of the mind. First, when beautiful objects are either perceived or imagined, "they produce a certain agreeable emotion or feeling in the mind." Second, the agreeable emotion is accompanied by a judgment that the objects have "some perfection or excellence belonging to them." According to this definition, everything in existence at least potentially houses the beautiful, but Reid and his followers apply the category of beauty primarily to persons and only secondarily to other parts of the creation. The beauty that most readily calls forth the highest agreeable emotion and the most excellent judgment, that of love, belongs to virtuous minds. "As grandeur naturally produces admiration, beauty naturally produces love. We may, therefore, justly ascribe beauty to those qualities which are the natural objects of love and kind affection."[76] Whether directed to natural or moral objects, aesthetic taste entails objective judgments, and it is possible, indeed necessary, to cultivate the judgments of that taste. "Good taste" is developed by opening our senses increasingly to physical nature, by cultivating our contacts with virtuous persons, by expanding our intellects so that more intellectual beauties fall within our view, by attending to and participating in the arts, by the improvement of our virtuous habits—and by good breeding.[77]

"Good taste implies Lively Imagination,"[78] James Beattie wrote, and the other Scottish philosophers agreed that imagination, rather than being the exclusive province of the artistic genius, is germane to every life lived to the fullest. Imagination is the faculty of selecting concepts, perceptions, and tastes from among the welter of human experience in order to form them into new combinations.[79] Imagination is thus man's creative capacity, and it involves the crucial and very difficult judgments of selection and arrangement. Unlike the judgments of perception or memory, however, those of the imagination consider something as present to the mind "without any view to real existence, or to past experience."[80] The imagination is essentially fanciful, and so it is to be carefully regulated by the other powers of the mind which do make judgments about "real existence." While exalting the role of the imagination in the cultivation of good taste, therefore, the Scottish philosophers also warned of the dangers of an imagination run wild. Uncontrolled by the powers of reason and morality, the dreams of poetry and the romance of novels result in inaction and social dislocation, and in the unrestrained passions of enthusiasm. Finally, however, the hope is held out that the imagination and the regulatory powers of reason are not incompatible. "Even supposing the pleasures of imagination to be greatest when the pleasures of reason are not felt, still the former would not last beyond the season of youth, without being combined with the latter. . . . The pleasure of imagination may be prolonged if subjected to reason beyond the season of youth and made to continue during the remainder of life."[81]

For the Scottish Common Sense Philosophy, the whole of human life—knowledge, action, imagination—was founded on a unifying principle: the "fixed and steady course of nature." Apart from that elementary principle, experience could not connect present with past; the objective truths of perception and conscience would disappear; aesthetic taste of something outside the self would be impossible.[82] Setting out from that principle, the Scottish philosophers proposed an inductive method of accounting for the laws of the human mind, laws, they were persuaded, that were as certain and stable as those of the material world. The Scots inspired American theologians to undertake a similar task, and to reach similar conclusions, in their own spheres of labor. Perhaps even more than Butler or Paley, the Scottish philosophers "enlightened" American theologians by awakening their confidence in an approach to the whole of reality that could illuminate the fixed and steady laws of nature, mental and physical. American theologians were thereby further encouraged to turn from ontology to moral philosophy, from nature's symbols to nature's facts, from the mind's act of symboling to the mind's grasp of moral laws.

NOTES

1. See Ralph Henry Gabriel, *Religion and Learning at Yale* (New Haven: Yale University Press, 1958), p. 21; Samuel Eliot Morison, *Three Centuries of Harvard, 1636–1936* (Cambridge: Harvard University Press, 1946), pp. 58–59, 89–93; Henry F. May, *The Enlightenment in America* (New York:

Oxford University Press, 1976), pp. 33–34; Robert Middlekauf, *The Mathers: Three Generations of Puritan Intellectuals, 1596–1728* (New York: Oxford University Press, 1971), pp. 284–89.

2. Frederick Copleston, *A History of Philosophy* (Westminster, Md.: Newman Press), vol. 4, *Descartes to Leibniz* (1960): 8–14; vol. 5, *Hobbes to Hume* (1961): 149.

3. Frank E. Manuel, *The Religion of Isaac Newton* (Oxford: Clarendon Press, 1974), pp. 16, 21.

4. On Butler's reputation in Britain, see Ernest C. Mossner, "Introduction" to Joseph Butler, *The Analogy of Religion* (New York: Frederick Ungar Publishing Co., 1961), pp. vii–x; and D. H. Meyer, *The Instructed Conscience* (Philadelphia: University of Pennsylvania Press, 1972), p. 40. All following references to Butler's *Analogy* are to the Mossner edition.

5. On Butler's influence in America, see Meyer, *Instructed Conscience,* p. 44; Daniel W. Howe, *The Unitarian Conscience* (Cambridge: Harvard University Press, 1970), p. 85; Kenneth Walter Cameron, *Transcendental Climate* (Hartford, Conn.: Transcendental Books, 1963), 1:15–16, 142; *The Works of W. E. Channing* (Boston: American Unitarian Association, 1900), p. 560; George H. Williams, ed., *The Harvard Divinity School* (Boston: Beacon Press, 1954), pp. 58, 129; *The Autobiography of Lyman Beecher,* ed. Barbara Cross (Cambridge: Belknap Press of Harvard University Press, 1961), 2:426; Noah Porter, "Introduction" to Nathaniel W. Taylor, *Lectures on the Moral Government of God* (New York: Clark, Austin & Smith, 1859), 1:v; Horace Bushnell, *Christ in Theology* (Hartford, Conn.: Brown & Parsons, 1851), pp. 282–83, 288–89.

6. Butler, *Analogy*, p. 254

7. Ibid., pp. 1–2.

8. Ibid., p. 12.

9. Ibid., p. 4.

10. Ibid., p. 17.

11. Ibid., pp. 133–39, 207–21.

12. Ibid., pp. 108, 165.

13. Ibid., p. 161.

14. Ibid., p. 179.

15. Ibid., p. 39.

16. Ibid., pp. 186–87.

17. Ibid., p. 109.

18. Ibid., pp. 40, 61–62, 81, 101–3, 151–52.

19. Ibid., p. 249.

20. D. L. LeMahieu, *The Mind of William Paley, A Philosopher and His Age* (Lincoln: University of Nebraska Press, 1976), p. 153.

21. Ibid., pp. 157, 177–79.

22. Wilson Smith, *Professors and Public Ethics* (Ithaca, N.Y.: Cornell University Press, 1956), p. 44.

23. Ibid., pp. 47–48, 61.

24. Gabriel, *Religion and Learning at Yale,* p. 110.

25. "Moral and Political Philosophy," *The Works of William Paley in One Volume* (Philadelphia: Crissy & Markley, n.d.), p. 34.

26. Ibid., pp. 30–34.

27. Ibid., p. 39.

28. LeMahieu, *Mind of Paley*, p. 123.

29. "Moral and Political Philosophy," *Works*, pp. 38–39.

30. Howe, *Unitarian Conscience*, p. 67; Timothy Dwight, *Theology, Explained and Defended*, (Middletown, Conn.: Clark & Lyman, 1818), 3:450–51.

31. "A View of the Evidences of Christianity," *Works*, pp. 272–73.

32. Ibid., p. 318.

33. LeMahieu, *Mind of Paley*, p. x.

34. "Natural Theology," *Works*, pp. 387–88.

35. LeMahieu, *Mind of Paley*, p. 61.

36. "Natural Theology," *Works*, pp. 401–2, 456.

37. Ibid., p. 401.

38. Ibid., pp. 469–70.

39. Ibid., p. 462.

40. Ibid., pp. 470–72.

41. Ibid., p. 476.

42. Ibid., p. 478.

43. LeMahieu, *Mind of Paley*, p. 85.

44. "Natural Theology," *Works*, p. 479.

45. Ibid., p. 486.

46. "The Present State of Ethical Philosophy," Cameron, *Transcendental Climate*, 1:19.

47. Merrell R. Davis, "Emerson's 'Reason' and the Scottish Philosophers," *The New England Quarterly*, 17 (1944): 209–28.

48. Howe, *Unitarian Conscience*, pp. 32–33. For discussions of the impact of Scottish philosophy on American college curricula, see Douglas Sloan, *The Scottish Enlightenment and the American College Ideal* (New York: Teacher's College Press, Columbia University, 1971). The availability of Scottish philosophy to the American reading public is documented by David Lundberg and Henry F. May, "The Enlightened Reader in America," *American Quarterly*, 28 (1976): 269–71. The influence of the Scots on American thinkers is treated in May, *Enlightenment in America*, pp. 346–47; Sydney E. Ahlstrom, "The Scottish Philosophy and American Theology," *Church History*, 24 (1955): 257–69; Theodore Dwight Bozeman, *Protestants in An Age of Science* (Chapel Hill: University of North Carolina Press, 1977); E. Brooks Holifield, *The Gentlemen Theologians* (Durham, N.C.: Duke University Press, 1978); Herbert Hovenkamp, *Science and Religion in America, 1800–1860* (Philadelphia: University of Pennsylvania Press, 1978).

49. Ahlstrom, "Scottish Philosophy and American Theology," pp. 257–59.

50. Thomas Reid, *An Inquiry into the Human Mind on the Principles of Common Sense*, 4th ed. (London: T. Cadell, 1785), pp. v, x.

51. Ibid., p. 474.

52. Ibid., pp. 369–70.

53. James Beattie, "An Essay on the Nature and Immutability of Truth," *The Philosophical and Critical Works of James Beattie* (Hildesheim & New York: Georg Olms Verlag, 1975), 1:18–31.

54. Thomas Reid, "Essays on the Intellectual Powers of Man," *The Works of Thomas Reid*, 8th ed. (London: Longmans, Green & Co., 1895), 1:425.

55. Cited in S.A. Grave, *The Scottish Philosophy of Common Sense* (Oxford: Clarendon Press, 1960), p. 109.

56. May, *Enlightenment in America*, p. 121; Lundberg and May, "Enlightened Reader in America," pp. 268–71.

57. Dugald Stewart, *Lectures on Moral Philosophy* (student notes for 1808–1809, Library of the University of Edinburgh), 1:23–28.

58. Thomas Reid, *Lectures on Pneumatology, Ethics and Politics* (student notes of Robert Jack for 1774–76, Library of the University of Glasgow), 1:39–40.

59. Thomas Reid, "Critical Remarks Upon the First Volume of Stewart's Elements" (MS 2131.4, Birkwood MSS, Library of King's College, Aberdeen), p. 1; Reid, "Essays on Intellectual Powers," *Works*, 1:231; Dugald Stewart, *Elements of the Philosophy of the Human Mind* (New York: Garland Publishing, 1971), pp. 5–13; Beattie, "Essay on Truth," *Works*, 1:5.

60. Stewart, *Elements of the Mind*, pp. 13–14.

61. James Beattie, "Notes on Various Subjects" (MS B.22, Library of King's College, Aberdeen), pp. 3–5.

62. Reid, "Essays on Intellectual Powers," *Works*, 1:345.

63. Reid, *Inquiry into the Human Mind*, pp. 55–56.

64. Grave, *Scottish Philosophy,*, p. 209.

65. Thomas Reid, "Essays on the Active Powers of Man," *Works*, 2:608–9.

66. Ibid., p. 603.

67. Ibid., pp. 613–22.

68. Dugald Stewart, *Outlines of Moral Philosophy* (New York: Garland Publishing, 1976), pp. 203–4, 233–26. Cf. Reid, *Lectures on Pneumatology*, Lecture LVI ff. and "Essays on Active Powers," *Works*, 2:615–16.

69. Howe, *Unitarian Conscience*, pp. 65–66.

70. Reid, "Essays on Active Powers," *Works*, 2:584.

71. Stewart, *Lectures on Moral Philosophy*, 1:62–64.

72. Reid, "Essays on Active Powers," *Works*, 2:590.

73. Ibid., pp. 590–91.

74. Thomas Reid, "Whether Moral Determinations Are Real Judgments" (MS 2131.3, Birkwood MSS, Library of King's College, Aberdeen), p. 4.

75. Thomas Reid, "Letter to the Rev. Archibald Alison," *Works*, 1:89.

76. Reid, "Essays on Intellectual Powers," *Works*, 1:498, 502.

77. Ibid., pp. 490–91, 507–8; Stewart, *Elements of the Mind,* pp. 36ff.; Thomas Reid, "Lectures on the Fine Arts" (MS, Library of the University of Edinburgh, 1774), pp. 43–46, 70–71.

78. James Beattie, "On Memory and Imagination," *Works*, 2:166.

79. Ibid., pp. 72–74; Stewart, *Elements of the Mind*, pp. 475–77.

80. Beattie, "On Memory and Imagination," *Works*, 2:72. Cf. Reid, *Lectures on Pneumatology*, pp. 20–21 and Stewart, *Elements of the Mind*, p. 477.

81. Stewart, *Lectures on Moral Philosophy*, 1:107–8. Cf. Stewart, *Elements of the Mind*, pp. 513–22 and Beattie, "On Memory and Imagination," *Works*, 2:168.

82. Reid, *Inquiry into the Human Mind*, pp. 437–38; Stewart, *Lectures on Moral Philosophy*, 1: 8–11.

6

The New Haven Theology

In the year 1800 an article appeared in the American Deist weekly, *The Temple of Reason*, that typified Enlightenment enthusiasm for modern science, especially astronomy. The article drew a striking contrast between the religion awakened by physical nature and that stimulated by Scripture:

> To form a grand idea of the Omnipotence and Wisdom of the One God, we must contemplate his works in the Heavens, by means of telescopes; and then our pride shall be humbled with the dust. One view of these stupendous works infinitely dispersed probably, through boundless space, will give us a more exalted and sublime idea of the divinity, than all the childish tricks and puny miracles recorded, or rather invented, by all the priests and imposters that ever existed.[1]

The conviction expressed here, that the wonders of God's creation evoke more genuine religious awe than the "inventions" of sacred history, was widely held among American Deists. The conviction was clearly and forthrightly proclaimed in Thomas Paine's *The Age of Reason*, the most extensively circulated and the most severely attacked Deist tract during the last quarter of the eighteenth century. Paine and other radical Deists minced no words: institutional Christianity is a priestcraft that employs scriptural conceits to enslave human minds; Deism frees the mind to make an unbiased response to the Creator of the universe. Even those more moderate American Deists, like Jefferson and Franklin, who could muster tolerance for institutional religion as a positive moral force for the masses, believed physical nature to be the superior means of God's revelation that could liberate the mind from the parochial features of Christianity. As Perry Miller has said, Enlightenment Americans often thought natural science included "an aesthetic contemplation of a perfected universe," and they saluted "the comprehension of this universe (mainly through a grasp of Newton's system) as providing an entrance into the cosmopolitan culture of the West."[2] To be cosmopolitan meant, in part, to be free of the constrictive medieval assumptions of institutional Christianity.

In a churchly American culture long reared not only on the teachings of scriptural and Christian history but also on the parallels between its own and previous "sacred events," the Deist sentiment could not win wide support. A more acceptable version of rationalism established itself in the culture in the form that Henry May has called the "didactic Enlightenment." Committed to institutional Christianity and to the validity of scriptural revelation, proponents of this form of the Enlightenment set out to snatch Newton's intelligible and perfected universe from the grasp of Deism and skepticism.[3] Two movements will serve to illustrate the didactic Enlightenment in this book—the New Haven Theology and early Unitarianism. Although at a number of critical theological points these movements were at cross-purposes, both drew upon the Enlightenment apologetics of Butler, Paley, and the Scottish philosophers in order to hold together Newton's perfected universe with institutional Christianity and to elaborate, in their own distinctive fashions, the didactic meaning of nature.

Timothy Dwight, founder of the New Haven Theology, was an ardent Federalist and a scathing critic of Jeffersonianism. Dwight and his students, Lyman Beecher and Nathaniel Taylor, invoked the authority of Scripture and creed as an alternative to Deism's self-sufficient natural revelation. They hurled in the teeth of religious rationalism defenses of the necessity of sentiment, feeling, and the traditional trappings of religion. Their revivals were aimed as much at defeating Deism as at converting the individual to faith. Yet, for all of that, the New Haven theologians were as persuaded as any Deist of the value of Newtonian science—of its discoveries, its methods, and its implications for religion. That meant that they decried speculative metaphysics and advocated induction, fact, and law as the touchstones of theological reflection. It meant that they believed God's universe to consist of the connected worlds of material and moral government. Finally, and here they were the most "practical" of Enlightenment Americans, it meant for them that nature and nature's laws provided the grounds for converting individual and American Republic to Protestant Christianity.

Timothy Dwight (1758–1817), grandson of Jonathan Edwards, served as an army chaplain, then as a pastor of the Congregational church at Greenfield Hill, Connecticut. He was elected president of Yale in 1795, and over the next two decades he taught the senior class rhetoric, logic, metaphysics, and ethics; supplied the college pulpit; served as professor of theology; and brought the college curriculum into line with the latest scientific thought. As a tutor at Yale, Dwight had carried his students into a study of Newton's *Principia*, and later as college president his promotion of scientific study testified to his conviction that evangelical Protestantism had nothing to lose and everything to gain from the science of Newton and Boyle. In his own lectures he appealed to the works of Locke, Butler, and Paley, and his theories of aesthetic taste and rational judgment depended upon the ideas of the Scottish philosophers. Dwight was a leader in the Eastern wing of the revivalist movement known as the Second Great Awakening and is reputed, as a contributor to the movement, to have checked the progress of Deism at Yale by defeating free thinking students in open debate.[4]

By the time he gave up his role as tutor at Yale, Dwight was nearly blind, a condition doubtless brought on by his discipline of parsing a hundred lines of Homer each dawn, studying fourteen hours daily, and confining himself to twelve mouthfuls of vegetables at dinner. As college president he had to employ an amanuensis. Dwight's favorite secretary was his prize pupil, Nathaniel William Taylor (1786–1858). Taylor inherited from Dwight a dedication to study, a love of preaching, and an abiding interest in the theme of God's moral government. Minister at First Church of Christ, New Haven, from 1812 to 1822, Taylor was according to all accounts one of the most powerful and respected preachers of his day. In 1822, he was appointed Dwight Professor of Didactic Theology at the newly established Yale Divinity School, a post he held until his death. A long and steady stream of future ministers flowed through Taylor's classroom to hear him lecture on moral government and to be challenged with his motto, "Follow the truth if it carries you over Niagara." His complex lectures drew critically upon the thoughts of Edwards, Butler, Paley, and the Scottish philosophers.[5]

Lyman Beecher (1775–1863), another of Dwight's students and a close friend to Taylor, was minister at East Hampton, Long Island, from 1799 to 1810, at Litchfield, Connecticut, from 1810 to 1826, and at Hanover Street Church in Boston from 1826 to 1832. In 1832, Beecher was named the first president of Lane Seminary in Ohio, where he stayed until 1850. Feckless in the recognition of theological subtleties, Beecher was the least scholarly of this group of ministers. Yet he was in fundamental agreement with the theological positions of Dwight and Taylor, and as a dynamic preacher, lucid popularizer, and tireless activist he set about to convert American minds and institutions to the moral and religious principles of the New Haven Theology. As Barbara Cross has said, Lyman Beecher was the prototype of the evangelical minister in the first half of nineteenth-century America. "No longer the 'teacher' of an inquiring congregation," the minister now became a healer, "an expert in states of the soul, able to diagnose men's spiritual illnesses and carry them through the critical stages of their disease."[6] For Beecher the processes of diagnosis and cure were served by the same instrument—a psychology of conversion thought to be as scientific and precise as any implement wielded by a physician. The philosophy of mind borrowed from the Scots was put to a very practical use by Beecher and his kind. But the healing of the individual was only a part of the remedy that these evangelicals envisioned; they also intended to heal the nation, a challenge that called for associations as well as psychology. Beecher and his contemporaries organized a host of interdenominational societies designed for promoting religion and saving the Republic from the diseases of immorality which threatened her undoing. The American Bible Society, the Temperance Society, many missionary societies, the Sabbath-Day Society were founded for just this purpose. Using both revivals and associations, the new minister of the day sought to mold individual and nation according to laws of human nature as clear and as certain as the laws of the physical world.

Such attention to nature and nature's laws by no means entailed repudiation of biblical history. The New Haven theologians appealed to the Bible as a sacred authority, interpreted the American Republic with biblical precedent, and beheld events of contemporary history through the lenses of scriptural prophecy. Rejecting the Founding Fathers' effort to locate the origins of the American Republic in the classical world, Beecher insisted that the new republic "is of heavenly origin. It was not borrowed from Greece or Rome, but from the Bible." Beecher found in the Old Testament all of the major features of a sound republic: personal liberty, elections, the right of appeal to higher courts, private property.[7] In his interpretation of the events of the late eighteenth and early nineteenth century, Timothy Dwight, like numerous other theologians of his time, turned to the Book of Revelation. The pouring of the sixth vial in the Apocalypse represented the rise of Deism, the chaos of the French Revolution, and the ensuing European rush to despotism, while the Second Great Awakening and the appearance of missionary societies signified America's first steps in the defeat of the powers of Satan.[8] Beecher forecast the culmination of the reign of Christ in the spread of American liberties and the defeat of feudal institutions.[9] The thought of the New Haven theologians, like that of their seventeenth-century New England predecessors, was immersed in scriptural history and prophecy. But their historical perspectives were set within a larger cosmic picture: the picture of history, the nation, the individual, and God himself acting according to the laws of the universe. Within this view of things, the laws which defined the individual and hence controlled the making of history were analogous to, and at crucial points were connected with, the laws of matter.

Nature, understood as New England's physical environment, was for the New Haven men a collection of moral lessons and a stimulus to the human will. Beecher, renowned for his indefatigability, looked upon his environment as both a spring of health and a place to spend his enormous energies. An avid fisherman, hunter, and gardener, Beecher constantly counseled his children on the restorative qualities of hard exercise and sport, himself sawed his neighbors' wood when he had finished his own, and shoveled a load of sand from one side of his cellar to the other to work off his nervous energy.[10] While applauding the capacity of steam power to subdue the American wilderness and thereby relax "the curse on beast and man," Beecher nonetheless bemoaned the effeminacy which loss of hard labor through technology was sure to bring, a vice that could result in the ruin of civilization in a few generations.[11] The physical environment was less a stimulus to Beecher's imagination than a challenge to his will and a medicine to his body.

Timothy Dwight's imagination *was* captured by the landscape of New England, but in such a way that moral lessons rather than symbols dominated his thinking. Seeking to establish a reputation as the new nation's epic poet, Dwight published a number of collections of verse celebrating America's destined rise to greatness, the most ambitious of which was *The Conquest of Canaan*. But it was his pastoral poem of 1794, *Greenfield Hill*, that most clearly reflected his response to the nature of New England. In that poem Dwight described his residence in Connecticut as the perfect model for American society as a whole.[12] In flourishing oats and Indian corn, he found signs of ordered industriousness; in the cold climate and rough soil, assurances of sturdy human frames and of ingenuity; in the practicality of the inhabitants, "philosophy bowing to common sense" and politics learning from the facts of "real life."[13] Dwight celebrated the pastoral conditions for the virtues of the Protestant Ethic. The highest form of physical nature—New England farm country—was that which elicited and supported the Yankee duties of practicality, thriftiness, and hard work.

The New Haven theologians interpreted the end of the whole of creation in equally practical, dutiful terms. Their initial definition of the end of creation was Edwardean. "The glory of God is his benevolence, and his natural attributes for the manifestation of it," according to Beecher, and "it was to manifest this glory, that the worlds were created." The universe is thus a storehouse of God's exhibitions of his benevolence, "and when he speaks, every intelligence and every atom flies to execute his pleasure."[14] It was as evident to these theologians as it was to Paley that only a benevolent Designer could have fashioned the intelligent and the material worlds.[15] But the benevolence and design of the Creator were chiefly displayed in laws of government, a government intended to "embrace as much good as in the nature of things is possible."[16] That is to say, God is a benevolent governor whose end is "the production of well-being, even the highest well-being of all, and the prevention of misery, even the highest misery of all."[17] God's glory consists above all in the laws of his government which operate for the well-being of the creation but especially for the happiness of the moral creature, man. To be sure, man has demonstrated his resolve to disobey the laws of that government and to choose misery rather than true happiness, but the design of God's government remains: the happy harmony of the whole. In support of that design, God has added scriptural revelation to natural revelation. Following Butler's teaching, Taylor and his fellows held that Scripture extends our knowledge of God's moral dictates in nature and makes known moral truths otherwise unavailable to us.[18]

The theme of moral government was the organizing motif of the New Haven Theology. Despite the immense precedent for treating the theme as theologically central, Taylor deemed theologies prior to his own to be largely failures because they did not give sufficient systematic attention to moral government.[19] Beecher summarized the chief components of a system of moral government that were to serve as the building blocks of the New Haven Theology: "A moral government is the influence of law upon accountable creatures. It includes a law giver, accountable subjects, and laws intelligibly revealed, and maintained by rewards and punishments, according to the character and deeds of the subject."[20] Within the scheme defined by those basic components, the Christian religion was described as a system of moral government. God's superior wisdom is his administrative capacity, his "competence and disposition to govern in the best manner." In fact, God cannot break the rules of his own government; he must act within a scheme of law constitutive of "the nature of things." The Bible is a "code of laws," the gospel a set of "precepts enforced by sanctions." The redemptive role of Christ is to safeguard justice under the laws of government: "What the atonement does, and all that it does as an atonement, is to render it *consistent* with justice to pardon the sinner, by fully sustaining even in such a case, the authority and the justice of the law-giver in the best manner possible to him."[21] Christianity's events of redemptive history were thus consistently interpreted according to the laws of moral government.

On the one hand, the New Haven men were eager to preserve a distinction between the moral and the material governments of the world. Like the philosophers of Common Sense, they pled for the clear differentiation between laws governing the physical realm and those regulating mind and moral responsibility. In the physical world, God effects his laws directly and ineluctably; in the realm of mind, God influences but does not coerce the keeping of laws by the human agent. Thus material and moral governments "differ entirely as to their subjects, and the manner of producing their results.

Natural government is direct, irresistible impulse. Moral government is persuasion." God's omnipotent, irresistible control of his moral creatures is "as irrelevant to the government of mind, as moral influence would be to the government of the material universe."[22] By maintaining this distinction between material and moral governments, the New Haven theologians could appeal directly to free men in a free republic who would not be governed, religiously or politically, by any means other than persuasion. And their attempt to preserve the freedom of the voluntary human agent led these theologians to be accused by strict Calvinists of having denied the consequences of Adam's fall. (Taylor's famous theory was that though all men in fact sin, they sin voluntarily and hence have a "power to the contrary," a power that makes them transcendent over the determining laws of the material world.)[23]

On the other hand, spokesmen for the New Haven Theology found significant points of connection between the moral and the material governments. The two were connected, first of all, by the principle of order or uniformity. This principle is the upshot of the iron law of cause and effect which applies to mind as well as to matter. "The maxim, that *the same cause, in the same circumstances, will produce the same effect*, is as true in the moral as in the natural world; the laws of mind, and the operation of moral causes, being just as uniform as the laws of matter."[24] The distinction between mind and matter is not abandoned here, for the law of causation differs in its subjects and in its mode of operation in the realms of mind and matter, but the principle of uniformity to which causation testifies is the same in the two realms. Uniform order is the precondition of identity, freedom, and moral accountability just as it is the precondition of certainty in nature. "Material causes, while upheld by Heaven, are adequate to their proper effects; and the mind of man, though fallen, is, while upheld, a cause of action sufficient in respect to the possibility of obedience, to create infinite obligation to obey."[25]

Natural and moral governments are also joined inasmuch as God presses the former into the service of the latter. "Every event of Providence in the natural world, from the opening of the flower of the field to the sweep of the tornado," Taylor told his New Haven congregation, "every event in the moral world, from the admonition of a friend to the heavens opened above us in showers of grace and salvation, is an effort to save the soul of man." All events of nature and history are joined into a grand conspiracy to move the sinner to his highest end: "The whole system of events, is a system of experiment on the heart of the sinner to bring him to God and life again."[26] Specifically, the events of the natural world are "experiments on the heart" through their didactic import: their majesty awakens us to our creaturely weakness; their overall design instructs us in the benevolence of God the Designer; their unremitting power to cause variation in the world reminds us of God as the Source of continuity and stability amidst change. Although such providential events in the natural world are not to be identified with the laws of moral government, they do bespeak that government and its laws, for "all that God does in all the varying modes of dispensation, has a bearing, more or less direct, on moral action in creatures."[27]

The whole of creation is one interconnected system of law, and the proper approach to that system, in its moral or mental as well as in its material dimension, is one that probes empirically for laws and their basis in fact. Like the Scottish philosophers of Common Sense, the New Haven theologians sought to understand the human mind as inductively as the natural scientist understood nature and thereby discover laws regulative of human decision and action. But these evangelical theologians were determined to do more than *understand* the laws of the mind; they also wanted to *put those laws to work* in such a way that men were led to given courses of action. The laws of the mind were the means of persuading voluntary agents to perform the duties of repentance, faith, and good works. "Persuade" is really too soft a word for what they intended. They would "cause" the religious duties as certainly as gravity pulls objects to the earth. The coercive omnipotence of God was believed to be irrelevant to a system of moral government that rests on the free accountability of the human creature, but the sure, scientific powers of the revivalist were thought to be quite relevant and appropriate. If only the preacher could discover the mental causes that lead to specific decisions and actions, he could shape human affairs as certainly as material causes determine events in the natural world. What William McLoughlin has said of revivalist Charles Grandison Finney is equally descriptive of the New Haven preachers; for both, "Revivalism was as much a science as bridge building."[28] Indeed, long before Finney had entered the revivalist scene, Timothy Dwight and Lyman Beecher had developed and used their evangelical science of the mind.

The conversionist psychology consisted of three parts: precepts, motives, and sanctions. The precepts were the legal directives, disclosures of what one must do in order to live up to God's system of moral government. The precepts were available in nature and conscience, but they were most clearly revealed in the commandments of the Bible. The motives were the spurs to decision and action, the mental impulses or the driving forces of human existence. The sanctions were the influences that made the motives effective and were of two types: the promise of reward and the threat of punishment. The key component for the revivalist was the sanction; it was his instrument for leading men to follow the right motives when choosing to follow God's precepts.

As Dwight told his Yale students, this entire psychology depends on the "common sense" truth that each person is possessed of the "natural ability" to choose to obey or to disobey the precepts. Motives by definition "are addressed to beings, supposed to be capable of being moved, or influenced, by them." Common-sense reasoning thus excludes the possibility of the human mind being either a collection of ideas or a material object moved deterministically by physical forces. This common-sense judgment regarding freedom of the will and moral accountability occurs when we attend to "the facts" of human volition instead of invoking at the outset "abstract principles" regarding unknown or unseen causes.[29] But it is equally a truth of common sense that sanctions are necessary to spur the right decision. Even the professing Christian must continually be promised eternal life and warned of his impending doom if he is to exercise faithful motives and reject sinful ones. "In this situation, the hope, which he enjoys, allures, and encourages him, to obedience" while the fears of damnation simultaneously "intervene, alarm him concerning the uncertainty of his condition, and compel him to new and more vigorous exertions for the performance of his duty."[30] Dwight and his followers were utterly convinced that the individual's teetering on the narrow edge between these conflicting sanctions would lead to resolute action rather than to psychological paralysis. As Beecher said, the mental principle that the promise of reward and the threat of punishment are necessary to legal obedience is as certain as any law in the natural world: "A law without rewards and punishments cannot *be made* as influential on moral beings as a law with sanctions, any more than vacuity in the scales can *be made* as weighty as lead." The conflicting sanctions "are as essential to secure evangelical affections as fire to heat, or any natural cause to its appropriate effect."[31]

The New Haven men believed the sanction of eternal torment to be an especially effective evangelical measure. Beecher thought it was a sanction not frequently enough employed in his day, an unfortunate turn of events since it was as scientifically derived as any natural law:

> There is a uniformity of action in the natural and moral world, from which the Most High does not depart; and which is the foundation of experimental knowledge, and teaches the adaptation of means to ends. Fire does not drown; and water does not burn; and fear is not excited by sentiments which exclude danger; nor repentance, by those which preclude guilt.[32]

Beecher himself was not averse to playing on the sentiment of mother-love as a sanction for arousing guilt and promoting virtuous obedience in his children. His daughter Harriet Beecher Stowe wrote of the manner in which Lyman used the memory of his saintly first wife (Harriet's mother), Roxana:

> There was one passage of Scripture always associated with her in our minds in childhood: it was this: "Ye are come unto Mount Zion, the city of the living God, to the heavenly Jerusalem, and to an innumerable company of angels; to the general assembly and Church of the first-born, and to the spirits of just men made perfect."
> We all knew that this was what our father repeated to her when she was dying, and we often repeated it to each other. It was to that we felt we *must* attain, though we scarcely knew how. In every scene of family joy or sorrow, or when father wished to make an appeal to our hearts which he knew we could not resist, he spoke of mother.[33]

The New Haven theologians viewed their conversionist psychology, including the candid exploitation of human sentiment, as a scientific alternative to metaphysical speculation. According to Taylor, "The Bible is a plain book" which speaks "directly to human consciousness" the facts, dictates, and sanctions of moral government.[34] There was no need for the biblical theologian to engage in arcane speculation. Sidney Mead has aptly observed that Nathaniel Taylor "supposed that only correct definition and inexorable logic had forced him to his conclusions," so it followed "that other intelligent persons must yield to the same irresistible forces. Small wonder, then, that both his preaching and his teaching revealed 'an instinctive and ineradicable confidence in the power of logic to convince' and that, having presented the 'truth,' he *demanded acceptance of it*."[35] The same attitude led Lyman Beecher to boast that if only he and his friend Taylor could have talked with Lord Byron, they could have argued the poet out of his prodigal life-style.[36] For neither Taylor nor Beecher did logical argument preclude appeal to sentiment; to their way of thinking, the sentimental sanction was quite as scientific as logic. Plain facts, direct appeal to sentiment, simple language, and tightly advanced argument about common-sense truths—these were the marks of a preaching and a theology based on the psychology of precepts, motives, and sanctions.

The New Haven men highly valued their psychology for its practicality. In fact, they esteemed most highly all human enterprises that had a practical bent: useful science, useful religion, useful branches of knowledge of all kinds. One characteristic of George Washington which Timothy Dwight most admired was the utility of Washington's knowledge. As president of Yale, Dwight ridiculed the scholar who remained aloof from the practical implications of his learning, and as a theologian he professed more interest in the "moral tendency" of his work than in its correctness of rational principle. Nathaniel Taylor vigorously pursued the theme of moral government out of an interest in its "practical usefulness" of turning men to the gospel. Lyman Beecher, most practical of them all, believed and acted upon the rule that all "truth is based on evidence, reason, and utility," and that the facts of religion, no less than those of natural science, reveal their truth in their "practical influences on man."[37] It is hardly surprising, therefore, that these men found the whole system of the government of the universe directed to a most practical end—the happiness of man.

Law itself, the foundation of government in the material and moral worlds, was designed to produce harmony. In moral government, the consequence of obedience to the law was the harmony of human happiness. The legal sanctions were to be applied to persons in order to produce motivations toward eternal happiness. At one point the New Haven men celebrated the human moral response that Jonathan Edwards had placed at the very center of his dynamic universe. For they declared that eternal happiness "arises from the disinterested love of God, communicated in various blessings to his children; in their disinterested communications of good to each other; and in the enjoyment, derived by their minds from the exercises of virtue."[38] Virtue was benevolence, a flow out of the creature of God's own love of his creation. From this virtue sprang eternal happiness. Yet for the New Haven theologians benevolence became something that it never was for Edwards—a means to a higher end. The foundation of the virtue of benevolence for these theologians was not to be found "in the Will of God, but in the Nature of things," or in man's motive to seek his own well-being implanted by God in the creation. This natural motive made benevolence the chief means to man's "ultimate good," which was happiness. The whole of God's glory displayed in his creation could be summarized as the expression of his desire to make men happy. In Dwight's words, "The original, and essential, Glory of God is his Ability, and Disposition, to accomplish perfect happiness. This is his inherent, unchangeable, and eternal perfection."[39] And the happiness which God is disposed to accomplish was not the Edwardean joyful appropriation and reflection of the power of God's majestic presence; it was, instead, "the love of doing good," the human mind's "own approbation of its conduct, and the delightful nature of its affections," the human "disposition voluntarily employed in doing good," the human action of "voluntary usefulness."[40]

The ultimate aim in human life was to be happy: to enjoy the approval of one's own conduct and to delight in voluntary usefulness to oneself and one's neighbors. Law within the system of moral government was meant to serve this highest end. As Taylor put it, the sanctions of moral law "proffer the highest good of which man is capable—the happiness of being good and doing good." When, therefore, he told his fellow clergy that the purpose of preaching was to urge the sinner "to his duty—*to his duty*—*to his duty*—, as a point-blank direction to business now on hand and now to be done," Taylor meant in no way to imply that duty to the law is devoid of its rewards. Law and obedience serve the happiness of the dutiful.[41] Nothing could have been farther from the spirit of the New Haven theologians than the New Divinity principle that if men have as their highest end the glory of God, they should be willing to be damned for that glory. As Beecher sniffed, if damnation could serve God's glory, He certainly wasted considerable divine energy urging sinners to choose heaven and providing means for the pursuit of their own happiness.[42]

Had not the New Haven spokesmen appealed to gross human selfishness in their definition of man's highest end and in their insistence that law serves human happiness? Their answer to this charge hinged on a distinction between a selfish and an unselfish interest in happiness. When we quest for our own well-being in preference to the well-being of others, our pursuit of happiness is selfish and sinful. But if we aim at our own happiness as a part of the well-being of the whole universe, our pursuit of happiness is not selfish but natural. The latter, though not the former, is included in the "utility" of God's plan to promote the happiness of all sentient beings.[43] It is the purpose of legal sanctions to assure that every man's natural desire for his own happiness will include more than his own well-being. Given the facts of human nature, it is far more reasonable to turn man to a sense of duty to God and neighbor through an appeal to his desire for his own happiness, than it is to urge him to his duty in ignorance of that natural desire.[44]

Perry Miller has remarked that at the time the New Haven theologians were spelling out the details of their theory of moral government, most Americans had little respect for the formalities of law. It was not that the masses of Americans were deliberately resolved on becoming lawless; they simply looked upon legal structures as artificial impositions on their native intelligence and integrity. Hence they gravitated to heroes such as David Crockett who were virtuous but relatively independent of the artificial features of American culture.[45] Miller's remark suggests one reason why American theology of the time may have been so preoccupied with the theme of moral government, the sanctions of the law, and the importance of duty. In Cincinnati, where mob violence often ruled, Lyman Beecher had firsthand acquaintance with what disrespect for the formalities of law could mean. And in all parts of the country, Beecher and other legalistic theologians saw evidence of lawlessness in the code of dueling, widespread disrespect for the Sabbath, and the practices of unscrupulous politicians. Beecher and his colleagues did everything in their power, therefore, to prove that law was both necessary to all order and germane to the integrity of the common man. Unruly Americans must be made to feel accountable before the Moral Governor of the universe and indeed before all legally constituted authority. But the evangelicals promised that obedience to the law and human happiness were inseparable. If threats of anarchy could not persuade Americans to be dutiful, the attraction of human happiness, individual and social, should do the job. So they sought to demonstrate, in Dwight's language, that "a disposition voluntarily employed in doing good is productive of more Personal and Public happiness, than any other can be."[46]

There was another social reason that the theme of moral government became increasingly dear to American theologians. The sanctions of this government provided the means of converting the public to Protestant Christianity after the disestablishment of the church. As New Englanders of Federalist persuasion were forced to accept the fact of institutional separation of church and state, they opted for a different form of religious establishment, one based on public opinion rather than on state support. As John Bodo has put it, "No longer able or willing to fight for the *status quo ante*, they endeavored to Christianize" the public life of the nation "by every means short of a reunion of church and state."[47] The adoption of the new task was reflected in the life of Lyman Beecher. As Connecticut elected to abolish the Standing Church Order, Beecher sank into a deep state of despair. When his daughter asked what troubled him, he replied solemnly, "The Church of God." Shortly afterward, however, he recovered from his gloom to announce that disestablishment was "the best thing that ever happened to the State of Connecticut." For now the churches were forced to depend "wholly on their own resources and on God." Through "voluntary efforts, societies, missions, and revivals," the churches could exert more influence on society than they ever could with "cocked hats and gold-headed canes."[48] Human government in its largest sense—the rule of law from family to state—could be rendered moral by churches thrown back on their own resources.

Rejecting the social-contract theory of government, Dwight and his followers argued that government *per se* is founded by God. Men by nature are uneasy under the restraints of social law and would never so limit themselves on their own initiative.[49] The only particular form of government ordained by God is the republican sort, provided first of all to the Israelites; it, more than any other

127

system of government, is *moral* because it operates through persuasion rather than force.[50] Highly critical though they were of Jeffersonian republicanism, the New England theologians nonetheless defended quite as much as any Jeffersonian the virtues of popular government. Nathaniel Taylor held, for example, that human rights, defined as the means to an individual's happiness that accord with the general good, are basic to the principles of justice in a system of moral government. In one sense human rights are not inalienable: they may be relinquished in changed circumstances or for equivalents to their objects; but in another sense they are inalienable: no one can justly give up a personal right at the expense of the general good of society.[51] All of the New Haven men defended the right of private property, especially land, as an indispensable stimulus to the virtues of industriousness, inventiveness, common-sense wisdom, and concern for the common good. "As the attraction of gravity is the great principle of motion in the material world," Beecher theorized, "so the possession of the earth in fee simple by the cultivator is the great principle of action in the moral world."[52]

Yet these theologians insisted that the institutions of a democratic republic and their legal underpinnings could not, by themselves, assure either their own morality or their perpetuity. Such an assurance must be provided by religion. Lyman Beecher had merely to observe the failure of civil government to check the use of alcohol—spirits which he felt were destroying the national spirit—to conclude that religiously inspired voluntary associations must step in to deliver the nation from intemperance. Religious influences, brought to bear on free institutions from the family outward, were the only factors that could hold together an extensive republic because *they* were the factors, not the civil laws, that reached the springs of action in the people.[53] So Beecher argued that the American Republic stood in constant need of revivals and voluntary associations directed to such moral causes as the preservation of the Sabbath as a holy day, the elimination of dueling from the land, the election of principled national leaders, and the promotion of total abstinence.

The nation as a whole, then, and not simply the individual citizen, was to be converted to the duties of moral government. And the nation was to be converted with sanctions as scientific as those aimed at the individual. Just as the New Haven preachers employed the sanction of eternal punishment to arouse in the individual the feelings of guilt and fear, so they sought to arouse in the public at large similar motives in their doomsday sketches of the collapse of family, church, school, and every civil liberty before the march of "aetheistic government."[54] The remedy for "infidels" in government positions was ridicule as well as reason, public fear as well as public hope. But the sanction of eternal reward also had its civic counterpart. The American opportunities for life, liberty, and the pursuit of happiness were promised as the fruits of a morality born of true religion.[55] The sanctions of the threat of social discord and the promise of social happiness were the causes thought to effect the moral posture of a nation built on the voluntary principle.

The defenders of moral government intended these methods to determine public opinion, or what they called "public sentiment." With particular churches no longer favored by the state, public sentiment was the only sure handle the churches had on the morals of the nation. Lyman Beecher said, for example, that the most powerful check against public leaders who repudiate a system of moral government is "the united and emphatic decision of public sentiment."[56] So he and preachers like him bent their revivals and their associations, their precepts and their sanctions, to the shaping of the motives of public opinion, in the belief that the duties of moral government would become habitual, "natural feeling."[57] At that point God's governments, moral and natural, public and private, were closely joined. God's providential activity in physical nature served his moral government of the individual and the nation, and the revivalist's application of sanctions to personal and public sentiments would assure the keeping of the moral laws.

In both its personal and its public dimensions, the religion of the New Haven theologians was thoroughly governmental and legal. Nature, understood as physical environment and as mental constitution, was a realm of law. And God's revelation through nature, physical and mental, was a display of the "ought." When these preachers appealed to physical nature in their sermons, therefore, they did so in order to point the didactic moral and apply the sanction. The preaching of Nathaniel Taylor, for example, sometimes borrowed natural metaphors from Scripture, but unlike Jonathan Edwards's natural imagery, the metaphors were not employed to lead the beholder into a symbolic participation in the immediate events of human experience. They were used as illustrations and sanctions.[58] In a sermon entitled "God Angry with the Wicked," Taylor depicts a scene reminiscent of the one that dominated Edwards's "Sinners in the Hands of an Angry God":

> How awful is the situation of the stupid sinner! . . . Here, fellow-sinners, you are. Your life is a vapor—you cannot prolong it a moment. That supporting, forgotten hand of an angry God withdrawn, and you sink to death and hell in a moment. You have no means of appeasing the divine anger, none of preventing its immediate and full expression in the lake of fire.[59]

The threat, the terror, the Edwardean sense of precariousness are certainly conveyed by this scene. But Taylor does not pursue the symbolic parallels between the slippery places of New England and the slide into hell, or between the fires of human experience and those of eternal torment. Rather, he paints the scene in order to move directly to the future "facts" of the sinner's predicament. The imagery is a sanction rather than a symbol:

> But stop, sinner. God is angry with you. The fact—the awful fact, has been proved. You know it; your stupidity and unconcern will not alter it.[60]

The sin of which fallen man is guilty is his failure to live up to God's moral government, his defilement of law. And the only method of correcting that situation, and avoiding the fires of hell, is to adopt the duty of faith.[61] The preaching of Beecher and Dwight was equally direct, "factual" and legal, with metaphors kept to a minimum and used only as occasions for exhortations to duty.[62]

The exhortations of the New Haven evangelicals were scarcely dull. These were no preachers of the stripe of Samuel Hopkins: gestureless, rambling, and abstract. Their contemporaries testified that they were exciting, concrete, pointed, and urgent in their delivery.[63] But were they imaginative? In one sense they were. Their imagination was that of Common Sense Philosophy. They took the facts and ideas of Scripture, nature, and human experience and formed them into new combinations, without reference to the real status of their constructions in present or past existence. Their sanctions were a future heaven and a future hell, fanciful constructs brought to bear on present decision. To their direct moral mandate, "Do, because you must," they added their futuristic sanction, "Do, or else!" In their preaching as well as in their theology and psychology, the New Haven men were representatives of the didactic Enlightenment. They intended their revivalist technique to be as scientific, empirical, and pragmatic as their meditations on the meaning of the universe, Scripture, and the human mind. And in their homiletical repertory, nature's metaphors, like nature's facts, were collections of moral teachings and warnings that one should "do good." The symbolic imagination of Edwards, which yielded new perspectives on given realities, was replaced by a fancy which apprehended facts about future worlds.

NOTES

1. Cited in G. Adolf Koch, *Religion of the American Enlightenment* (New York: Thomas Y. Crowell Co., 1968), p. 89.

2. Perry Miller, *The Life of the Mind in America: From the Revolution to the Civil War* (New York: Harcourt, Brace & World, 1965), p. 277.

3. Henry F. May, *The Enlightenment in America* (New York: Oxford University Press, 1976), pp. xvi, 307ff.

4. Edmund Morgan has advanced the compelling argument that historians, relying upon the biased reminiscences of Lyman Beecher and other enthusiastic supporters of Dwight, have overestimated Dwight's leadership in the Second Great Awakening and his deliverance of Yale from the chaos of "infidelity" he allegedly inherited from his predecessor, President Ezra Stiles. Yet, as Morgan acknowledges, if Dwight's contributions to the Awakening and to the intellectual and religious life of his students have been overestimated, they were nonetheless substantial. Edmund Morgan, "Ezra Stiles and Timothy Dwight," *Proceedings of the Massachusetts Historical Society*, 72 (1963): 101–17. For discussions of Dwight's role as college president and his intellectual sources, see "Memoir of the Life of President Dwight," Timothy Dwight, *Theology, Explained and Defended* (Middletown, Conn.: Clark & Lyman, 1818), 1:xii, lx; Ralph Henry Gabriel, *Religion and Learning at Yale* (New Haven: Yale University Press, 1958), pp. 55–56; Roland H. Bainton, *Yale and the Ministry* (New York: Harper & Brothers, 1957), pp. 73–78; Leon Howard, *The Connecticut Wits* (Chicago: University of Chicago Press, 1943), pp. 28–29, 108–9.

5. For surveys of Taylor's career and the influences on his thought, see Noah Porter, "Introduction" to Nathaniel W. Taylor, *Lectures on the Moral Government of God* (New York: Clark, Austin & Smith, 1859), 1:iii–viii; Sidney Earl Mead, *Nathaniel William Taylor* (Chicago: University of Chicago Press, 1942); Bainton, *Yale and the Ministry*, pp. 96–101.

6. Barbara M. Cross, "Introduction" to *The Autobiography of Lyman Beecher* (Cambridge: Belknap Press, 1961), 1:xxvi.

7. Lyman Beecher, "The Republican Elements of the Old Testament," *Lectures on Political Atheism* (Boston: John P. Jewett & Co., 1852), pp. 176–90.

8. Timothy Dwight, *A Discourse in Two Parts, Delivered July 23, 1812, on the Public Fast* (New Haven: Howe & Deforest, 1812). For a discussion of the convergence of republicanism and millennialism in the thought of Dwight and other New Englanders during the Revolutionary Period, see Nathan O. Hatch, *The Sacred Cause of Liberty* (New Haven: Yale University Press, 1977), especially chap. 3.

9. Lyman Beecher, *A Plea for the West* (Cincinnati: Truman & Smith, 1835).

10. *Autobiography of Beecher*, 2:84, 379, 422.

11. Beecher, "Perils of Atheism to Our Nation," *Political Atheism*, p. 113.

12. Kenneth Silverman, *Timothy Dwight* (New York: Twayne Publishers, Inc., 1969), p. 53.

13. *The Major Poems of Timothy Dwight* (Gainesville, Fla.: Scholars' Facsimiles & Reprints, 1969), pp. 378–80, 383, 509–10.

14. Lyman Beecher, "The Government of God Desirable," *Sermons Delivered on Various Occasions* (Boston: John P. Jewett & Co., 1852), pp. 6–7.

15. Taylor, *Moral Government*, 1:9–10; Beecher, "The Being of a God," *Political Atheism*, pp. 26–38.

16. Beecher, "Government of God Desirable," *Sermons*, pp. 9–16.

17. Taylor, *Moral Government*, 1:9.

18. Ibid., 1:9, 353–64.

19. Ibid., 2:2.

20. Beecher, "The Bible a Code of Laws," *Sermons*, p. 155.

21. Beecher, "Government of God Desirable" and "Bible a Code of Laws," *Sermons*, pp. 9, 20, 159; Taylor, *Moral Government*, 2:147; Nathaniel W. Taylor, "Concio ad Clerum," in Sydney Ahlstrom, ed., *Theology in America* (New York: Bobbs-Merrill Co., 1967), p. 246.

22. Beecher, "Bible a Code of Laws" and "Resources of the Adversary," *Sermons*, pp. 157–58, 415–16. Cf. Dwight, *Theology*, 2:386.

23. Taylor, "Concio ad Clerum," pp. 217–37. Cf. Dwight, *Theology*, 1:445–57; 2:1–15 and Lyman Beecher, *Views of Theology* (Boston: John P. Jewett & Co., 1853), p. 214.

24. Beecher, "The Faith Once Delivered to the Saints," *Sermons*, p. 252.

25. Beecher, *Views of Theology*, p. 213.

26. Nathaniel W. Taylor, *Practical Sermons* (New York: Austin & Smith, 1858), p. 447.

27. Taylor, *Moral Government*, 2:298. Cf. Beecher, "The Being of a God," *Political Atheism*, p. 24.

28. William G. McLoughlin, *Modern Revivalism: Charles Grandison Finney to Billy Graham* (New York: Ronald Press, 1959), p. 84.

29. Dwight, *Theology*, 1:407, 457.

30. Ibid., 2:601–2.

31. Beecher, "Bible a Code of Laws" and "Faith Once Delivered to the Saints," *Sermons*, pp. 178, 288.

32. Beecher, "Bible a Code of Laws," *Sermons*, p. 178.

33. *Autobiography of Beecher*, 1:225–26. For an illuminating study of the survival and modification of the themes of moral government in three members of the Beecher family, see John Goodell, "The Triumph of Moralism in New England Piety: A Study of Lyman Beecher, Harriet Beecher Stowe, and Henry Ward Beecher" (Ph.D. diss., Pennsylvania State University, 1976).

34. Taylor, "Concio ad Clerum," pp. 213, 229–30.

35. Mead, *Taylor*, p. 160.

36. *Autobiography of Beecher*, 1:394.

37. Timothy Dwight, *A Discourse on the Character of George Washington* (New Haven: Thomas Green, 1800), p. 23; Gabriel, *Religion and Learning at Yale*, p. 55; "Introduction" to Taylor, *Moral Government*, 1:v; Mead, *Taylor*, p. 45; Beecher, "Perils of Atheism to the Nation," *Political Atheism*, p. 132 and "Bible a Code of Laws," *Sermons*, p. 191.

38. Dwight, *Theology*, 3:159. Cf. Taylor, *Moral Government*, 1:49; Beecher, "Government of God Desirable," *Sermons*, pp. 6–8.

39. Dwight, *Theology*, 3:318, 447–48.

40. Ibid., pp. 319–20, 439, 454.

41. Taylor, *Moral Government*, 1:153 and "Concio ad Clerum," p. 241.

42. Beecher, "Government of God Desirable," *Sermons*, pp. 29–30.

43. Dwight, *Theology*, 3:163; Taylor, *Moral Government*, 1:49.

44. Taylor, *Practical Sermons*, pp. 259–60 and *Moral Government*, 1:153.

45. Miller, *Life of the Mind*, pp. 101–2.

46. Dwight, *Theology*, 3:439.

47. John R. Bodo, *The Protestant Clergy and Public Issues, 1812–1848* (Princeton: Princeton University Press, 1954), p. 34.

48. *Autobiography of Beecher*, 1:252–53.

49. Dwight, *Theology*, 4:133–34.

50. Ibid., pp. 137, 139. Cf. Beecher, "Republican Elements of the Old Testament," *Political Atheism*, pp. 176–90.

51. Taylor, *Moral Government*, 2:265–67.

52. Beecher, "The Memory of Our Fathers," *Political Atheism*, p. 318. Cf. *Major Poems of Dwight*, p. 511.

53. Beecher, "Memory of Our Fathers" and "The Remedy for Intemperance," *Political Atheism*, pp. 324, 391–92; "Duties of Local Churches," *Sermons*, p. 218.

54. Beecher, "Remedy for Duelling" and "Reformation of Morals," *Sermons*, pp. 33–74, 75–113; "Perils of Atheism to the Nation," *Political Atheism*, pp. 91ff.; Dwight, *Discourse in Two Parts*, pp. 1–54.

55. Dwight, *Character of Washington*, p. 49; Beecher, "The Building of Waste Places," *Sermons*, pp. 142–43.

56. Beecher, "Perils of Atheism to Our Nation," *Political Atheism*, p. 135.

57. Beecher, "The Decrees of God," *Political Atheism*, pp. 306, 308.

58. See Taylor, "Their Rock, Not as Our Rock," "Sinners Hate the Light," "The Harvest Past," *Practical Sermons*, pp. 1–23, 171–85, 441–55.

59. Taylor, "God Angry with the Wicked," *Practical Sermons*, p. 225.

60. Ibid., p. 226.

61. Ibid., p. 218.

62. See "Memoir of Dwight," *Theology*, 1:1xiii, lxviii; *Autobiography of Beecher*, 1:324–25, 2:84–86.

63. See "Memoir of Dwight," *Theology*, 1:lxvii–lxviii; Mead, *Taylor*, pp. 61, 158–59; Stuart C. Henry, *Unvanquished Puritan: A Portrait of Lyman Beecher* (Grand Rapids, Mich.: William B. Eerdmans Publishing Co., 1973), pp. 15, 125.

7

Unitarianism

When Lyman Beecher proclaimed his gospel of moral government in Boston, he discovered that some religious citizens of that city had no ears for his message. They found his style coarse, his content convoluted, and his modified Calvinism repulsive. Beecher had encountered Boston Unitarians. Given to a dramatic interpretation of events in which he was involved, and leaning toward a conspiratorial view of history, Beecher believed that the "Cambridge College folk" and other Unitarians of "political, literary, and social influence" had unleashed a "persecuting power" against him.[1] The truth of the matter was that Beecher's preaching simply appealed to a different class than the highly literate, upper-class Boston Unitarians. Unitarians were not receptive to his message because they adhered to a moralistic Christianity more in keeping with the sensitivities and outlook of their class than anything Beecher could offer. Boston Unitarianism had developed an alternative form of Enlightened religion and an alternative reading of nature's moral lessons.

The roots of American Unitarianism stretched back into the early eighteenth century. Setting themselves against both the revivalism of the Great Awakening and many of the doctrines of strict Calvinism, a number of highly respected eighteenth-century Congregational ministers began to develop ideas designed to create a more liberal Protestantism. They were Arminian defenders of man's freedom to choose between sin and holiness, anti-Trinitarian debunkers of the notion that Jesus was a part of the Godhead, and rationalist proponents of the view that every person's reason can establish the essentials of religion which scriptural revelation supplements.[2] The open breach between these liberal Congregationalists and their orthodox Calvinist counterparts occurred in 1805, when Henry Ware, a liberal, was elected Hollis Professor of Divinity at Harvard, an event that created a storm of protest among the orthodox. Systematically excluded from fellowship with their orthodox brethren, the liberals were forced, by 1819, to admit that they were a separate religious group. By that time Harvard and the influential churches of Boston were under the control of the liberals. Less than two decades later, liberal New England Protestants were squabbling among themselves, the chief occasion of controversy being the rise of the Transcendentalist Unitarians. Theodore Parker, in particular, shocked conservative Unitarians with his questioning of the stable authority of the Bible and his claim that Christian truth was independent of the historical Jesus. That controversy, however, could not obscure what Harvard moral philosophers and conservative Unitarian ministers were able to achieve: the development of an Enlightenment Christianity fully as ethical in import and a view of nature quite as didactic in meaning as anything proposed by Hopkinsians or New Haven theologians.

The central figure in early American Unitarianism was unquestionably William Ellery Channing (1780–1842). "Both for his contemporaries and for subsequent historians," as Sydney Ahlstrom has said, Channing "was the Luther of the Boston reformation."[3] In his famous sermon of 1819, "Unitarian Christianity," Channing encouraged liberal Congregationalists to admit that they were a separate, "Unitarian" religious body. And in that sermon he posted the theses which American Unitarians were to defend: that the Bible is a book written by men for men which calls for methods of exegesis suitable to any piece of literature; that the Bible precludes the Trinity in its teachings about God's unity; and that all theological doctrine is to be measured by the yardstick of the human moral sense. For forty years as pastor of the Federal Street Church in Boston, Channing stood watch over a Congregationalism which had freed itself from Calvinism, criticized the positions of the Transcendentalist Unitarians, and kept in close touch with Harvard, the educational bastion of the Unitarian reformation. Drawing upon many of the same British sources as his Calvinist opponents, Channing proposed another option to Enlightenment skepticism and Deism. Channing's nature taught law and duty but in the genteel tones and eloquent rhetoric of cultured Boston. And the teachings of that nature were deciphered by a reason which was, at base, an inward voice of refined moral sentiments.

During his early years Channing's moral sentiments were nurtured by conversionist Protestantism. In New London, Connecticut, where as a boy he lived with his uncle and prepared for college, Channing was touched by a religious revival. The event made such an impression on him that he later looked back on it as that which decisively turned him to a life devoted to religion.[4] And during a two-year period in Richmond, Virginia, where following college he served as a private tutor, he reported a religious experience in language reminiscent of that of Jonathan Edwards. Finding Virginian Christianity tepid at best and lacking any friend willing to talk with him seriously about religion, Channing clung tightly to the importance of a heartfelt Christianity and eventually passed through a critical inward change. He wrote to his uncle:

> I believe that I never experienced that *change of heart* which is necessary to constitute a Christian, till within a few months past. The worldling would laugh at me; he would call conversion a farce. But the man who has felt the influences of the Holy Spirit can oppose fact and experience to empty declaration and contemptuous sneers. . . . Once, and not long ago, I was blind, blind to my own condition, blind to the goodness of God, and blind to the love of my Redeemer. Now I behold with shame and confusion the depravity and rottenness of my heart. Now I behold with love and admiration the long-suffering and infinite benevolence of Deity.[5]

As a college student at Harvard, Channing absorbed the ideas of the Scottish philosophers Thomas Reid, David Hume, Adam Ferguson, and Francis Hutcheson. Hutcheson convinced him of something that would sustain him for the remainder of his days—that an innate human dignity resides in every man's capacity for disinterested love. The Scottish Common Sense philosophers taught him to trust his perceptions as apprehensions of God's ways in nature and to attend in his thinking first and foremost to the truths of his moral consciousness. Also in college the writings of the British Unitarian Richard Price saved him from Lockean materialism by persuading him of the truth of the Platonic theory of ideas. During his busy years as a minister Channing's time was, as a friend remarked, "more occupied in writing than in reading," but he did manage to pay particular attention to the works of Butler, Paley, and William Law. He believed Jonathan Edwards's dissertation on the will to be acute, if misguided, and he is reported to have read to a friend the account of Edwards's conversion "with a voice trembling in its tenderness and eyes softened with emotion," believing it to be "one of the most pathetic and beautiful sketches ever given of the deeper workings of the soul." As a native of Newport, Rhode Island, Channing in his youth had attended the church of Samuel Hopkins, and he later recalled Hopkins as a boring preacher of appalling doctrines, but he respected Hopkins for his nobility of character and his independence of thought. He also credited Hopkins for "turning my thoughts and heart to the claims and majesty of impartial, universal benevolence." Channing attained some familiarity with the German philosophers Kant, Schelling, and Fichte, expressed delight with the poetry of Coleridge, and heaped special praise on Wordsworth. During a trip abroad, where he obtained appointments with the romantic poets, his conversation with Wordsworth was "free, various, animated," with the meeting climaxed by Wordsworth reciting poetry as the two descended into Grasmere at sunset. After talking with Channing, Coleridge wrote a friend that his American visitor was "a philosopher in both possible meanings of the word. He has the love of wisdom and the wisdom of love." And Coleridge suggested that the differences between Channing and himself amounted to "the same truth seen in different relations. Perhaps I have been more absorbed in the depth of the mystery of the spiritual life, he more engrossed by the loveliness of its manifestations."[6]

Channing's religious experiences in New London and Richmond, his exposure to the New Divinity in Newport, and his sympathetic response to Edwards's conversion bear out the truth of Herbert Schneider's claim that a strong stream of evangelical pietism ran through the life and thought of the Father of American Unitarianism.[7] Yet it was a stream with its own twists and turns. Once asked if he had ever experienced conversion, Channing answered, "I should say not, unless the whole of my life may be called, as it truly has been, a *process* of conversion."[8] Turning points, crucial religious events, had shaped his life, but the underlying piety of that life was religious process. Indeed, the process of attaining perfection was the central doctrine in Channing's theology, and the process of gently cultivating a sense of moral duty was the aim of his warm preaching. The flow of Channing's piety ran within the banks of Enlightenment moralism. Those were the boundaries of his idealism and romanticism, as well. Coleridge's tribute to Channing, and Channing's fascination with German philosophy and romantic poetry, should not be overestimated. As one of Coleridge's American disciples, James Marsh, remarked in a letter to his English master, Channing's knowledge of German philosophy was superficial and derived from secondary sources, and his metaphysics were not the speculative idealism of Coleridge.[9] Like most other American Unitarians of the first half of the nineteenth century, Channing was attracted to German and English romantics neither because of their metaphysics nor because of their poetic symbols but because of their noble sentiments and their seeming blending of morality and religion. As Daniel Howe has pointed out, to the American Unitarians the role of the artist was principally the hortatory task of enlivening virtue, and the nature poet like Wordsworth was thought to stimulate the moral emotion of sublimity. To these American moralists, "emotions of the sublime, by drawing out man's own spiritual nature, developed a Christian character."[10] Channing turned to romantic poetry and to German and Platonic idealism in order to give his Christian moralism an aura of sublimity. But he remained firmly rooted in the traditions of the didactic Enlightenment.

Channing held that nature embodies a set of rules governing the just actions of both God and men and that those rules are also instructions in the meaning of human duty. Nature's chief spiritual function is its mirroring of innate human virtues which every person is called to perfect. According to Channing, the religious significance of nature is available not to a symbolic imagination which discerns the holy character of God in physical images but to a reason, inspired by sublime sentiments, which detects the virtuous character of man reflected in the physical world. In his Enlightenment moralism, Channing was no Hopkinsian or New Haven Calvinist. He defended the unity of God against their alleged tritheism. He replaced their complex system of moral government with a theology reducible to a few clear ideas. He preferred to speak of God as a loving Father rather than as a forensic Governor. And he carried the human sense of fairness as a theological criterion well beyond the limits imposed by the new breed of Calvinist. Yet Channing shared with the Calvinists of his day a thoroughly moralized and legalized Christianity. Nature for him was less a collection of symbols of the divine life than a set of moral laws and lessons. God was above all else a father figure who demanded the performance of duties. And theology was an enterprise of moral reasoning. Channing's Unitarianism was Enlightened Christianity with a distinctive hue, one in which nature was tinted by sentiment and moral reason was imbued with the genteel spirit of liberal Boston.

As Conrad Wright has observed, it was partly an accident of history that liberal New England Congregationalists came to be known as Unitarians. They were certainly anti-Trinitarian, but unlike the more radical Unitarians of Great Britain and the Continent they ascribed semidivine moral and spiritual qualities to Jesus. Furthermore, the label "Unitarianism" tended to obscure the fact that their basic disagreement with orthodox Calvinism was over the nature of man and the meaning of grace.[11] Channing nonetheless made clear the major points of contention in his sermon "Unitarian Christianity." For there he asserted that "it is not because [God's] will is irresistible, but because his will is the perfection of virtue, that we pay him allegiance." And the doctrine of the Trinity is to be rejected not only because it is unscriptural but also because it offends human reason and obstructs the human mind's efforts to reach communion with the one God.[12] The test of the legitimacy of any doctrine, in other words, is its conformity with man's virtuous sense of fair play and its promotion of man's natural religious yearnings. God cannot predestine persons to salvation or damnation; He cannot restrict the effects of Christ's atonement to the elect; He cannot grant forgiveness irrespective of human decision and obedience—all such divine acts would fail to conform to the universal principles which differentiate moral authority from tyranny and which are evident to the virtuous human creature.

Channing insisted that all of his writings were "distinguished by nothing more than by the high estimate which they express of human nature." That high estimate of man derived from Channing's belief in a human "intellectual energy which discerns absolute, universal truth, in the idea of God, in freedom of will and moral power, in disinterestedness and self-sacrifice, in the boundlessness of love, in aspirations after perfection, in desires and affections, which time and space cannot confine, and the world cannot fill."[13] The *magnum opus* which Channing envisioned writing was to have been a portrayal of moral perfectibility as something that comes as naturally to man as eating and sleeping.[14] Although he never completed that work, the rough copy of it, his essays, and his sermons indicate that moral perfectibility was his burning intellectual and spiritual passion.

Growth into perfection is a matter of self-culture. Every person owes it to himself to direct his life toward its highest natural ends. The highest ends of man are moral and religious. The human being's moral purpose is the "idea of duty," given through the conscience. And that idea of duty is a call to exercise disinterested benevolence or "impartial justice and universal good will." This call to benevolence is simultaneously a principle of action, an end of action, and a supreme power within each person. "There are no limits to the growth of this moral force in man, if he will cherish it faithfully." The religious end of man is to enjoy communion with God. It, like the voice of conscience, is a power as well as a principle and goal. God "could not require us to devote our entire being to himself, if he had not endowed it with powers which fit us for such devotion." Although the moral and the religious dimensions of human perfectibility are analytically separable, they in fact function as one principle and one end in the unfolding of the highest forms of human existence. The moral and the religious ends of man are connected by disinterested benevolence:

> The religious principle and the moral are intimately connected, and grow together. The former is indeed the perfection and highest manifestation of the latter. They are both disinterested. It is the essence of true religion to recognize and adore in God the attributes of Impartial Justice and Universal Love, and to hear his commanding us in the conscience to become what we adore.[15]

Sin is the obstacle to man's growth into moral and religious perfection, but it is an obstacle which man himself throws in his way. Sin is "voluntary wrongdoing," not "some mysterious thing wrought into our souls at birth." Nonetheless, if sin is not mysteriously predetermined, the reasons for man's freely choosing the course of sin are mysterious. Though persons for various reasons fall into the habit of sin, the desire to sin does not spring from human nature, from a corrupt will, from the environment, or from an inborn habit. Sin is simply the inexplicable violation of the duty dictated by conscience. It is a violation of our duty to God as we withhold our reverence and love of him; it is a rejection of our duty to our fellow man as we transgress the law of disinterested benevolence; and it is a repudiation of our duty to our higher selves as we yield to beastly appetites. Human wrongdoing brings the sinner suffering in this life; "indeed no wrong deed ever failed to bring it." But the miseries of sin are also extended beyond the grave. Channing said that for himself he saw "no need of a local hell for the sinner after death" since the fruits of sin in this life were hell enough. But he did adhere to the teaching of Scripture about future punishment and, with Butler, thought it a teaching reasonably inferred from human experience. Channing's descriptions of the horrors of the future state of punishment, if mild in comparison with those detailed by Edwards or Taylor, were nonetheless sanctions appropriate to his cultured Boston congregation:

> The circumstances which in this life prevent vice, sin, wrongdoing, from inflicting pain, will not operate hereafter. . . . sleep is a function of our present animal frame, and let not the transgressor anticipate this boon in the world of retribution before him. It may be, and he has reason to fear, that conscience will not slumber there, that night and day the same reproaching voice is to cry within, that unrepented sin will fasten with unrelaxing grasp on the ever-waking soul.[16]

Channing's inclusive term for the conjoined principles of morality and religion, principles voluntarily rejected by the sinner, is man's "rational nature." God's revelation of his will in nature and Scripture is but a means of encouraging man to develop his rational powers. Reason performs two basic functions: it grasps universal truths, and it reduces thoughts to consistency. Reason thus defined is the measure of all religion. "I ought not to sacrifice to any religion that reason which lifts me above the brute." Channing is certain that Christianity calls for no *sacrificium intellectus;* it is a religion that teaches the highest universal truths, and it calls for no assent to contradictory ideas.[17] Both the moral drive to disinterested benevolence and communion with God, the essential ethical and religious ingredients of Christianity, are thoroughly reasonable ends. The same cannot be said of the doctrine of the Trinity, for that unscriptural human invention is a mathematical riddle composed of contradictory and ignoble ideas. "Men call it a mystery; but it is mysterious, not like the great truths of religion, by its vastness and grandeur, but by the irreconcilable ideas which it involves."[18] Such "mystery" has no place within the boundaries of a rational religion. Equally irrational is the Calvinism which, in its doctrines of predestination, irresistible grace, and original sin, "contradicts our best ideas of goodness and justice."[19]

Channing acknowledged that human reason has its limits. It neither grasps everything nor always avoids error. Above all, the infinite being and character of God are beyond our rational comprehension. Yet the limits of reason are no excuse for turning to an irrational religion. Reason remains our highest gift, and we can know enough things comprehensively and correctly to get on with the pursuit of our moral and religious ends and to test claims that men make about God:

> Knowledge is not the less real because confined. The man who has never set foot beyond his native village, knows its scenery and inhabitants as undoubtedly as if he had travelled to the poles. We indeed see very little; but that little is as true as if every thing else were seen. . . . We grant that God is *incomprehensible*. . . . But He is not therefore *unintelligible*. . . . We do not pretend to know the *whole* nature and properties of God, but still we can form some *clear ideas* of him, and can reason from these ideas as justly as from any other. . . . God's goodness, because infinite, does not cease to be goodness, or essentially differ from the same attribute in man; nor does justice change its nature, so that it cannot be understood, because it is seated in an unbounded mind.[20]

Reason is for Channing essentially moral reason. It is the consistent grasp of those ideas that are appropriate to voluntary actions of beings possessed of intellect and will. The aim of reason is quite practical: it turns us to the duties of conscience, to the ends of moral and religious perfection. And when employed by the professional theologian who must measure competing religious claims, reason is also practical: it provides access to those truths that are morally responsible. As a young man Channing vowed to avoid abstruse speculation and to attend to a few important truths relevant to a life of action.[21] His later theologizing and preaching reflected that early vow. Channing sought a religious wisdom that was simple, orderly, ethical, and based upon the facts of nature and human consciousness. His definition of faith summarized his religious vision and placed him securely in the religious traditions of the didactic Enlightenment: "True faith is essentially a moral conviction; a confidence in the reality and immutableness of moral distinctions."[22]

In keeping with this nonspeculative, morally practical view of religion, Channing's God was a supreme moral being who called man to his duty. Channing endlessly invoked the Father-God, the loving Deity of New Testament Christianity, whom he believed Calvinism had replaced with a tyrannical Ruler. But for all of his warm benevolence, Channing's divine Father was scarcely a twentieth-century permissive parent. He was a God of command and government. In a catechism for children, which Channing composed jointly with a friend and former student, God's presence was made to quicken the feeling of guilt, to support obedience to authority, and to assure unhappiness to the wicked:

III. Q. *Does God always see you?*
    A. 1. He sees me at all times all the night and all the day.
       2. He sees me when I am alone, when no other person sees me.
    Q. *How must you feel and act towards those around you?*
    A. 1. I must love and obey my parents, and be thankful to them for the tender care they take of me.
       2. I must treat with respect those, who are older than myself.
XX. Q. *But what if you are wicked?*
    A. 1. I can then never be happy. The wicked must always be miserable.[23]

Although the drab tone of the catechism was not typical of Channing's style,[24] in his sermons he conveyed the same heavy sense of duty bound up with a belief in God as Father. To refer to God as "Father," he told his congregation, is to remind oneself that God is a being who loves his creatures with an unbounded benevolence and who draws near to his children in a spirit of care. But the term should remind us as well that God exercises authority over his rational creatures and calls them to their duties. "Authority is the essential attribute of a father. A parent, worthy of that name, embodies and expresses, both in commands and actions, the everlasting law of duty." God never speaks more truly as a loving parent, therefore, than when through conscience he utters "that inward voice which teaches duty, and excites and cheers to its performance."[25]

Channing's rational Christianity was a religion of duty inspired by the sentiment of love. Channing called for a balance between light and heat, intellect and affection, law and feeling. But there was about this balance no mutual influence of head and heart, no fires of the affections igniting the ideas of the intellect, or understanding illuminating feeling. More in the line of the "Old Light" critics of revivalism than in the tradition of the "New Light" Edwards, Channing had in mind the ideal of balanced self-mastery. For Channing, as for the Unitarian moral philosophers at Harvard, the superior religious man was a person of taste and refinement who carefully regulated his feelings.[26] Obedience to the authority of the Father was not to be lifeless, but neither was it to be fervid; religion was not to be heartless, but its affections were to be carefully regulated by a reasoned approach to God and his mandates.

Channing's understanding of disinterested benevolence was also quite different from the benevolence which Edwards and Hopkins hailed as the highest ethical principle. For Channing benevolence was a prompting of human nature itself, the voice of conscience given to every man. All virtue "has its foundation in the moral nature of man, that is, in conscience, or his sense of duty," and so the naturally virtuous person stands in no need of a special infusion of divine grace.[27] Furthermore, self-love or concern for my own self-interest "is not to be warned against and destroyed," for it can act as a stimulus to disinterested benevolence. Like his New Haven opponents, Channing claimed that self-love need not be narrowly selfish. When combined with the higher principle of disinterested benevolence, it forms the dynamics of human decision making.[28] Finally, Channing transformed Edwardean benevolence into the performance of duty and the love of doing good. Instead of human love becoming beautiful and holy by virtue of a supremely beautiful and holy object, it was beautiful and holy because of the moral, dutiful posture of man himself.[29] Channing humanized benevolence even more thoroughly than the Calvinists who interpreted it within the framework of moral government.

When Channing turned his moral reason upon physical nature, he discovered emblems of man's virtuous nature. Like knows like: what the human mind discerns first of all in nature is a revelation of the qualities of the human mind itself; by extension it discovers qualities of the divine mind which are held in common with the human. "God is another name for human intelligence raised above all error and imperfection," and so the emblematic extension is justified.[30] Nature neither mirrors God to himself through man's symboling activity nor speaks directly to man of divine truths.

Rather, it directly symbolizes human virtue, and by implication it points to the divine life:

> The beauty of the outward creation is intimately related to the lovely, grand, interesting attributes of the soul. It is the emblem or expression of these. Matter becomes beautiful to us when it seems to lose its material aspect, its inertness, finiteness, and grossness, and by the ethereal lightness of its forms and motions seems to approach spirit; when it images to us pure and gentle affections; when it spreads out into a vastness which is a shadow of the Infinite.[31]

Channing developed no metaphysic which would establish the analogical differences and similarities between the divine mind and the human soul, or which would specify nature's capacity to function symbolically. Such a metaphysic he would have considered needless, abstract speculation. But he did assert that in the great chain of being everything material subserves mind. That, he believed, was apparent on the surface of things. Human beings, possessed of the elevating faculties of intellect and will, most desire communion with beings of their own kind. Nature's images of spiritual truth serve that desire by awakening awareness of the mental virtues of man and God.[32] The lawful regularities of physical nature are also means to a higher end: they stimulate the human mind to engage in its own orderly operations of reasoning from effect to cause, inferring general from specific truths, adapting means to ends, and discovering the principles internal to the mind itself. But as means rather than ends, nature's laws may be suspended by God for the sake of revelation. With Paley, Channing held that since the orderly universe operates under the disposal of God, He may miraculously break into that universe in order to reveal himself to human minds.[33] Finally, nature is subservient to mind as a machine is subservient to its user. Channing agreed with the Scottish philosophers of Common Sense that the laws of matter are not the laws of mind. "Man must never be confounded with the material, mechanical world around him. He is Spirit." Man is a spirit of free will who transcends and uses the world of matter, even as God does so to an infinite degree.[34]

Nature thus subordinated to mental ends and signifying innate moral virtues hardly ever spoke a harsh word. Jack Mendelsohn is certainly justified in pointing out that Channing was not callous to life's tragedies, that "the pain of the human condition was seldom out of his thoughts." Furthermore, despite his focus on the beauties of human existence, he constantly called the attention of his Federal Street congregation to the limitations of man and the tragic failures of human history.[35] Yet Channing's universe remained that of Paley—beneficent in its overall design and fundamentally kind in its treatment of man. Channing's understanding of sin as "voluntary wrongdoing" could allow for no possibility of destructive tendencies lurking deep within the heart of the human race. And his sanguine view of nature could include no symbols of man's evil drives. Even the power of the ocean contained no hint of rage or destruction. A journal entry which Channing made while crossing the Atlantic was typical of his treatment of nature's threatening aspects:

> Nature breathes nothing unkind. It expands, or calms, or softens us . . . .
> The ocean is said to rage, but never so to me. I see life, joy, in its wild billows, rather than rage. It is full of spirit, eagerness. In a storm, we are not free to look at the ocean as an object of sentiment. Danger then locks up the soul to its true influence. At a distance from it, we might contemplate it as a solemn minister of Divine justice and witness of God's power to a thoughtless world; but we could associate with it only moral ideas,—not a blind rage. At least, I have seen nothing which gives nature an unkind expression.[36]

Physical nature could on occasion represent something to be mastered by the human will. Holland diked from the ocean, Venice sitting amidst the waves, New England's fields rising from their rockbound setting witnessed to the manner in which physical nature could be subordinated to a higher end—"the culture of man."[37] But Channing more commonly went to the sublime beauties of the natural world to discover "kind expressions" of refined moral feelings, displays of "mental and moral perfections."[38]

Channing's perspective on the Newtonian universe was, like that of other American Enlightenment thinkers, an aesthetic contemplation of perfection. Yet unlike the Deist who has humbled in the dust before the immensity of space, Channing found his sentiments aroused by nature's soft appearances. The universe was to him less awesome than sublime. He believed with most American Unitarians of his day that more emotional stimulation appropriate to religion could be found in natural poetry than in natural science, that more religious sentiment was awakened through the lines of a Wordsworth than through the lens of a telescope.[39] For it was a nature in its beneficent proportions that best betokened a loving Father-God and enticed man dutifully to obey the Father. Duty was man's highest religious calling, but it was a duty which arose as much from sentiment as from mandate. Nature taught moral lessons, but its teachings were gentle. Genial didacticism was also the purpose of Channing's preaching.

Unitarians were the first New England ministers of Congregational background to concern themselves with preaching as an "art." Although they agreed with their seventeenth- and eighteenth-century predecessors that pulpit rhetoric was an instrument for reaching men's minds and hearts, and not an end in itself, American Unitarians were outspoken about the need to make preaching an appealing, interesting form of communication. Because Unitarian ministers had no interest in inculcating a fixed body of complex dogma and because they held that there was a close correlation between religious and aesthetic sentiment, they were in a position to elevate preaching to the status of an art. But in adopting that task they were also responding to a number of social pressures: increasing complaints among New Englanders about the dullness of preaching, competition from secular forms of spiritual gratification in a cultured Boston, and the rhetorical vacuum created by revivalist pyrotechnics on the one hand and orthodox abstractions on the other. To meet these pressures, Unitarian preaching became the art of gentle persuasion. Its aim was neither enthusiastic exhortation nor doctrinal teaching but the persuasive cultivation of moral impressions. Avoiding both drama and speculation, the Unitarian preachers were typically dignified, reasonable, eloquent, and sentimental. And they introduced a number of innovations into the technique of homiletics: a looser structuring of the sermon to replace the old text-doctrine-application pattern; allusions to classical and modern literature and to all kinds of secular subjects; the use of Scripture more for analogy and illustration than for authoritative endorsement of ideas.[40]

No Unitarian preacher was more revered than William Ellery Channing. Even Emerson, who in abandoning his Unitarian ministry thought it necessary to sever ties with cold New England rationalism, said on Channing's death that the pastor of the Federal Street Church took Unitarianism close to "the flowering of genius."[41] Channing became the model preacher for other Unitarian ministers, and the attractions of his pulpit performance resulted in his congregation's outgrowing its sanctuary. Lawrence Buell has captured the reason for Channing's success as a preacher: "Channing was able to furnish his hearers with the mixture of enthusiasm and restraint they wanted. Unitarians wanted to be moved, they wanted heart-stirring eloquence almost as much as any sect, but they did not want it at the expense of dignity and reason. Within these limits, none could surpass Channing."[42]

Channing sought, in his own words, "to preach striking, rather than melting, sermons."[43] He believed the purpose of preaching to be the quickening of man's innate virtue, the provision of aid to every man who assumed responsibility for developing the germ of moral and religious perfection which lay within his soul. To achieve that purpose, the preacher must address the heart as well as the head. "Some preachers," Channing complained, "from observing the pernicious effects of violent and exclusive appeals to the passions, have fallen into an opposite error" of making a warm gospel icy cold and dull. Christianity is a religion of life; its appeal is to intellect, will, and affections; and it teaches that "without moral feeling, there can be no moral purpose." Hence the proclaimers of the Christian religion must make moral feeling vivid, though always restrained by the "clear discoveries of reason." Just enough emotion, just the right amount of controlled feeling should be introduced by the minister into his sermon in order "to touch and to soften his hearers, to draw them to God and duty."[44] Preaching should also be direct and plain without being coarse, refined without being unnatural; and it should create distinct impressions rather than complex arguments or ostentatious embellishments.[45] Channing himself lived up to his stated aims of preaching. In the pulpit he appeared serious but approachable, fervent but earnestly devout. His sentences were graceful and clear. "With no flights of mystic exaltation, forgetful in raptures of the earth, with no abstract systems of metaphysical theology," he spoke of "facts with which he was conversant," urged his hearers "to fix their attention on the concerns of eternity," and gently persuaded his congregation to devote themselves to the performance of their daily duties.[46]

Channing made frequent use of metaphor in his sermons, but he avoided the florid metaphorical language which characterized some Unitarian appeals to human sentiment. Unitarian minister

F. W. P. Greenwood, for example, offered this "Lesson of Autumn":

> Go into the fields and woods, when "the wind of the Lord" has blown upon them; when the blasts and the frosts of autumn have been dealing with them. A change has passed over everything, from the loftiest and broadest tree of the forest down to the little wild plants at its roots. Winged seeds are borne about by fitful gusts. Leaves descend in dark showers. Dry and bare stems and stalks hoarsely rattle against each other, the skeletons of what they were. You cannot raise your eyes, but you look upon the dying; you cannot move, but you step upon the dead. Leaves and flowers are returning to the dust;—can you forbear thinking, that in this universal destiny they are like yourself? Dust *thou* art, and unto dust thou shalt return.[47]

The effusive nature-language of Transcendentalist minister Theodore Parker dripped with sentimentalism, as in his observations on "The Material World and Man's Relation Thereto":

> [Nature] is the home of us all, and the dear God is the great housekeeper and the ever-present mother therein. He lights the fires every morning, and puts them out every night; yea, hangs up the lamps, and makes it all snug for the family to sleep in, beneath His motherly watchfulness all night long, till the morning fire awakes again, and glittering along the east, shines into His children's brightening eyes.[48]

By contrast, the natural metaphors of Channing were simple and direct, and the sentiment surrounding them restrained. The following reflection on the material world is representative of the metaphors in his sermons:

> How much of God may be seen in the structure of a single leaf, which, though so frail as to tremble in every wind, yet holds connections and living communications with the earth, the air, the clouds, and the distant sun, and, through these sympathies with the universe, is itself a revelation of an omnipotent mind! . . . How far the Supreme Being may communicate his attributes to his intelligent offspring, I stop not to inquire. But that his almightly goodness will impart to them powers and glories of which the material universe is but a faint emblem, I cannot doubt.[49]

One of Channing's favorite natural images was the sun, and like Edwards he was especially attracted to those passages of Scripture which employ metaphors of light and which play on the contrasts of illumination and darkness. Yet Channing gave the imagery a very un-Edwardean turn. Light symbolized primarily man's innate moral virtue, and darkness his voluntary wrongdoing. "The Infinite Light would be ever hidden from us did not kindred rays dawn and brighten within us. God is another name for human intelligence raised above all error and imperfection." And sin is to be understood as voluntarily darkening "a light brighter than the sun, as carrying discord, bondage, disease and death into a mind framed for perpetual progress towards its Author."[50] To express his view of man's capacity to progress to perfection, Channing frequently turned to the organic metaphor: the principles of human nature are meant to unfold together like all parts of a plant.[51] Both the metaphors of light and the organic symbols only indirectly served as "images or shadows of divine things" outside the human self; their primary reference was to divine inclinations within the heart of every man.

Within Channing's theological perspective, scriptural revelation "is not intended to supersede God's other modes of instruction; it is not intended to drown, but to make more audible, the voice of nature."[52] What moral reason discovers, what physical nature betokens, what Scripture makes most audible is man's duty—and his capacity—to achieve the supreme virtue of disinterested benevolence. That was the distinct impression, more than any other, which Channing sought to create through the benign moralism and the refined emotion of his sermons. The purpose of the natural metaphor, indeed the purpose of all rhetoric, was to enlist human sentiments in the service of moral resolve and the struggle for religious perfection. In time, Channing concluded that he must turn his rhetorical powers to that darkest of "voluntary wrong-doings"—slavery.

Although both his own and his wife's parents had been implicated in the slave trade, Channing in his youth had been persuaded of the evil of slavery by the preaching of Samuel Hopkins and by his firsthand encounter with Southern slavery during the two-year stay in Virginia.[53] Yet as a minister Channing was reluctant to launch a sustained attack on slavery, not wanting to identify himself with strident abolitionists, fearing the alienation of influential proslavery Bostonians, and believing that he would make "poor material for a reformer." Finally, after an acquaintance convinced him that in the silence created by responsible men would always arise the shrill voices of the irresponsible, Channing made his position clear.[54] In his book of 1835, *Slavery*, and in a number of essays and sermons, Channing advanced an argument that evoked bitter protest from the South and resulted in his being systematically shunned by parishioners and friends in Boston. His attack on the peculiar institution did not accuse the slaveholders of evil—the evil resided in the institution itself. He did not propose a plan of emancipation—Southerners must be persuaded morally to find the solution. He did not join the national antislavery societies. And he died in 1842 confident that the progressive, providential actions of God in history would in time cleanse the land of slavery. But drawing upon his understanding of human nature, Channing scored the practice of slavery for denying human beings their rights and the origin of those rights, the sense of duty. "Man's rights belong to him as a moral being, as capable of perceiving moral distinctions, as a subject of moral obligation. As soon as he becomes conscious of duty, a kindred consciousness springs up that he has a right to do what the sense of duty enjoins." All specific rights are comprised in the general right "which belongs to every rational being, to exercise his powers for the promotion of his own and others' happiness and virtue."[55] Slavery strips humans of that right and of the freedom to act on the basis of the call of duty.

Just as the God of moral government and his command of disinterested benevolence had led Samuel Hopkins to argue that slavery was the most wicked of sins because it denied the black man the essence of his humanity, so man's innate potential for achieving perfection by dutifully obeying the inner voice of moral reason led Channing to the same argument. Channing offered even less theological explanation than Hopkins for the rise of the sin of slavery, and his perception of its evil depths was blunted by his progressivistic view of mankind. But Channing's gentle sense of duty, quite as much as Hopkins's vigorous legalism, issued in a public attack on the most noxious of America's social maladies. Didactic religion had once again achieved pointed social significance.

In his assessment of the religious contributions to changes in the American Character after the framing of the Constitution, Henry Adams described a yawning abyss separating the theology of William Ellery Channing from that of Edwards and Hopkins:

> Between the theology of Jonathan Edwards and that of William Ellery Channing was an enormous gap, not only in doctrines but also in methods. Whatever might be thought of the conclusions reached by

Edwards and Hopkins, the force of their reasoning commanded respect. Not often had a more strenuous effort than theirs been made to ascertain God's will, and to follow it without regard to weaknesses of the flesh. The idea that the nature of God's attributes was to be preached only as subordinate to the improvement of man, agreed little with the spirit of their religion. The Unitarian and Universalist movements marked the beginning of an epoch when ethical and humanitarian ideas took the place of metaphysics, and even New England turned from contemplating the omnipotence of the Deity in order to praise the perfections of his creatures.[56]

Adams clearly saw the transformations which theology in New England had undergone in a short span of time. The strenuous efforts to ascertain God's will had indeed been replaced by the tasks of improving human nature. The omnipotence of God had been eclipsed by the perfection of man, metaphysical inquiry superceded by moral philosophy. In the process, the religious meaning of nature had been substantially altered. Nature, understood as an image of divine things by Edwards and as a set of strict divine precepts by Hopkins, had been transformed by Channing into a kindly token of human perfection. And the human activity appropriate to the religious import of nature—Edwards's spiritual perception of divine holiness or Hopkins's faithful obedience to the Moral Governor—had been supplanted by the reasonable cultivation of the innate human virtues mirrored by the natural world.

Yet over the wide gulf there stretched bridges connecting Channing with his New England predecessors. Seizing upon the didactic and legalistic ingredients in Edwards's thought, Hopkins had introduced a thoroughly moralistic theology into New England. And the New Haven theologians had further emphasized human duty and moral government as the tests of religious and theological truth. As a consequence, the symbolic qualities of nature were overshadowed by the didactic, the symbolic consciousness by an awareness of duty. In his praise of human perfectibility, the sense of fair play, and the innate laws of duty, Channing took the implications of New England moralism to their ultimate humanistic conclusion.

Enlightenment moralism, despite its defenses of human liberty, its techniques of rational persuasion, and its subjection of God to the rules of a just government, did not always have deep religious appeal to Americans of the eighteenth and nineteenth centuries.

Nature and nature's laws, even when set within Channing's benign universe or within Beecher's system of voluntaryism, could strike Americans as forbiddingly legalistic. That was the complaint of another New Englander who cast a critical eye upon the culture's theological traditions. Harriet Beecher Stowe confessed a profound respect for the rugged character of the New England Calvinism which ran from Edwards to Hopkins to her father Lyman Beecher. "While I fully sympathize with the causes which incline many fine and beautiful minds against the system" of Calvinism, she said, it "will never cease from the earth, because the great fundamental facts of nature are Calvinistic, and men with strong minds and wills always discover it."[57] In addition to admiring the Calvinists' bold confrontation with the giant forces of human guilt and evil, and their unwavering commitment to the towering sovereignty of the biblical God, Mrs. Stowe esteemed their willingness to try their strength by the forces and laws of an unsympathetic nature. Yet she was herself one of those "fine and beautiful minds" repulsed by New England Calvinism. She felt that Edwards and Hopkins in particular had offered us a rungless ladder to heaven, an approach to the ethereal heights of true virtue devoid of the steps of ascent through "tender instincts, symbolic feelings, sacraments of love."[58] There must be, as she said in her novel *Oldtown Folks*, a Father's heart, a divine helping hand, else the ruthless laws of nature over-power the sensitive person lacking the tough courage or the confi-dent virtue of the Calvinist.

Mrs. Stowe found her own consolation in the symbolic rites of Episcopalianism and in the love of Christ which swallows up the mysteries of God and the difficulties of nature and history. She found no comfort in the liberal optimism of Unitarianism. It did not, she thought, deal realistically with death, and its urbane preaching did not touch other sinewy themes of human existence. In its own way, however, Unitarianism had also set out to dis-cover the divine helping hand that would rescue the human spirit from the labyrinth of nature's laws. Toward that end, Channing preached a religion of sentiment, sweet reasonableness, and fair play. God himself, in fact, must conform to the gentle principles of virtue apprehended by moral reason at the center of things. Yet Channing ultimately was frustrated in his task of liberating the human spirit from the maze of natural law because his religious vision was framed by the New England heritage of moral theology. Religion was still for him a matter essentially of rules and duties, and religious awareness a grasping of virtue to be achieved. Physical nature still taught lessons about moral duty. The Father's heart still throbbed mechanically—to the beat of nature's laws.

NOTES

1. *The Autobiography of Lyman Beecher*, ed. Barbara Cross, (Cambridge: Belknap Press, 1961), 2:55–56.

2. Conrad Wright has traced the emergence of these ideas in liberal Congregationalism in *The Beginnings of Unitarianism in America* (Boston: Beacon Press, 1966).

3. Sydney E. Ahlstrom, *A Religious History of the American People* (New Haven: Yale University Press, 1972), p. 398.

4. *Memoir of William Ellery Channing*, ed. W. H. Channing (Boston: W. Crosby & H. P. Nichols, 1848), 1:43–44.

5. Ibid., pp. 126–27.

6. Coleridge's impressions of Channing were recorded in a letter of June 13, 1823, to Washington Allston, reprinted in *Memoir of Channing*, 2:218–19. Channing's background of reading and reports of his relations with Hopkins and Wordsworth are also found in the *Memoir*, 1:63–66, 136–42, 147–54; 2:95, 216–18. A long, critical tribute is paid to Hopkins in Channing's "Christian Worship," *The Works of William E. Channing* (Boston: American Unitarian Association, 1900), pp. 423–28.

7. Herbert Wallace Schneider, "The Intellectual Background of William Ellery Channing," *Church History*, 7 (1938): 3–7.

8. *Memoir of Channing*, 1:129.

9. *Coleridge's American Disciples: The Selected Correspondence of James Marsh*, ed. John J. Duffy (Amherst: University of Massachusetts Press, 1973), p. 110.

10. Daniel W. Howe, *The Unitarian Conscience* (Cambridge: Harvard University Press, 1970), pp. 194–99.

11. Conrad Wright, "Introduction," *Three Prophets of Religious Liberalism: Channing-Emerson-Parker* (Boston: Beacon Press, 1961), p. 7.

12. Channing, "Unitarian Christianity," ibid., pp. 60–61, 70.

13. Channing, "Introductory Remarks," *Works*, p. 1.

14. Jack Mendelsohn, *Channing, The Reluctant Radical: A Biography* (Boston: Little, Brown & Co., 1971), p. 200; Channing, "The Perfect Life," *Works*, pp. 931–38.

15. Channing, "Self-Culture" and "The Perfect Life," *Works*, pp. 14–16, 931.

16. Channing, "The Evil of Sin," *Works*, pp. 347–50, 352–53.

17. Channing, "Christianity a Rational Religion," *Works*, pp. 233–46.

18. Channing, "Unitarian Christianity Most Favorable to Piety," *Works*, p. 390.

19. Channing, "The Moral Argument Against Calvinism," *Works,* p. 461.

20. Ibid., pp. 463–64.

21. *Memoir of Channing,* 1:154–58.

22. Channing, "Remarks on National Literature," *Works,* p. 136.

23. Cited in Mendelsohn, *Channing,* p. 90.

24. See Mendelsohn, ibid.

25. Channing, "Christian Worship," *Works,* pp. 416–17.

26. Channing, "Unitarian Christianity Most Favorable to Piety," *Works,* p. 399; Howe, *Unitarian Conscience,* pp. 60–63, 153.

27. Channing, "Unitarian Christianity," *Three Prophets,* ed. Wright, p. 79.

28. Channing, "Remarks on the Character and Writings of Fénelon," *Works,* pp. 568–70.

29. This is a point developed by Schneider, "The Intellectual Background of William Ellery Channing," p. 20. Cf. Channing, "Writings of Fénelon," *Works,* pp. 571–72.

30. Channing, "Spiritual Freedom" and "Likeness to God," *Works,* pp. 172, 292–93.

31. Channing, "Self-Culture," *Works,* p. 19. Cf. Channing, "The Perfect Life," p. 1001.

32. Channing, "Likeness to God" and "The Perfect Life," *Works,* pp. 298–99, 1003.

33. Channing, "The Evidences of Revealed Religion," *Works,* pp. 223–26, 230.

34. Channing, "Introductory Remarks" and "Christian Worship," *Works,* pp. 4–5, 416.

35. Mendelsohn, *Channing,* pp. 9, 148.

36. *Memoir of Channing,* 2:203.

37. Channing, "National Literature," *Works,* p. 125.

38. *Memoir of Channing,* 3:408–9.

39. See Howe, *Unitarian Conscience,* pp. 197–201.

40. My paragraph summarizes Lawrence Buell's excellent study of Unitarian preaching in its social context, "The Unitarian Movement and the Art of Preaching in 19th Century America," *American Quarterly,* 24 (1972): 166–90.

41. Howe, *Unitarian Conscience,* p. 19.

42. Buell, "Unitarian Movement and Art of Preaching," p. 188.

43. *Memoir of Channing,* 1:209.

44. Channing, "Preaching Christ," *Works,* pp. 329–34.

45. Channing, "Moral Argument Against Calvinism," *Works,* pp. 460–61.

46. *Memoir of Channing,* 1:204–6, 244; 2:285–89.

47. Cited in Buell, "Unitarian Movement and Art of Preaching," p. 184.

48. *The Collected Works of Theodore Parker* (London: Trübner & Co., 1872), 14:3.

49. Channing, "Likeness to God," *Works,* p. 295.

50. Ibid., pp. 293, 300. Cf. Channing, "The Perfect Life," *Works,* p. 1001.

51. Channing, "Self-Culture" and "Spiritual Freedom," *Works,* pp. 15, 175.

52. Channing, "Unitarian Christianity Most Favorable to Piety," *Works*, p. 384.

53. *Memoir of Channing*, 1:85; Channing, "Christian Worship," *Works*, p. 426.

54. *Memoir of Channing*, 3:155–58.

55. Channing, "Slavery," *Works*, pp. 697–98.

56. Henry Adams, *History of the United States of America During the Second Administration of James Madison* (New York: Charles Scribner's Sons, 1891), 3:239.

57. Harriet Beecher Stowe, *Sunny Memories of Foreign Lands* (Boston: Phillips, Sampson, and Co., 1854), 2:277.

58. See Charles H. Foster, *The Rungless Ladder: Harriet Beecher Stowe and New England Puritanism* (Durham, N.C.: Duke University Press, 1954).

PART THREE

Nature's Symbols: Horace Bushnell

The material universe, saith a Greek philosopher, is but one vast complex mythus, *that is, symbolical representation, and mythology the* apex *and complement of all genuine physiology. But as this principle cannot be implanted by the discipline of logic, so neither can it be excited or evolved by the arts of rhetoric. For it is an immutable truth, that what comes from the heart, that alone goes to the heart: what proceeds from a divine impulse, that the godlike alone can awaken.*

Samuel Taylor Coleridge
The Friend

8

Symbolic Imagination

Ideas that mark turning points in intellectual history are linked with the established ideas that they are designed to replace. Twentieth-century historians have carefully observed the connections that Renaissance and Reformation thought maintained with medieval ways of thinking, that the Enlightenment had with the Middle Ages and the Renaissance, that Romanticism shared with the Enlightenment. As convenient, and as accurate, as it is to name movements in order to denote shifts in human consciousness and changes in the presuppositions underlying reflection, each movement grows out of that which it replaces. And the creative individuals who provide leadership in each movement have their thinking shaped in part by the ideas they are so eager to repudiate. Horace Bushnell (1802–76) introduced a number of romantic innovations into the theology of New England,[1] but his thought retained vital links with that theological heritage.

Convinced that New England trinitarian theology had degenerated to a lifeless rationalism and Unitarianism to a humanistic project of self-culture, Bushnell proposed that Christian theology has more in common with poetic sensitivity than with scientific reason and that its doctrines are symbols of God's own truth rather than emblems of human perfection. Sensing that Christ had been made by theologians of moral government into a mere makeweight in a vast legal scale and by Unitarians into just another moral example, Bushnell set out to interpret Christ as God's central metaphor, a symbol calling for a response of imagination rather than a feeling of duty. Persuaded that most of the wrangling among his theological contemporaries could be traced to their misunderstanding of the nature and limits of religious language, he sought to

158

develop a theology based on the language of nature and history as a collection of symbolic hints about a formless truth. Believing that Paley's version of physical design in nature was wishful thinking and that the Enlightenment emphasis on the law of cause and effect obscured the dynamism of God's creation, he thought it necessary to point to the discord in nature, to replace mechanical models of thinking with organic ones, and to insist that at the heart of the universe resides a supernatural dimension unexplained by nature's law of cause and effect. Horace Bushnell thus cut behind many of the presuppositions that had gained wide acceptance among his theological contemporaries, and in the process he recovered a symbolic view of religious truth very much like that of Jonathan Edwards. He also gave American theology an important new turn for the future, inspiring the development of "Christocentric liberalism" and many of the ideas of the "Social Gospel" during the latter part of the nineteenth century. And, along with nineteenth-century thinkers in England and Germany, he set the precedent for twentieth-century theologians' making symbol the essence of religious language.

Yet Bushnell was also very much a man of his time, and his thought bore traces of the New England tradition which he so effectively transformed. He shared with the Enlightenment and with the successors of Edwards a distrust of speculative metaphysics. Despite his transmoral view of religious truth, at points he subjected God to general moral principles. For all of his organicism, he understood nature itself mechanistically. And his symbolic sensitivity did not altogether rid him of didacticism in his approach to nature. Bushnell introduced some critical new meanings into American theology's axial language of "nature" and "imagination," but his words betrayed the accents of his immediate past.

Horace Bushnell's early life did not signal his later career in the church. His youth was a period of religious doubt and skepticism; he was nineteen years of age when he finally joined the church, and the fire of the religious experience which ignited that decision soon died. He entered Yale College in 1823 and there attended chapel and communion services, but "the growing spirit of doubt which he had so early cherished took strong possession of his mind as he advanced in college life."[2] Upon graduation from college, he taught school for a while in Connecticut and then worked for a New York daily newspaper, but two years after graduation he had returned to Yale as a tutor and a student in the law school. In 1831 Yale was swept by a religious revival. At first Bushnell held himself aloof from the movement, but eventually he was won over to a renewal of faith that resulted in a vocational change. Completing theological studies at Yale Divinity School, he became minister of the North (Congregational) Church in Hartford, Connecticut, the only parish he would serve. Ill health prevented his full participation in the ministry of North Church from the 1850s on; he made repeated travels for his health, retreated to his books, and became an occasional minister-at-large. When he first entered the ministry he discovered that his experience of 1831 was not an enduring one. His decisive religious experience occurred in 1848, following a series of mental struggles prompted in part by the death of his son. This turning point was a quiet one; according to his wife, it was the gaining of a perspective in which the gospel of the New Testament seemed to open before him in a fresh way. As late as 1871, Bushnell looked back on this event as pivotal for his life and thought:

> I seemed to pass a boundary. I had never been very legal in my Christian life, but now I passed from these partial seeings, glimpses and doubts, into a clearer knowledge of God and into his inspirations, which I have never wholly lost. The change was into faith,—a sense of the freeness of God and the ease of approach to him.[3]

During his career Bushnell was under repeated attack from his fellow ministers and theologians. His first book, *Christian Nurture*, an argument for the child's steady development as a Christian within the organic structures of family and church, engendered charges that he had denied the consequences of original sin; the book was quickly suppressed. His *God in Christ,* consisting of three lectures which sought to break the deadlock between Calvinists and Unitarians, satisfied neither party and induced a neighboring ministerial association to call for a heresy trial. His later books and essays prompted similar charges. Although he was never officially convicted of heresy, Bushnell's church at Hartford was constantly in the position of having to defend and safeguard their minister.

As a student at Yale Divinity School, Bushnell studied with Nathaniel William Taylor. He was critical of his teacher's theological perspective, and in his student essays he sketched ideas alternative to Taylor's which he would develop in his later works. He decided, for example, that moral philosophy cannot be a systematic science after the manner of natural philosophy because that would entail reducing free human powers to mechanical laws. And he concluded that a Moral Governor could not be proved by the arguments from physical design because those arguments "prove either an infinite series of subordinate causes or of designing agents or else they fail to prove any cause or designing agent prior to things sensible." Yet in his Yale days Bushnell admired the way in which Taylor encouraged independent thinking among his pupils, and as a student he adopted a number of Taylor's notions: that there is a coincidence of duty and happiness, that God is a Moral Governor (provable from conscience), and that speculative metaphysics is obscurantism.[4]

While at Yale Bushnell also came under the influence of Josiah Gibbs, a comparative philologist who taught Greek and Hebrew. Gibbs convinced Bushnell that there is "a secret analogy between the intellectual and physical worlds," an analogy underlying metaphorical language which transfers meaning from realm of sense to realm of intellect.[5] Bushnell later expanded his understanding of the metaphorical import of language through a study of Plato, Swedenborg, Goethe, Humboldt, and Schleiermacher.[6] After the religious turning point of 1848, Jonathan Edwards's reflections on the "sense of the heart" as a means of detecting the spiritual meaning of types in nature and history took on special significance. And Bushnell's thinking on these matters was influenced by the Scottish Common Sense Philosophy, at least indirectly. Bushnell made substantial use of the work of Victor Cousin, whose "Eclectic Philosophy" carried many of the ideas of the Scots into France and whose works were quite popular in America. Bushnell was especially attracted to Cousin's view of "spontaneous reason" or the intuition of an outer world and its first principles, and to Cousin's Hegelian theory that antithesis in conflicting creeds is an aspect of comprehensive, synthetic truth.[7] No single influence was more crucial in the development of Bushnell's theology, however, than a book by Samuel Taylor Coleridge—*Aids to Reflection*. Bushnell had begun his reading of Coleridge at Yale, but it was only after he had taken up residence in Hartford that the ideas in *Aids* inspired his own thinking.

In 1829 James Marsh edited and introduced the first American edition of the *Aids to Reflection*, and within a decade the book was so quickly snatched up that bookstores found it difficult to keep the volume stocked.[8] Most New England theologians influenced by Locke and the Common Sense Philosophy found Coleridge's book, if pious and provocative, foggy and lacking in the admirable New England qualities of clear reasoning, earnestness and practicality.[9] Marsh had anticipated this reaction, for in his "Preliminary Essay" to the *Aids* he had lamented the stranglehold that Locke, Paley, and the Scottish philosophers exerted on New England theology.[10] Yet Transcendentalists and literary figures by the score discovered in the book illumination of a new world, and Marsh saw to it that younger theologians in his own Vermont and throughout New England were introduced to Coleridge's perspectives. In the 1830s Coleridge remarked, with only a touch of irony, that "I am a poor poet in England, but I am a great philosopher in America." When Bushnell first read *Aids to Reflection*, he found the book terribly unclear, but eventually it became the writing, second only to the Bible, to which he was most indebted.[11]

Coleridge's *Aids to Reflection* was a collection of aphorisms and discourses directed particularly to young men completing their education and about to assume the duties of the world, but more particularly to students about to enter the ministry. Its overall purpose was to show that "the Christian Faith is the perfection of human intelligence," and its method was to generate in the reader the "art of reflection" and the confidence of self-knowledge.[12] Horace Bushnell made his own the following arguments from Coleridge's book:

1. *Language is the key to human thought and to religious belief.* Language is "not only the vehicle of thought but the wheels," the very means of thinking. The philosopher or the theologian should seek to attain a knowledge of his words' "primary, derivative, and metaphorical senses" in order to think straight and to discover the intention of religious claims. The linguistic task means, furthermore, inquiring into the visual image that forms the primary meaning of any word.[13]

2. *The highest form of language is symbolic, and the symbol is to be differentiated from the bare sign and the allegory.* Symbol is a part that participates in the greater whole which it signifies; it is "a sign included in the idea which it represents;—that is, an actual part

chosen to represent the whole, as a lip with a chin prominent is a symbol of man." Unlike the allegory and the literal sign which point away from themselves to something at the same time different from and similar to themselves, the symbol is transparent to the represented reality. The symbol is a "word," the greater meaning of which is present in and with it. One of the purposes of Christianity is to deliver man into the symbolic meaning of language, beyond that level of language which simply teaches *about* truth. "Did Christ come from Heaven, did the Son of God leave the glory *which he had with his Father before the world began*, only to show us a way to life, to teach truths, to tell us of a resurrection? Or saith he not, *I am the way—I am the truth—I am the resurrection and the life?*"[14] The Christ is the Incarnate Word, the central symbol of Christianity, who in his person and words is transparent to the power and reality of God. Knowledge of symbolic religious language requires a metaphorical awareness which thinks along with the symbol and the thing symbolized, rather than an allegorical consciousness which separates symbol from reality symbolized. In the words of Owen Barfield, for Coleridge,

> the meaning-content of a metaphor is destroyed if we look in it, as Aristotle did, for a *tertium comparationis*; that is to say, if we force it into the molds of the understanding by analysing the likeness, on which it is based, into sameness on the one hand and difference on the other. To experience metaphor *as* metaphor, on the other hand, is to experience likeness as a *polarity* between sameness and difference; and there is a similar contrast underlying the distinction between allegory and symbol, or allegory and myth.[15]

3. *Christian doctrines of redemption are metaphorical or symbolic expressions rather than literal statements.* Theologians' refusal or inability to appreciate the symbolic role of doctrine has led to the disastrous consequence, for example, of making the atonement of Christ a literal matter of the payment of debts. They have literally imputed to the divine causality what is meant to be expressive of the consequences of divine activity in human affairs. The divine causality itself is transcendent; available to the human symbolic consciousness are the fact of the divine act, the effect of that act (man's being born anew), and the consequences of that effect ("sanctification from sin, and liberation from the inherent and penal consequences of sin"). A common theological error has been that the symboling of God's redemptive activity with metaphors of

debt, drawn from the effects and consequences of God's activity, "has been mistaken for an intended designation of the essential character of the causative act itself; and thus divines have inter- preted *de omni* what was spoken of *de singulo*, and magnified a partial equation into a total identity." The symbolic consciousness, on the other hand, while grasping a whole (redemption) through the symbolic part (effects), will avoid confusing the part with the fullness of the whole (God's being).[16]

Any symbolic reading of doctrine will resist the attempt to dis- solve the mystery of the reality that is symbolized, quite as much as it will avoid the separation of symbol and thing symbolized. Indis- soluble mystery, one exhausted neither by literal sign nor by sym- bol, is the foundation of all thinking and the hedge against all dogmatizing.

> *Omnia exeunt in mysterium*, says a schoolman: that is, There is nothing, the absolute ground of which is not a mystery. The contrary were indeed a contradiction in terms: for how can that, which is to explain all things, be susceptible of an explanation? It would be to suppose the same thing first and second at the same time.[17]

Symbolic doctrines partake of the mystery of the divine life, but they do not, short of the elimination of the grounds of all theological thinking, dissolve the mystery of the divine life.

4. *Symbolic consciousness is an act of the imagination; the difference between it and literal consciousness rests on the distinction between Reason and Understanding.* Coleridge defines Reason as "the power of universal and necessary convictions, the source and substance of truths above sense, and having their evidence in themselves." Reason has both a speculative function, which is the grasping of necessary formal or abstract truth, and a practical operation, which is the intuition of actual or moral truth. Practical Reason "is reason in the full and substantive sense" since it is an independent source of ideas; speculative Reason is closely linked with Understanding. The Understanding emerges from the attention of the mind to objects of sense and consists of three activities: the giving of our attention to sense objects, abstraction or voluntarily withholding our attention, and generalization of information gained from atten- tion to the world of sense. Understanding connects us with the beasts. It is a superior form of what other sentient beings possess— the capacity to respond to sense experience. Reason is a distinc-

tively human endowment in its capacity to grasp universal truth that is irreducible to objects of sense and the experience of them. In one respect, therefore, Reason, unlike the Understanding, is analogous to sense experience, for Reason is "a direct aspect of truth, an inward beholding, having a similar relation to the intelligible or spiritual, as sense has to the material or phenomenal."[18]

As different as Reason and Understanding are, they are not unrelated. Reason is "the light that lighteth every man's individual understanding," the grasping of the *logos* or meaning-structure of the universe which enables the Understanding to reflect upon and generalize objects of sense. Both the difference and the relation between Reason and Understanding are apparent in the operations of the imagination. Imagination is Reason's becoming creatively conscious of itself; it is "a repetition in the finite mind of the eternal act of the creation in the infinite *I am*." It is thus transcendent of Understanding. Yet the imagination also actively dissolves and re-creates objects available to the Understanding. Hence although the imagination differs from the "fancy" which passively receives "fixities and definites" ready-made from the memory, "imagination must have fancy. In short the higher intellectual powers can only act through a corresponding energy of the lower."[19] Thus the imaginative response to Christianity does not ignore religion's "facts" or even its fanciful modification of facts, but it sees in and through them to the whole, mysterious truth which they symbolize. The myths and legends of Scripture, the dreams and miracles of prophets, the facts and events of history all stand before the human imagination as symbols.

5. *The Christian religion is a "life" governed by practical Reason; theology is its speculative helpmeet.* Christianity is "not a theory, or a speculation; but a life;—not a philosophy of life, but a life and a living process." The proof of the truth of this life lies in the living of it: "Try it." Proof of the truth of Christianity is simply unavailable to the Understanding, for the categories of the Understanding can no more gather up a life process than the skin "though sensible of the warmth of the sun" can convey the "notion of its figure or its joyous light." Nonetheless, the trying of the life of Christianity is reasonable; it is an application of the practical Reason. Coleridge had only the most unkind things to say of the religious fanaticism and enthusiasm which turn Christianity into a matter of private

feelings and inward sensations. Living the Christian religion means grasping the truths of practical Reason—universal "moral" truths, or those worth living, truths available through symbols and adopted as projects by the human will.[20] Speculative Reason, closely associated with the sense data of the Understanding, is secondary to religion and its practical wisdom. But speculative Reason does have a role to perform on religion's behalf:

> Do I then utterly exclude the speculative reason from theology? No! It is its office and rightful privilege to determine on the negative truth of whatever we are required to believe. The doctrine must not contradict any universal principle: for this would be a doctrine that contradicted itself. Or philosophy? No. It may be and has been the servant and pioneer of faith by convincing the mind that a doctrine is cogitable, that the soul can present the idea to itself.[21]

6. *Nature is the mechanical system of cause and effect; the spiritual or the supernatural is the realm of the will, which is inexplicable within mechanistic categories.* "Nature" designates the deterministic chain of cause and effect. It also indicates whatever appears in the forms of time and space. "But whatever is comprehended in time and space, is included in the mechanism of cause and effect. And conversely, whatever, by whatever means, has its principle in itself, so far as to originate its actions, cannot be contemplated in any of the forms of space and time." Humans have the principle of will from themselves; our power to originate actions is "the principle of our personality," our supernatural capacity that distinguishes us from things. A theory of the will such as that of Jonathan Edwards casts humans within the same class as things, locks them firmly within the iron mechanism of cause and effect, and hence obscures the difference between the human and the material worlds.[22] Only viewing the will as transcendent of nature's categories can safeguard the necessary distinction:

> Where there is no discontinuity there can be no origination, and every appearance of origination in nature is but a shadow of our own casting. It is a reflection from our own will or spirit. Herein, indeed, the will consists. This is the essential character by which will is opposed to nature, as spirit, and raised above nature, as self-determining spirit— this namely, that it is a power of originating an act or state.[23]

Like the Scottish philosophers of Common Sense, Coleridge understood the will as the power to originate acts, a power which nature lacks. But unlike those philosophers, Coleridge denied that that power obeyed the law of cause and effect. Freedom of the will for Coleridge was an absolute ground of thought and action that is prior to law: "In irrational agents the law constitutes the will. In moral and rational agents the will constitutes, or ought to constitute, the law: I speak of moral agents, unfallen."[24]

Coleridge believed, however, that moral agents *are* fallen, that their wills are diseased. But he would not exaggerate the disease to the extent of depriving fallen creatures of all freedom, thereby erasing the distinction between person and thing. Nor would he press to a logical conclusion of the Understanding (absolute predestination) the truth of Reason that fallen creatures cannot rescue themselves from sin. For sin and the reason for its rise are shrouded in a mystery beyond the categories of cause and effect. "The moment we assume an origin in nature, a true beginning, an actual first—that moment we rise above nature, and are compelled to assume a supernatural power." Sin's origin lies in the power of man's nature-transcending will; it is an "original," an "actual first," a rebellion against God and a rejection of his glory that is "beyond time." Man's free fall into sin "is a mystery, that is, a fact, which we see, but cannot explain."[25]

7. *Taken together, nature and supernature constitute an organic system; reflection on nature, man, and God is most properly a form of thinking that preserves organic connections.* Although the power of the will renders the human being transcendent of the material world, he is connected on the scale of being with entities above and below him. Typologically, all beings strive to ascend the scale. Thus the muscular structure of the insect and the wings of the bird anticipate and prefigure the higher "adaptive understanding" of man. And through his Reason man reaches after the heights of the Divine Mind. But it is also the case that man is linked with beings below him through his Understanding, and even his supernatural will functions in concert with the system of nature to which he belongs. In such an interconnected system of persons and things, the law of cause and effect is severely limited as an explanation of the universe; it is concerned only with the effect that one part has on another. Much more satisfactory are categories of organic connection, in which the reciprocal relation of parts is set within the unity

of a whole.[26] Mechanical thinking dissects persons and things and thereby loses sight of the whole; organic thinking attends to the unified identity of the whole and understands the parts as symbols of it:

> Detach this eye from the body. Look steadily at it—as it might lie on the marble slab of a dissecting room. Say it were the eye of a murderer, a Bellingham: or the eye of a murdered patriot, a Sydney!—Behold it, handle it, with its various accompaniments or constituent parts, of tendon, ligament, membrane, blood-vessel, gland, humors; its nerves of sense, of sensation, and of motion. Alas! all these names like that of the organ itself, are so many anachronisms, figures of speech, to express that which has been: as when the guide points with his finger to a heap of stones, and tells the traveller, "That is Babylon, or Persepolis,"—Is this cold jelly *the light of the body?* . . . herein consists the essential difference, the contra-distinction, of an organ from a machine; that not only the characteristic shape is evolved from the invisible central power, but the material mass itself is acquired by assimilation.[27]

When organicism is taken as the model of thinking, ethics will study the whole self in its moral acts, rather than isolated, outward deeds. Apologetic theology will attempt to awaken persons to self-knowledge and to the power of Christianity to restore human wholeness, instead of adopting Paley's "evidences" which are mechanical devices that succeed only in making religion a rigid legalism and God a lifeless *anima mundi*.[28]

Horace Bushnell adopted uncritically most of these ideas of Coleridge; he brought all of them to bear upon his own American theological situation. He agreed with Coleridge, first of all, that the starting point for reflection is the nature of language. As a student at Yale Divinity School he had already done some thinking on symbolic language, and in 1839, in a hurriedly written speech which he delivered in Andover, he had suggested that the problem of the meaning of God's revelation is a problem of the "forms and figures" of language.[29] By 1848 Bushnell's theory of language was fully developed. In that year he prefaced his book *God in Christ* with "A Preliminary Dissertation on the Nature of Language," convinced that his departures from both Calvinists and Unitarians were due to his understanding of language. Most of the books which he would later write were predicated on views expressed in the "Dissertation" or followed out the implications of those views. As Bushnell's daughter observed, the theory of language was *"the key to Horace Bushnell*, to the whole scheme of his thought, to that peculiar manner of expression which marked his individuality,—in a word, to the man."[30]

Indeed, language itself was for Bushnell the key to *all* thought, not simply to his own. He believed words to be the instruments of all thinking and the source of all contention among theologians. It was imperative to arrive at an understanding of the nature of language both in order to think upon the meaning of thinking and to assess competing religious claims. The beginnings of such an understanding could be made if we would recognize "two departments" of language, as well as the origin of words. Every language is made up of the "physical department—that which provides names for things; and the intellectual department—that which provides names for thought and spirit."[31] Humans share the mental capacity inherent in the first department with some animals, which can learn the names of things. Only humans, however, can use objects of sense as images of thought. Although we cannot always detect the precise origin of spiritual language, or the precise reason for a given correlation between idea and physical image, Bushnell believed it was certain that all language has its origin in the facts of the material world. "In one word, the outer world, which envelops our being, is itself language, the power of all language."[32] The physical world is the source of all language expressive of ideas. The origin of "faith" in "ligature," the origin of "right" in "straight," the origin of "expectation" in "looking forth" are examples of how our thought-language is rooted in images of the physical world.

Donald Crosby has appropriately remarked that Bushnell's theory of the origin of language is much too sweeping, for "only an exhaustive philological investigation into the history of nearly every word in every language of the world could prove conclusively Bushnell's contention that all mental and spiritual words are of sensible origin." Bushnell would have been in a better position, Crosby concludes, if he had avoided a general theory of the departments of language and a general view of the origin of words and had limited himself to the intent of religious discourse.[33] Crosby's criticism is quite to the point. Yet, as he recognizes, Bushnell's chief concern was the meaning of religious language. His general theories were but springboards into an examination of what occurs in symbolic religious language and, as a correlate, an analysis of the reasons for the theological stalemate in his day.

Bushnell's main point is this: religious language is metaphorical and hence lacks the precision of literal "naming." Both Calvinism and Unitarianism fail to appreciate this characteristic of religious language. Bushnell is hopeful that the liberal Unitarians will prove to be more responsive to a vital, symbolic view of religious discourse than the dull, literalistic conservatives. But in their endless debates Unitarians as well as their conservative opponents are preoccupied with arriving at the precise literal meaning of a word or dogma. The orthodox of the day "seize upon one symbol as the real form of the truth, and compel all the others to submit to it," while the Unitarians are inclined "to decoct the whole mass of [biblical] symbol, and draw off the extract into pitchers of our own; fine, consistent, nicely-rounded pitchers."[34] Both parties fail to recognize that religious language is figurative utterance. Unlike the "naming" of the first department of language, religious words and doctrines are inexact "hints, or images, held up before the mind of another, to put *him* on generating or reproducing the same thought."[35] The hints of metaphorical language neither directly convey ideas from one mind to another nor capture the truth to which they attest. Rather they are words that may expand self-consciousness and partially participate in a truth greater than themselves. In one sense, all religious and theological affirmations may be said to contain falsehoods, for they are not identical with the truth which they affirm. "They impute form to that which is really out of form"; they are at best mere earthern vessels bearing eternal truth. "Bunyan beautifully represents their insufficiency and earthiness when he says—

> 'My dark and cloudy words, they do but hold
> The truth, as cabinets inclose the gold.'"[36]

The divine truth at which religious words hint evades comprehension by any individual image or by numerous images taken collectively. It is a truth that remains an inexhaustible mystery, one that can be symbolized but never unraveled or fully explained. In the place of a theologian who pretends to be scientifically precise or literally true, Bushnell asks for a theologian who sets out "from a background of mystery" and employs "a symbolism, through which the infinite and the unknown are looking out upon us, and by kind significances, tempting us to struggle into that holy, but dark profound, which they are opening."[37] Bushnell insists that this is no invitation to obscurantism, for figurative language, if less precise, is more concrete and less frequently misunderstood than abstract propositions. Explicitly figurative theological language makes clear, in other words, that its images are just that, images, and not the truth which they symbolize. So Bushnell calls for theologians closely to align themselves with poets, for "poetic forms of utterance are closer to the fires of religion within us, more adequate revelations of consciousness because they reveal it in flame," and yet poetry makes no literal claims and hence preserves the necessary distance between the forms of language and formless truth.[38]

Language springing from the fires of the religious consciousness is also organic. That means that its words should not be lifted out of the context of their user or dissected without reference to the overall intention of his utterance.

> It is the right of every author, who deserves attention at all, to claim a certain liberty, and even to have it for a merit that he cannot be judged exactly by old uses and formulas. Life is organic; and if there be life in his work, it will be found not in some noun or verb that he uses, but in the organic whole of his creations. Hence, it is clear that he must be apprehended in some sense, as a whole, before his full import can be received in paragraphs and sentences.[39]

Bushnell obviously meant this organic view of language to be a defense against his critics: they should take him as a whole thinker rather than preoccupying themselves with his use of particular words. But organicism was also his principle for interpreting historic Christian beliefs. He thought that a misguided approach is taken to such beliefs when theologians debate whether faith precedes and causes repentance or vice versa, or whether justification gives rise to sanctification, or sanctification to justification. This way of framing questions is an attempt to understand an organic whole with mechanistic concepts. The questions are inappropriate. In properly observing the organic functions of the human body, we do not ask if the heart causes the heaving of the lungs or the lungs effect the pumping of the heart, for all parts of a living body are mutual conditions of one another. "And so it is in spiritual life. Every grace supposes every other as its condition," with faith and repentance, justification and sanctification joined into a living whole rather than into a machine with part causing part.[40]

By virtue of the same organic principle, living religious language will contain contradictions or "antagonistic forms of assertion." Religious claims are best understood when they are seen coalescing to constitute a whole linguistic scene—"a kind of painting, in which the speaker, or the writer, leads on through a gallery of pictures or forms, while we attend him, catching at the thoughts suggested by his forms." Within that larger scene, claims may appear that seem logically to contradict each other. But when taken as a whole they are forms hinting at various sides of the same truth, forms struggling with the difficult task of symbolizing an organic whole. Such apparent contradictions—those in Scripture, for example—are not to be blinked but accepted, allowing our minds to gravitate toward that whole truth in which the antagonistic assertions ultimately coalesce.[41] At times this perspective led Bushnell to an irenic blurring of irreconcilable theological differences. "Unite the Arminian and the Calvinist," he could say, "comprehend both doctrines, and we have the Christian truth."[42] That synthetic comprehension, heavily dependent upon the views of Victor Cousin, too simply disposes of real and serious contradictions regarding grace and human nature between Calvinists and Arminians. Their antagonistic forms of assertion disrupt the vast religious painting; they do not coalesce. Yet Bushnell's chief point was larger—and truer: apparent contradictions should be measured by the whole of what a person or religious tradition has to say.

Although religious language lacks the precision and exactness of scientific language, Bushnell looked forward to the day when it would gain in exactitude. Without ceasing to be poetic, religious language would then benefit from the advances of modern science in the "first department" of language. In fact, he believed that physical science was already "leading the way, setting outward things in their true proportions, opening up their true contents, revealing their genesis and final causes and laws, and weaving all into the unity of a real universe." This could "so perfect our knowledges and conceptions" of the things of nature that we could "use them, in the second department of language, with more exactness."[43] Bushnell did warn the theologian and the religious devotee against worshiping at the feet of modern science—against thinking that all "Bible impressions" must conform to every new scientific theory, or assuming that nothing could be true unless proved by the scientific method.[44] But short of idolizing science, one could expect the improvement of religious discourse as it was joined with improved scientific insight and language. For one thing, the eventual joining of the languages could act as a check against the tendency of religious expressions to run into "visionary flights, erratic fancies, and wild hallucinations." Science could, in other words, keep the poetry of religious language tangible. So Bushnell eagerly anticipated the time when astronomy and Christian doctrine would be so united that "the God of Calvary and of the firmament, the love of one and the grandeur of the other" would melt into one linguistic form.[45] That day would mark a kind of "third chapter of revelation" in which the outward laws of the universe and the inner images of the spiritual world would blend into one symbolic expression of the Author of creation.[46]

Although science could improve religious imagery, religious language would remain symbolic expression, and the proper response to such language would still be symbolic knowledge. The mental activity appropriate to religious symbol Bushnell variously designated "imagination," the "aesthetic apprehension of faith," the "supernatural sense," the "union of head and heart," the "reason of faith."[47] All of these terms indicated, first of all, this characteristic of symbolic knowledge: finding meaning within a symbol, rather than either speculating behind the symbol or puzzling over the symbol as a separate object. The first function of the imagination is, therefore, a passive or receptive one. Instead of aiming at getting the meaning of symbols out of its symbolic forms into literal propositions, the imagination stays "by the symbols and in them." This means "ceasing to be busied *about* and *upon* truth, as a dead body offered to the scalpels of logic" in order to give ourselves "*to* truth as set before us in living expression." The imaginative response to religious symbol is analogous to standing in the presence of a friend, finding in his face his mood or "state of soul."[48] But this receptive function of the imagination also avoids probing the facticity of the symbol itself, looking at a face as a face rather than as an image of the friend's mood. Concern over the symbolic medium in and of itself would be "as if Moses, when he saw the burning bush, had fallen at once to speculating about the fire. . . . it was better, methinks, to take the bush as it was meant, to see God in it, and let the chemists look after the fire!"[49]

Imaginative receptivity to the meaning of symbols is the epistemological dimension of redemption; it results from the illumination of the mind of man by God's Spirit. Inspiration "contempers" the person to God; it is a communication of God himself to the human mind which establishes an inward correspondence between the imagination and the truth of God revealed through symbols. "Mere revelation, or a word of truth that has gotten form as in language, has by itself no effectually quickening or regenerative power in character. It stands before the mind, glassing truth in a way to act upon it, but it can accomplish nothing save as another kind of power acting in the mind makes it impressible under and by the truth."[50] Bushnell's understanding of spiritual illumination is identical to that of Jonathan Edwards: illumination is a quickening principle which conforms the whole heart or mind of man to God's truth available through symbols. The new principle awakens a love and knowledge of God's glory displayed in outward forms. The human mind must first be conformed to the mind of God by an act of God himself; the mind must participate in the holiness of the Spirit of God within, before the holiness of God's truth can be known and loved. According to Bushnell, Christ then becomes the "form of the soul." The "de-formity" of sin—man's loss of the form or image of God that could put him in intimate contact with God's outward glory—is overcome by God's own "form," the Christ. By his Spirit God makes Christ as form to dwell imperfectly but redemptively within the mind of man. Receptive imagination is thus one's becoming symboled by God's Spirit, formed into an image of God's own image.[51] This transformation elevates the imagination above the level of notional understanding; it inspires a love of what is known, a "transactional trust" in the revealed God, and a commitment of will even to the mystery of God behind revelation.[52] And now the object of imaginative love and knowledge shapes the character of the lover. For imagination "delights in truth, more as a concrete, vital nature, incarnated in all fact and symbol around us—a vast, mysterious, incomprehensible power, which best we know, when most we love."[53]

The passive function of the imagination, though primary, does not preclude a more aggressive, active response to symbols. Bushnell followed Coleridge in ascribing to imagination the role of dissolving and reconstructing outward forms. The active imagination is neither a speculation behind symbols nor a preoccupation with symbols themselves. Nor does it totally abandon passive reception. Rather, it is the effort to discern what is symbolic about symbols in order to expand their symbolic meaning. Active imagination is close to what Paul Ricoeur has called "a second naiveté." Unlike the naiveté of the primitive mind which dwells within an undifferentiated and uninterpreted world of symbols, second naiveté engages in critical interpretation, "an interpretation that respects the original enigma [or multiple meaning] of the symbols, that lets itself be taught by them, but that, beginning from there, promotes the meaning, forms the meaning in the full responsibility of autonomous thought." Then the symbols are allowed to perform two functions: they can give meaning through themselves, and they can become the occasion for "something to think about."[54] In Bushnell's terms, religious symbols call for both a passive reception of symbolic meaning and a "handling of thoughts by their forms" in order further to promote that meaning.[55]

Active imagination is crucial to the task of the theologian because he must come to grips with religious language that has a way of settling into a literalism. Forms of language used in creeds, for example, tend to lose their original figurative meaning as they are repeated through many generations and as they are often offered by the church as bare statements of fact. "What was true at the beginning," that is, the symbolic meaning, "has now become untrue." The fundamental error of New England rationalism—indeed, the mistake of all dogmatism—is its refusal to appreciate the temporality of language, its change of context over time, and the incapacity of language ever, in any context, to capture religious truth. Unitarianism, on the other hand, errs in the opposite direction, but on the same grounds. Unitarians are unwilling to plumb imaginatively for the symbolic meaning of past forms of expression because they also assume that creeds declare bare, and for them now antiquated, facts. The imaginative alternative is to subject the symbolism of the creeds to "the deepest chemistry of thought, that which descends to the point of relationship between the form of the

truth and its interior formless nature."[56] Although that act of thinking will never fully discern the formless truth, it can attain empathy
with the authors of the creeds and their historical context, recon-
struct a meaning for the interpreter, and keep one alert to the
temptation of confusing the form with its truth.[57] The imagination,
therefore, is an active power as well as a passive receptacle; it is a
"power that distinguishes truths in their images, and seizes hold of
images for the expression of truths."[58]

Theology at its best promotes or expands the metaphorical meaning of religious language. Theology as a "scientific metaphysic" is
of very limited value. Bushnell was once asked to write a letter of
reference on behalf of an acquaintance's application for a college
post in metaphysics. Bushnell replied that he was the wrong person
to write the recommendation since he had long ago lost interest in
the field of metaphysics, finding that it "established nothing."
Teachers of metaphysics, he wrote to the applicant, "are all building what they call the 'science,' but science does not fare in that
way. There is, in fact, no science here, and never will be,—language
is too light-winged and too competent of right uses to be harnessed
in this mill." Bushnell could find only three possible uses for scientific metaphysics: "They show that metaphysics are impossible;
secondly, they are a good gymnastic; thirdly, they vary the old
questions, so as to enlarge the field."[59] Bushnell could add at
another time that metaphysical speculations could, like the operation of Coleridge's Understanding, expand our awareness by con-
ceptualizing the variety of words.[60] As we shall see, Bushnell himself engaged in metaphysics of one kind: he developed a theory of
the structures of being when reflecting upon the relations between
nature and supernature. But that theory grew out of attention to the
concreteness of language, involved no attempt to construct a complete system, and candidly employed metaphorical language without trying to reduce metaphor to nonsymbolic propositions.

The metaphysics that Bushnell found to be, at best, mental gym-
nastics was the propositional theology of New England, such as that
developed by Nathaniel Taylor. But in devaluating such theology
Bushnell was pushing to its logical conclusion one of Taylor's own
presuppositions. For if the theologian should attend only to the
"facts"—the facts of Scripture and human consciousness for Taylor,
the facts of language and its uses for Bushnell—he should know that

no systematic, propositional theological science is possible. All facts appropriate to the human spirit are laden with symbols that lose their metaphorical meanings when reduced to logical propositions. In their attempts to construct a science of the mind, a science of morals, a science of God, a science of the Trinity, New England theologians had replaced the rich welter of religious facts and their symbolic hints with a propositional, nonsymbolic system that was as pretentious and speculative as the old metaphysics which they rejected. New England's theology had become speculative in the worst sense: it had abstracted itself from the tangible world of the human spirit.

This was the argument which Bushnell advanced in his criticism of Edwards Amasa Park of Andover Seminary. Hoping to mediate between the rationalist and the revivalist factions in New England Protestantism, Park had described the proper, respective roles of the "theology of the intellect" and the "theology of the feelings." The theology of the intellect "comprehends the truth just as it is," sets out the truth in general propositions, "demands evidence," and prefers "the literal to the figurative" use of words. The theology of the feelings is a response of the heart, expresses itself in metaphors, and "is satisfied with vague, indefinite representations." Park insisted that the theological approaches could mutually benefit each other: that of the intellect illustrating and vivifying itself through the theology of the feelings; the theology of the feelings finding systematic clarification of its sentiments through the theology of the intellect. But Park clearly judged the theology of the intellect to be the superior, governing force in the union of the two: "the intellect must be the authoritative power, employing the sensibilities as indices of right doctrine, but surveying and superintending them from its commanding elevation" and framing into propositional form the one, consistent meaning symbolized by the various feelings.[61]

According to Bushnell, what Park had failed to understand is that all rational propositions are themselves "packed full of figures and images," that human language "has no exact blocks of meaning to build a science of." The attempt to hide that fact with claims about the intellect's ability to state truth "just as it is" can only serve to produce a pretentious theology even more ambiguous than its metaphorical language already makes it.[62] Furthermore, there is every indication that the allegedly "fixed and solid" language of propositions does not have the quality of endurance possessed by the palpable language of explicitly metaphorical theology. Who has endured as the master of Christian theology, Francis Turretin or John Bunyan? The "venerable dogmatizer" Turretin, seventeenth-century propositional systematizer of Reformed theology, "is already far gone by, and will ere long be rather a milestone of history than a living part of it." Bunyan survives and will long endure because of the living quality of his language: "the glorious Bunyan fire still burns, because it is fire, kindles the world's imagination more and more, and claims a right to live till the sun itself dies out in the sky." Bunyan correctly understood the fundamental question about language:

> But must I needs want solidness, because
> By metaphors I speak? Were not God's laws,
> His gospel laws, in olden time, set forth,
> By Shadows, Types, and Metaphors?[63]

At the very heart of Horace Bushnell's theories of language and imagination resided the conviction that religious truth is available "always by images metaphorically significant, never by any other possible means." God reveals his truth to the religious imagination, and that means "always in finite forms"—the forms of spoken and written language, historical events, persons, and physical nature.[64] Bushnell's commitment to the indispensability of outward forms for God's self-revelation was evident in his Christocentrism, or his holding as central to theology Christ as the chief metaphor or outward form of God's truth, in his probing of the metaphorical meanings of historic creeds and doctrines, and in his deliberations on nature's symbolic qualities. His adherence to the necessity of the outward forms of the imagination was also apparent in his suspicion of all types of subjectivism. As he once said upon reading Goethe, "I was never more struck than by the observation, that living in feeling and subjective thought, independent of outward objects and works, 'tends, as it were, to excavate us and to undermine the whole foundation of our being. As if it were a way to become hollow and finally vacant.'"[65] Yet there was another side to Bushnell, one that hungered for direct contact with God unmediated by finite forms.[66] This mystical union, for which he sometimes yearned, he also on occasion suggested was possible of realization. In a letter to his wife in 1852, he reported having attained, *after* the contemplation of the glories of nature, an experience of God in which "I seem to have gotten quite beyond all physical images and measures, even those of astronomy, and simply to think *God* is to find and bring into my feeling more than even the imagination can reach." Much later in life he wrote of a similar experience of God beyond the reaches of the imagination and its finite forms:

> O my God! what a fact to possess and know that he is! I have not seemed to compare him with anything, and set him in a higher value; but he has been the *all*, and the altogether, everywhere, lovely. There is nothing else to compete; there is nothing else, in fact. It has been as if all the revelations, through good men, nature, Christ, had been now through, and their cargo unloaded, the capital meaning produced, and the God set forth in his own proper day,—the good, the true, the perfect, the all-holy and benignant.[67]

These letters cannot be lightly dismissed as reports of isolated, totally unrepresentative "mountain top" experiences. In his sermons Bushnell sometimes urged his hearers to strive for an immediate experience of God, an experience unmediated by forms.[68] The clearest expression of that point of view was developed in the sermon, "The Immediate Knowledge of God," where Bushnell said that "God's internal activating presence" may be "immediately felt as such" quite independent of the outward forms of language. The purpose of all mediators—books, teachings, words, the Incarnate Word himself—is to lead us beyond themselves to unmediated knowledge.[69] Here imaginative knowledge is not the highest, much less the only, means of apprehending God; it is but a means to a higher form of knowledge.

This mystical strain in Bushnell's life and thought seriously contradicts and undermines his theories of religious language, imagination, and doctrine, all of which are founded on the utter necessity of finite forms for religious knowledge. No invocation of the need for "antagonistic forms of assertion" can deliver him from the seriousness of the contradiction. Either the highest form of religious knowledge is that which makes use of finite images, or it is that which transcends such images. Either knowledge is possible only in and through finite symbols, or it is possible also when symbols are unloaded as so much cargo. When Bushnell dispensed with the need for imagination's outward forms, his version of religious knowledge was very much like that of American Transcendentalism: a knowledge constituted by the divine Spirit's breathing directly through the human soul and hence rendering historic religious forms superfluous.[70] And it was precisely this feature of Bushnell's thought which prompted former-Transcendentalist-turned-Roman Catholic Orestes Brownson to charge Bushnell with a foggy, spiritualistic Quakerism.[71]

As undeniably as Bushnell showed a mystical side, a side that cannot be reconciled with his theory of symbolic imagination, his immediatism was not the guiding principle for his development of theological doctrine. Theology remained for him an imaginative response to the "art of God" in its outward forms in nature and history. History, he said, "is but a kind of figure, having its greatest value, not in what it is, but in what it signifies."[72] And before the theologian can adequately detect the symbols of nature, he must nurture his symbolic awareness on the metaphoric meaning of sacred and secular history. Toward that end, God has supplied Christ as a grand metaphor, the paradigm for the interpretation of all other symbols. Christ as metaphor also frees the theologian from the task of trying to prove what was literally true about the life and person of Jesus:

> And when we have gotten all the metaphoric meanings of his life and death, all that is expressed and bodied in his person of God's saving help and new-creating, sin-forgiving, reconciling love, the sooner we dismiss all speculations on the literalities of his incarnate miracles, his derivation, the composition of his person, his suffering,—plainly transcendent as regards our possible understanding,—the wiser shall we be in our discipleship. We shall have him as the express image of God's person.[73]

Thus the purpose of the traditional doctrine of the "two natures" of Christ "is not to raise a scientific problem" but to image forth the truth of God's active presence to us in history.[74] Bushnell's handling of two doctrines in particular, the Atonement and the Trinity, revealed his symbolic imagination at work on historic doctrine, the manner in which he departed from his own epistemological immediatism, and his attempt to break through the terms of theological debate in his time.

Bushnell found unacceptable both the "penal substitution" theory of the Atonement, which holds that Christ died to satisfy God's wrath and even up the score for sinful man, and its New

England equivalent, the moral government theory, which portrays Christ as the preserver of God's law. Both of these theories fail to depict the God of Christianity as he is—a God who takes the initiative in reconciling man to Himself. The art of God in the gospel can be preserved only if the Atonement be construed as an effective symbol of God's love. The death of Christ is the expression of God's character as love, a love that goes to the full extent of sacrifice and suffering, "vicarious in its own nature, identifying the subject with others, so as to suffer their adversities and pains, and taking on itself the burden of their evils."[75] Bushnell referred to this view of the Atonement as "moral" and "practical" because it focuses on the character of God, and because it holds that the purpose of the Atonement is the actual transformation of the character of human beings. The life and work of Christ terminate "not in the release of penalties by due compensation, but in the transformation of character, and the rescue, in that manner, of guilty men from the retributive causations provoked by their sin." The moral, practical meaning of the Atonement is therefore something quite different from the doctrine's teaching about how men might go about doing good. It is, rather, an effective expression of what God is, a symbol that transforms the life of the person who lives in the truth of the symbol. Nor is the Atonement designed to elicit some vague sentiment, some "mood of natural softness or merely instinctive sympathy"; it fully embodies the horrors of suffering and death that love requires.[76]

The Atonement is for Bushnell an energizing divine act that unites the subjective and the objective dimensions of a symbol. It is subjective in that "the work of Christ is operative wholly on man"—it does not "satisfy" God, respect God's desire for governmental order, or placate the divine wrath. But it is also objective in its representation, in its metaphorically ascribing the effects of atonement to God. The objective dimension of the Atonement is its "altar form," its use of the form of sacrifice. "We must transfer this subjective state or impression, this ground of justification, and produce it outwardly, if possible, in some objective form; as if it had some effect on the law or on God." This outward expression of an inward state is achieved in the ritual sacrifices of the Old Testament and in the New Testament portrayals of Christ's sacrifice. These images from sacred history provide what nature lacks: types "out of which, as roots, the words could grow, that would signify a matter so entirely supernatural, as the gracious work and incarnate mystery of Christ."[77] The objective images of ritual sacrifice, rather than being literal descriptions of effects on God, are forms that express the mysterious, redemptive activity of God in the life of man. The union of the subjective and the objective in the symbol avoids making Christian truth either a life of self-culture or a dogma cast into propositions:

> If the soul, then, is ever to get her health and freedom in goodness, she must have the gospel, not as a doctrine only, but as a rite before her, a righteousness, a ransom, a sacrifice, a lamb slain, a blood offered for her cleansing before Jehovah's altar. Then, reclining her broken heart on this, calling it her religion—hers by faith—she receives a grace broader than consciousness, loses herself in a love that is not imparted in the molds of self-culture, and, without making folly of Christ by her own vain self-applications, he is made *unto her*, wisdom, righteousness, sanctification, and redemption.[78]

The Atonement as a subjective-objective, character-transforming symbol preserves Christianity as a "life" while at the same time employing the outward forms of scriptural revelation.

Bushnell's symbolic interpretation of the Atonement was a decisive shift away from the legalism of the New England theory of moral government. It was his alternative to that theory's making Christ simply a part of God's "judicial machinery."[79] Yet Bushnell's view of the Atonement included a notion which linked him formally with the New England theological heritage which he so substantially modified. Like theologians from Dwight to Taylor and Channing, he measured God by a general principle common to Creator and creature. For Bushnell that principle was not harmony, duty, happiness, or disinterested commitment to law; it was love, suffering love. It is a moot point whether Bushnell discovered his universal principle in Christological revelation, in nature and history at large, or in his own experience. Given the importance that he attached to Christ as central paradigm, he probably would have insisted that it came to him from that source. The indisputable point is that, whatever the source, suffering love in general became for him the test of the goodness and wisdom of God. To be sure, God is bound only to obey the goodness and wisdom that is himself; his obligation to provide an atoning redeemer springs from within him, not from any source outside of him. Yet the principle of suffering love which God embodies is no higher and no other than that which is at the center of all intelligent existence and that is "commonly known."[80] God's virtue in the vicarious sacrifice of Christ can therefore be measured with that generally available ethical principle:

> What can we think, or know, of a goodness over and above all standards of good? We might as well talk of extensions beyond space, or truths beyond the true. Goodness, holy virtue, is the same in all worlds and beings, measured by the same universal and eternal standards; else it is nothing to us. Defect is sin; overplus is impossible. God himself is not any better than he ought to be, and the very essence and glory of his perfection is, that he is just as good as he ought to be. Nay it is the glory of our standards of goodness themselves, that they are able to fashion, or construct, all that is included in the complete beauty of God.[81]

It apparently escaped Bushnell's notice that there was an alternative to this position, one implicit in his own theory of symbol. The Atonement might be taken as an expression of God's suffering love that calls for "living in the symbol" and that cannot be formed into general principles. By making suffering love a general principle, he speculated behind the symbol to a nonsymbolic, universal standard of excellence. Bushnell was much more the student of Nathaniel William Taylor than he knew or cared to admit.[82] And on this particular point of interpretation, he was closer to Channing's penchant for subjecting God to the rules of fair play than his criticisms of Unitarianism's subjectivism and self-culture would indicate.

Nonetheless, in his interpretation of the Atonement Bushnell managed to push symbol to the forefront of doctrinal theology. He was more successful in that endeavor in his symbolic interpretation of the Trinity. That doctrine was, of course, at the center of debates between Unitarians and other Congregationalists, and Bushnell gave the doctrine his sustained attention over a period of several years. In fact, Bushnell's thought on the Trinity underwent expansion over time, but throughout the years the doctrine remained firmly tied to his symbolic view of language. The Trinity was a language of revelation addressed to the imagination, and, like the Atonement, it contained a moral or practical truth, a truth bearing upon human existence and its transformation. For "as by the use of language our understandings are adjusted, our feelings expressed, our information received, our mind itself developed, so by the

Christian Trinity it is that our sense of God is opened" and his action put to redemptive use in our lives.[83]

At first Bushnell was unwilling to say what, if anything, the Trinity symbolized of the nature of God himself. At the early stage of his thinking on the subject, he was content to believe that "the three persons are given to me for the sake of their external expression, not for the internal investigation of their contents. . . . I must not intrude upon their interior nature, either by assertion or denial." Living in the symbol as revelation meant refusing to engage in the impossible task of unraveling the mystery within the Trinity. In fact, the Trinity symbolized that very mystery while at the same time expressing our own experience of God's personal relations to us as Father, Son, and Spirit. But in themselves the three persons are "surfaces of the Infinite Person, boundaries and types of thought inclosing the vast unknown of solid being, otherwise only a dark, impersonal, unrepresentable abysm."[84] This interpretation of the Trinity provoked a thunderous charge from Bushnell's critics—Sabellianism.[85] It seemed to them that Bushnell had resurrected that ancient Christian heresy which held that the persons of the Trinity were three successive temporal modes of the revelation of God—that God was essentially one and only historically three. But Bushnell's view of the Trinity was not really a form of Sabellian modalism. He was quiet about God's essence, and although he expressed appreciation for some of Friedrich Schleiermacher's opinions on the Trinity, he explicitly rejected Schleiermacher's alleged Sabellianism.[86] A more telling criticism was brought by Orestes Brownson: in refusing to speak of the Trinity as symbolic of the nature of God, by holding that there is an unbridgeable gulf dividing the mystery of God's being and the trinitarian character of his revelation, Bushnell had rendered questionable that revelation reveals anything of God at all.[87] Indeed, the Trinity, by only hinting at the "surfaces of the Infinite Person," seemed to lack much objective content.

Bushnell began to move beyond the limits of this view of the Trinity, however, as he undertook a study of the Athanasian version of the Nicene Creed.[88] That study, plus the following out of his own theory of symbolic imagination, resulted in an interpretation of the Trinity in which the doctrine opens on the nature of the revealing God. Here the Trinity is still a symbol calling for imaginative insight rather than a fixed dogma inviting speculation about how one can be three, or three one. It is still a "practical" truth in that it is designed to keep alive in the human consciousness the depths of God's mystery and the experience of God as relational. Now, however, Bushnell claims that just as "person" is a symbol when applied to God, so the term "three persons" is a symbol with direct application to God:

> Literally, God is not a person; for the very word is finite in all its measures and implications, because it is derived from ourselves. Figuratively, he is a person; and beyond this, nothing can be said which is more definite, save that he is in some sense unconceived, a real agent who holds himself related personally to us. . . . we do exactly the same thing, as regards truth or intelligent comprehension, when we say that God is a person, that we do when we say that he is three persons, and there is really no difficulty in one case that does not exist in the other. As we can say that God is a person without any real denial of his infinity, so we can say that he is three persons without any breach of his unity.[89]

Figurative language, whether it be "person" or "three persons," though not literal, is symbolic of God; it refers beyond itself. The fact that the language is figurative does not mean that there is "nothing in God to meet and support the figure."[90]

That in God which does meet and support the figure of trinitarian language is the being-of-God-in-action. Bushnell is now in a position to affirm, in the words of Fred Kirschenmann, that "God *is* the way He *acts*."[91] God "does" in his revelation as Trinity what is "inherent in him."[92] The Trinity is therefore a symbol of God himself:

> If then we dare to assume what is the deepest, most adorable fact of God's nature, that he is a being infinite, *inherently related in act* to the finite, otherwise impossible ever to be found in that relation, thus and therefore a being who is everlastingly threeing himself in his action, to be and to be known as Father, Son, and Holy Ghost from eternity to eternity, we are brought out full upon the Christian Trinity, and that in the simple line of practical inquiry itself. It is nothing but the doctrine *that God is a being practically related to his creatures*.[93]

Although Bushnell is now willing to understand the Trinity as a symbol of God himself, he is unwilling to say that our knowledge of God through the trinitarian formula exhausts the mystery of God. The active imagination discovers in the Trinity something to think about—the being of God in his action of revelation—but it recognizes that the Trinity remains a paradox in affirming both the absoluteness of God's unity and the eternal threeness of his relation to creatures. So the Trinity remains a symbol to "live within" through the passive imagination: "We are only to love the grand abyss of God's majesty thus set before us and rejoice to fall into it, there to bathe and submerge our finite love, rejoicing the more that God is greater than we knew, taller than our reach can measure, wider than our finite thought can comprehend."[94]

Bushnell's mature interpretation of the Trinity gathered up and applied his theories of language and symbolic imagination—in a manner superior to his treatment of the Atonement. The Trinity led him to no attempt to state a universal ethical principle binding on both God and man. Rather, he took the doctrine as a symbol of God uniting the divine being and action. The Trinity betokened a truth about God and his character which no general truth about the relation between one and three, or about love in general, could possibly explain. And the Trinity elicited both the passive and the active functions of the imagination. The passive imagination received the trinitarian language as an image of God's personal relations with his creatures, with the inexhaustible mystery of the divine life ever in the background. The trinitarian symbol was also promoted in its symbolic meaning by the active imagination, as the doctrine's linguistic forms were treated as metaphors, the symbolic intention of past creedal formulations was recognized, and the Nicene Creed was reconstructed by the interpreter. Thus the interpretation of the Trinity could draw out the full range of powers inherent within the symbolic imagination and could illustrate the possibilities and limitations of religious language. Yet the Trinity was more than that for Bushnell. It was a revelation of God-in-action. As such, although it could not be framed in general laws, it was the divine realization of what the human imagination attains most imperfectly—an act of life within expression.

Bushnell consistently maintained that human "words"—the utterances in written and spoken language and expressions of the human will—were the highest forms of religious symbol. He believed that historical symbols were more appropriate than the images of physical nature to the drama of the Christian way of life. Yet the whole of creation was nonetheless a vast storehouse of religious symbols. God "fills the whole universe with actions and reactions, such as will bring us into lively acquaintance with Him."[95] The things of physical nature express the Infinite Intelligence in much the same way that our faces express our minds. "They are all so many physical word-forms given to make up images and vocables for religion."[96] Physical nature, therefore, invites probing by the religious, symbolic imagination. And the grounds of the material world's symbolic capacity require examination.

NOTES

1. A similar romantic theological movement appeared in Pennsylvania under the leadership of John Nevin and Philip Schaff. See James Hastings Nichols, *Romanticism in American Theology: Nevin and Schaff at Mercersburg* (Chicago: University of Chicago Press, 1961).

2. Noah Porter, "Horace Bushnell," *New Englander*, 36 (1877): 154.

3. *Life and Letters of Horace Bushnell*, ed. Mary Bushnell Cheney (New York: Harper & Brothers, 1880), p. 192.

4. Bushnell's early ideas on moral philosophy and moral government are contained in two unpublished essays: "Natural Science and Moral Philosophy," (MS in Yale Divinity School Library, 1832), and "There is a Moral Governor," (MS in Yale Divinity School Library, 1832). On Bushnell's relation to Taylor, see *Life and Letters*, pp. 62–65, and Theodore Munger, *Horace Bushnell: Preacher and Theologian* (Boston & New York: Houghton, Mifflin and Co., 1899), pp. 27–29.

5. Josiah W. Gibbs, *Philological Studies* (New Haven, Conn.: Durrie and Peck, 1857), pp. 197–98, 226. Cf. Jerry Wayne Brown, *The Rise of Biblical Criticism in America, 1800–1870* (Middletown, Conn.: Wesleyan University Press, 1969), pp. 171–79.

6. The influence of these and other thinkers on Bushnell's theory of language, as well as the larger picture of reflection on language in the nineteenth century, are discussed in rich detail by Donald A. Crosby, *Horace Bushnell's Theory of Language, In the Context of Other Nineteenth-Century Philosophies of Language* (The Hague: Mouton, 1975).

7. For the influence of Cousin on Bushnell, see H. Shelton Smith, *Horace Bushnell* (New York: Oxford University Press, 1965), pp. 28–29, 107–8.

8. John J. Duffy, "Introduction," *Coleridge's American Disciples: The Selected Correspondence of James Marsh* (Amherst: University of Massachusetts Press, 1973), pp. 1, 4.

9. See, for example, the letter of Leonard Woods, ibid., pp. 105–8, and Noah Porter, "Coleridge and His American Disciples," *Bibliotheca Sacra*, 4 (1847): 164–65.

10. James Marsh, "Preliminary Essay" to Samuel Taylor Coleridge, *Aids to Reflection*, from the 4th ed. of 1840 (Port Washington, N.Y.: Kennikat Press, 1971), pp. 31–34, 52–58.

11. *Life and Letters*, pp. 208, 499.

12. Coleridge, *Aids to Reflection*, pp. 61–65.

13. Ibid., pp. 62–63, 80–81.

14. Ibid., pp. 243, 284–85, 349.

15. Owen Barfield, *What Coleridge Thought* (Middletown, Conn.: Wesleyan University Press, 1971), p. 112.

16. Coleridge, *Aids to Reflection*, pp. 287–98.

17. Ibid., p. 156.

18. Ibid., pp. 211–12, 216–18, 353.

19. Ibid., pp. 212, 233; Barfield, *What Coleridge Thought*, pp. 74–77, 85.

20. Coleridge, *Aids to Reflection*, pp. 181, 201–3, 337ff.

21. Ibid., pp. 189–90.

22. Ibid., pp. 108, 110, 169.

23. Ibid., p. 246.

24. Ibid., pp. 109–10, 274.

25. Ibid., pp. 157–59, 177, 179, 245–48, 262–63.

26. Ibid., pp. 106, 140, 225ff.

27. Ibid., pp. 342–44.

28. Ibid., pp. 269, 346–49.

29. "There is a Moral Governor," pp. 3–8; "Revelation" (MS in Yale Divinity School Library, 1839); *Life and Letters*, pp. 88–90.

30. *Life and Letters*, p. 203.

31. *God in Christ* (Hartford, Conn.: Brown and Parsons, 1849), p. 24.

32. Ibid., p. 30.

33. Crosby, *Bushnell's Theory of Language*, pp. 233, 242.

34. *God in Christ*, p. 69. For Bushnell's belief that Unitarians were more likely than conservative Protestants to come around to a less literalistic piety, see his letter to Cyrus Bartol, 13 February 1849, in *Life and Letters*, p. 214.

35. *God in Christ*, p. 46.

36. Ibid., pp. 48–49.

37. Ibid., p. 88.

38. *Christ in Theology* (Hartford, Conn.: Brown and Parsons, 1851), pp. 42, 87, 150.

39. *God in Christ*, p. 85.

40. Ibid., pp. 63–64.

41. Ibid., pp. 49, 71.

42. "Christian Comprehensiveness," Smith, *Horace Bushnell,* p. 121.

43. *God in Christ*, p. 78.

44. "Science and Religon," *Putnam's Magazine*, 1 (1868):267; *Nature and the Supernatural* (New York: Charles Scribner's Sons, 1877), p. 20.

45. *God in Christ*, pp. 314–15.

46. "Revelation," pp. 78–84.

47. I agree with Donald Crosby that Bushnell was careless of close definition of his terms and never developed in one place a unified definition of imagination. But as my following paragraphs attempt to show, the meaning that Bushnell assigned to the same mental activity designated by various terms does emerge in his several writings as a largely coherent meaning. See Crosby, *Bushnell's Theory of Language*, pp. 117–20.

48. *Christ in Theology*, pp. 15–16, 32, 91; "The Gospel of the Face," *Sermons on Living Subjects* (New York: Scribner, Armstrong & Co., 1872), p. 72.

49. *God in Christ*, p. 158.

50. "Inspiration by the Holy Spirit," *The Spirit in Man, Sermons and Selections* (New York: Charles Scribner's Sons, 1903), pp. 8, 13, 22.

51. "Christ the Form of the Soul," *Spirit in Man*, pp. 40–41, 48–49.

52. "The Reason of Faith" and "Light on the Cloud," *Sermons for the New Life* (New York: Scribner, Armstrong & Co., 1873), pp. 94, 153–54; "Heaven Opened," *Christ and His Salvation* (New York: Charles Scribner, 1864), p. 450.

53. *God in Christ*, p. 94.

54. Paul Ricoeur, *The Symbolism of Evil* (Boston: Beacon Press, 1967), pp. 348–51.

55. *God in Christ*, p. 52.

56. Ibid., pp. 80–82.

57. "Christian Comprehensiveness," Smith, *Horace Bushnell*, p. 118; *Christ in Theology*, p. 18.

58. "Our Gospel a Gift to the Imagination," *Building Eras in Religon* (New York: Charles Scribner's Sons, 1881), p. 265.

59. Bushnell to an unnamed correspondent, 18 April 1867, *Life and Letters*, pp. 492–93.

60. "Gospel a Gift to the Imagination," *Building Eras*, p. 272.

61. Edwards Amasa Park, "The Theology of the Intellect and That of the Feelings," in *American Philosophic Addresses, 1700–1900*, ed. Joseph L. Blau (New York: Columbia University Press, 1946), pp. 627–58.

62. "Gospel a Gift to the Imagination," *Building Eras*, pp. 269–80.

63. Ibid., pp. 284–85. Cf. Roger Sharrock's "Introduction" to Bunyan's *The Pilgrim's Progress* (Baltimore, Md.: Penguin Books, 1965), pp. 16–18, 24–25, for an argument that Bunyan's metaphorical story is best understood as a myth rather than as a strict allegory.

64. "Gospel a Gift to the Imagination," *Building Eras*, p. 266; *God in Christ*, p. 141.

65. *Life and Letters*, pp. 523–24.

66. This feature of Bushnell's life and thought and the problems it creates for his symbolic view of knowledge were pointed out to me by Robert Alan Schneider. See Schneider's "Form, Symbol, and Spirit: Religious Knowledge in the Thought of Horace Bushnell" (M.A. thesis, The Pennsylvania State University, 1974), chap. 2.

67. *Life and Letters*, pp. 277, 516.

68. See, for example, "Present Relations of Christ with his Followers," *Christ and His Salvation*, pp. 343–44; "The Finite Demands the Infinite," *Spirit in Man*, pp. 210–11.

69. "The Immediate Knowledge of God," *Sermons on Living Subjects*, pp. 117–19.

70. See, for example, Ralph Waldo Emerson, "Nature" and "The Divinity School Address," *Selections from Ralph Waldo Emerson*, ed. Stephen E. Whicher (Boston: Houghton Mifflin Co., 1957), pp. 24, 112–13.

71. Orestes A. Brownson, "Bushnell's Discourses," *Works of Orestes Brownson* (New York: AMS Press, 1966), 7:11–15, 32.

72. "Gospel a Gift to the Imagination," *Building Eras*, p. 264; *The Vicarious Sacrifice* (New York: Charles Scribner & Co., 1866), p. 31.

73. "Gospel a Gift to the Imagination," *Building Eras*, p. 259.

74. *God in Christ*, pp. 156–60; *Christ in Theology*, pp. 99–100.

75. *Vicarious Sacrifice*, p. 42.

76. Ibid., pp. 171, 297, 449.

77. Ibid., p. 459; *God in Christ*, p. 254; *Christ in Theology*, pp. 241–48.

78. *God in Christ*, p. 266.

79. Ibid., p. 344.

80. *Vicarious Sacrifice*, p. 48.

81. Ibid., pp. 57–58.

82. For a similar point of connection between Bushnell and Taylor, see the former's discussion of the "law of Right" which precedes the exercise of God's governing will, *Vicarious Sacrifice*, pp. 234ff.

83. "The Christian Trinity a Practical Truth," *Building Eras*, p. 110. Cf. *God in Christ*, pp. 102, 175; *Christ in Theology*, pp. 120–22, 140.

84. *God in Christ*, pp. 175–79; *Christ in Theology*, pp. 126, 137, 140, 150.

85. See Review of *God in Christ* in *Christian Observatory* (1849), 3:251–52; Review of "Bushnell's Discourses," *Biblical Repertory and Princeton Review*, 21 (1849): 280.

86. *Christ in Theology*, pp. 119–20.

87. Brownson, "Bushnell's Discourses," pp. 32, 45.

88. See *Christ in Theology*, p. 177; George P. Fisher, "Horace Bushnell," *International Review*, 10 (1881): 19.

89. "Trinity a Practical Truth,"*Building Eras*, pp. 114–15.

90. Ibid., p. 133.

91. Fred Kirschenmann, "Horace Bushnell: Orthodox or Sabellian?" *Church History*, 33 (1964): 58. Kirschenmann's article carefully traces the development of Bushnell's understanding of the Trinity.

92. "Trinity a Practical Truth", *Building Eras*, p. 134.

93. Ibid., p. 136.

94. Ibid., pp. 147–48.

95. *God in Christ*, p. 180.

96. "In and By Things Temporal Are Given Things Eternal," *Sermons on Living Subjects*, pp. 273–75.

9

Nature

Early in his career, long before he had worked out to his satisfaction the relation between the mystery of God's being and the divine disclosure in the Trinity, Horace Bushnell proclaimed that God is most apparently a communicative being. "The highest aspect of grandeur in God," he told an audience in Andover in 1839, "is beheld not in his knowledge or in his power but in his publicity." Bushnell's theory of religious language included the idea that God so publishes himself abroad in the physical world that nature becomes a "temple of being" that is "laid and inlaid with types of thought" of the Infinite Mind itself. God's implanting of types of his own mind in the material world establishes the possibility of the connections between physical images and spiritual language.[1] As formless as the very truth of God may appear to the human mind which symbolizes that truth in finite forms, there resides with God from eternity his own Form, his Logos, by which he orders the universe into a Cosmos. The creation as a unified collection of entities and, as such, the source of all figurative language, is "manifestly possible, only on the ground of an originative power of Form, from which the created objects and frames of order deriving their mold, may issue as a true Cosmos; representing, as in a mirror, the thoughts of their Author." The types or figures in physical nature, which constitute the basis of all human thought and language, attest to an infinite creative imagination by which the author of creation "can produce Himself outwardly, or represent Himself in the finite."[2]

The ultimate purpose of God's own imaginative act, however, is neither the order of the cosmos itself nor the possibility of human communication. The end of the act, rather, is the holiness of God, the display of the infinite beauty and glory of the Creator. Reclaiming Edwards's version of the ultimate end of creation, Bushnell spurns the utilitarianism of those New England theologians who would make God's self-manifestation but a means to the higher end of human happiness or the "happiness of the whole system":

> For, if [God] were to value holiness only as the means of some other end, such as happiness, then he would even disrespect holiness, rating it only as a convenience; which is not the character of a holy being, but only an imposture in the name of such a character. Regarding holiness then as God's last end, his world-plan will be gathered round the end proposed, to fulfill it, and all his counsels will crystallize into order and system, subject to that end. For this nature will exist, in all her vast machinery of causes and laws; to this all the miracles and supernatural works of redemption will bring their contributions.[3]

The finite creation embraces two organizing factors: that of cause-and-effect relations and that of a freedom transcendent of cause and effect. Following the lead of Coleridge, Bushnell designates these two as forming the realm of nature and the realm of the supernatural. Nature is a dimension of reality in the process of coming to be according to the fixed laws of cause and effect. It is "a chain of causes and effects, or a scheme of orderly succession, determined from within the scheme itself." The supernatural is that dimension of reality "that is either not in the chain of natural cause and effect, or which acts on the chain of cause and effect, in nature, from without the chain." Bushnell believes that it is altogether unnecessary to cast around for instances of the supernatural in marvels and miracles. The clearest, most readily available instance is the human being. At the very center of the human personality is the will, a principle which renders the human a "being supernatural." The ground of all human action, the clearest message of the human consciousness, is that "we act from ourselves, uncaused in our actions." Deterministic views of the will succeed only in "carrying over into the world of mind a judgment formed in the world of matter"—they confuse supernature with nature. The transcendent power of the will, however, is not the power to suspend or abolish the laws of nature. Rather, supernature is the ability to "set the causes of nature at work, in new combinations otherwise never occurring, and produce, by our action upon nature, results which she, as nature, could never produce by her own internal acting." A person, not a law, lifts a weight from the ground, yet the laws of nature, such as those governing gravity, are not suspended in the act. The realm of cause and effect is subjected by human freedom to new circumstances that produce new results which natural laws in themselves cannot effect.[4]

Bushnell insisted that if the definitions and respective domains of nature and supernature were properly respected, the dangers of "naturalism" would be apparent. Bushnell felt that naturalism was "the new infidelity" spreading in Western civilization—in biblical scholarship, popular literature, and modern philosophies of science. In all of its manifestations, naturalism imprisons the universe in a system of natural law and disallows the possibility of the dynamism of freedom. The scheme of things denies not only God's continuing, personal action in his world; it also repudiates human liberty and the altogether unexpected events of history. The alternative to naturalism, as well as to a religious supernaturalism which defensively dwells only on divine and human transcendence, is a vision of the cosmos as one system embracing both the natural and the supernatural. The world is then seen as a true cosmos or unity. It is then understood in terms of the dynamic interplay between law and freedom, nature and will, thing and person, fixed cause and growing organism—in short, in terms of the relations between nature and supernature.[5]

The cosmos as a union of nature and supernature does not mean, however, that all parts of the universe are of equal standing on the scale of being. Nature is but the stage on which supernature is played out. The material realm of cause and effect is subordinate to the intentions and acts of will. Things totally devoid of the power of self-determining action fall to the bottom of the scale of being, with God as absolute originating power at the top. The degree of the possession of that power decides the status of animals and men midway on the scale.[6] Will is thus a decisive factor for explaining how the one system of nature and supernature holds together: it holds together for the sake of beings possessed of the power of self-originating action. The system coheres into a single system ultimately because it has as its end God as absolute will, but it also coheres penultimately because it has as its secondary end man, the finite creature with the greatest power of will.[7] Yet man stands at the height of the creaturely ladder of being not only because of his power over nature, but also because he is the one creature who can be awakened to God's revelation, the one creature who can receive God's communication within through inspiration and without through the images of nature:

> Not even the obedient worlds of heaven can so receive [God]. Following in the track of his will, and filling even immensity with their stupendous frame of order, they yet have nothing fellow to God in their substance, and can not, therefore do what the humblest soul is able; can not receive the communication of God. They can be shaken, melted, exploded, annihilated by his will, but they are not vast enough in quality to be inspired by him. Spirit only can be inspired.[8]

The universe has its penultimate unity as much through man's capacity for inspiration as through his power of will.

From Bushnell's perspective, there is a hierarchy of symbols as well as a scale of being. The purpose of God's communication of his own holiness is most notably attained when it is received and reflected back by intelligent beings.[9] The intelligent creature, when formed by God's own inspiring Logos, is thus the highest spiritual type or symbol. Those parts of the creation below man which share with him the principle of life and which manifest some semblance of will are types of human intelligence and thereby indirectly image forth the Divine Mind. The mechanical world, through its obedience to the laws of attraction, in turn symbolizes organic existence and indirectly images forth the realm of human spirit.[10] The organic realm is superior to the mechanical in its typological import, and within the organic realm the unpredictable exercises of will and spirit are superior to nature's regularity and harmony as tokens of the Divine Life. Nature's stability cannot begin to capture the freedom of God's imaginative act of creation. "The glory, the true sublimity of God's architectural wisdom is that, while his work stands fast in immutable order, it bends so gracefully to the humblest things, without damage or fracture, pliant to all free action, both His and ours." Only the spontaneous growth in the organic kingdom and the pliant freedom of beings of will can adequately symbolize that aspect of the Divine Wisdom.[11]

Taken as a whole, then, the creation as both a system of being and a system of symbols is more organic and flexible than a machine. Nature, the realm of mechanical cause and effect, is suffused with the spirit of the supernatural. Nature's regularity and nature's laws are fixities that are bent to the purposes of life, will, imagination, and action. And symbols most expressive of religious truth draw upon a nature shaped by those purposes. Because nature invaded by supernature is purposeful, the cosmos may be said to be making progress. The progress does not arise from nature herself, for new beginnings, which form the basis of all progress, presuppose supernatural agents who can introduce change into nature's mechanical scheme. Although Bushnell forecasts no time at which the progress of the cosmos will culminate in some omega point of perfection, he does believe that supernatural activity, especially that of God, works upon the natural world to bring it into ever higher levels of growth. Nature's rise up the scale of being from mechanical order to life to intelligence, in other words, is possible because "the supernatural is present always to nature, an imminent fomentation, working always in strict system with it, and doing, *pari passu*, just what nature at her given stage of progress may be ready for."[12]

Yet progress never meant for Bushnell an utterly smooth flow. Nor, for that matter, was nature's mechanical regularity a complete harmony, nor was the cosmos as a union of nature and supernature an unbroken unity. Bushnell thought that anyone who looked honestly at the world around him would know that the orderliness of that world is scarcely a fixed scheme, "otherwise it would flow in courses of order and harmony, without any such turbulence of conflict and mutual destruction as we now see."[13] There are simply too many instances of sheer waste in nature, too many natural and supernatural beings red in tooth and claw, to allow us to construe our cosmos as a world of perfect harmony. The union of nature and supernature and nature's own regularity have been disrupted by a supernatural act—human sin. Man's continuous rebellion against the Creator and his repudiation of himself as an image of God become "a shock of disorder and pain that unsettles the apparent harmony of things, and reduces the world to a state of imperfect, or questionable beauty."[14] Human sin throws nature's laws into new combinations and gives rise to new consequences. When a grain of sand falls into the eye, the eye functions under the same laws as before, only now as an organ of pain. Similarly when sin invades nature, nature's laws continue, but now nature becomes an organ of pain and a token of the tragedy of the human fall.[15] In fact, Bushnell claims that it is necessary to say that nature has been reduced to a

state of "unnature." Because it is joined with a disorderly supernatural act, nature possesses disorder as well as regularity. The
cosmos as a whole, including the natural realm of cause and effect,
groans and travails for a lost good. To be sure, the cosmos has not
fallen into total chaos. God continues to maintain order in his
universe, and fallen man continues to impose order upon his world.
But it is an order in the midst of disorder. The world's beauty is
"flecked by injury," its organic developments "carbuncled and
diseased." And just as a supernatural activity, human sin, has
plunged the world into disorder and diseased beauty, so only a
supernatural activity, God's redemption of the causative agent, can
deliver it again into order and the beauty of harmony.[16]

Given this perspective on the disharmonies in the universe, it is
hardly surprising that Bushnell dismissed as hopelessly naive and
myopic Paley's proof of God from the harmonious physical design
in nature. How could Paley and the authors of the Bridgewater
Treatises possibly argue that every part of nature serves some
physical end? What physical end is served, for example, by a devas-
tatingly severe winter? "Do animals and children grow faster because of the cold? Do we make up our supplies more easily, for
having a whole third part of the year given up to consumption,
while producing nothing?" A survivor of many bitter New England
winters, Bushnell could only conclude that "as far as we can see,
almost no single end of our mere physical life is at all advanced by"
the winter's cold.[17] Paley simply overlooked too much evidence to
the contrary in his claim that God benevolently arranges the whole
of the creation as an assurance of man's physical well-being. Nature
is too "interlarded with agues and miasmas, and all sorts of mineral
and vegetable poisons" to prove the hypothesis that God adapts
nature to human happiness.[18]

There is something about the human psyche that fixes upon an
earthly token of a private hell, something that returns our night-
mares to a given form of nature. Bushnell's own special symbol of
the bizarre disorder and the sinister forces within the universe was
the kingdom of insects. Nothing proved to him so manifestly the
lack of nature's economy than the sheer superfluity of bugs. Nothing so gave the lie to the claim that all of nature conspires for the
promotion of human happiness than his horror of being stung by
spiders, ants, scorpions, flies, mosquitoes, and centipedes. Noth-

ing made so clear that nature is an emblem of evil rather than a symbol of some "mollusc softness swimming in God's bosom" than the insect's indiscriminate use of its venom. "Whatever else may be true, God has created venom, and we must not scruple to say it. If we have any conception of goodness that forbids this kind of possibility in God, then our God plainly enough does not exist, or the God that does exist is not he."[19]

Bushnell's fixation upon insects recalls the predominance of the image of the spider in the writings of Jonathan Edwards. For both Edwards and Bushnell the insect was a vivid symbol of human sin. But in Bushnell's reflections it was also a token of nature's grotesque disorder, of beauty's ugly face, of God's hard presence. Bushnell's insect was thus closer in symbolic complexity to Melville's whale than to Edwards's spider. And it was closer still to a twentieth-century American's meditations on the kingdom of the insect. At her Walden-like retreat at Tinker Creek in Virginia's Blue Ridge, Annie Dillard finds constant reminders that "nature is as careless as it is bountiful," that the Creator "is apt to create *anything*." Insects are proof enough of that. "Fish gotta swim and bird gotta fly; insects, it seems, gotta do one horrible thing after another. I never ask why of a vulture or shark, but I ask why of almost every insect I see. More than one insect—the possibility of fertile reproduction—is an assault on all human value, all hope of a reasonable god."[20] This leads Dillard to challenge all forms of Paleyism:

> Nature is, above all, profligate. Don't believe them when they tell you how economical and thrifty nature is, whose leaves return to the soil. Wouldn't it be cheaper to leave them on the tree in the first place? This deciduous business alone is a radical scheme, the brainchild of a deranged manic-depressive with limitless capital. Extravagance! Nature will try anything once. This is what the sign of the insect says. No form is too gruesome, no behavior too grotesque.[21]

Bushnell would have agreed that if the end of creation were physical design, or if the purpose of a seriously flawed world were the direct disclosure of God's own beauty, Dillard's doubts about God's motivation would be none too radical. Bushnell would find the purpose of a fallen creation elsewhere—in what he called its "moral uses."

Even if Paleyism were not so insensitive to the grotesque forms of nature, it could prove at best only a God *of* nature, not a being with supernatural disposal over the natural order. Paley and his imitators had not only misread nature, they had also misunderstood religion, for they provided no access to a personal God:

> The evil in our present stage of thought, is that natural theology has the whole ground to itself, and the God established is not a being who meets the conditions of Christianity at all. We get, of course, no proofs out of nature, that go farther than to prove a God of nature, least of all do we get any that show him to be acting supernaturally, to restore the disorders of nature. What we discover is a God, who institutes, is revealed by, and, as many will suspect, *is* the causes of nature. A latent pantheism lurks in the argument. Calling the God we prove a personal being, and meaning it in good faith, we yet find ourselves living before causes, and looking for consequences.[22]

In this statement Bushnell not only scorned Paleyism; he also discounted any theology which would attempt to prove a personal God from nature's causes, he rejected all forms of Enlightened piety which would blend world of fact and world of value, and he repudiated any theological scheme which would reduce religious truth to the categories of moral and natural law. In short, he set himself against an entire theological method current in his own New England. His alternative was to take nature as most directly a symbol of human sin and to suggest what a redeemed symbolic imagination might detect about God in a disordered nature's images.

Bushnell considered every person's imagination, even that of the unredeemed, to be superior in its discoveries to those of the speculative natural theologian. There is a yearning for God within every human breast, and as each person lets his imagination play upon the natural world he manifests a desire to know its Unknown Creator. If he is honest in his imaginative vision, he may also see that the temple of nature is blackened by evil. Yet these uses of the natural imagination do not spring from a human spirit internally conformed to the Spirit of God, they do not issue from a character transformed by God's own Form, and so they are a mere grasping after God:

> What a sublime and almost appalling proof of the religious nature of man, feeling dimly, groping blindly after God, imagining that he is somewhere and everywhere; in the sun, in the moon, in the snakes of the ground, the beetles of the air, the poor tame vegetables of the garden, the many-headed monsters carved in wood or stone, that never were any where but in the crazy fancy of superstition. Look on these, and see how man feels after God: does he therefore find him?[23]

Natural imagination is essentially fancy, the idolatry of the pagan mind, which is incapable of breaking through nature's images to the religious truth within them. Although that imagination reveals the religious nature of man, or the finite's yearning for union with the infinite, it is not union with God. The union is achieved, God is found, only when the soul is created anew in God's image; then the imagination "dwells in light" and has illuminated the true intent of God's communication through nature.[24]

The illuminated imagination first of all and most directly apprehends physical nature as an image of human fallenness. It grasps the truth that diseased beauty, not God's own perfect beauty of holiness, is most immediately displayed in the creation. Physical nature is held before the human mind as a mirror; in it is beheld images of human disorder. Nature's attempts "to execute more than she can finish," her abortive growths and her diseased fruits, her destructive powers—all become symbols of aborted human plans, man's loss of the beauty of the *imago dei,* the impulses of destruction deep within human selfhood. And yet precisely by attending first of all to physical nature's reflections of human nature, the redeemed imagination apprehends the beauty of God's own holiness in the physical world. For nature is a reflection of a reflection. Physical nature reflects the nature of man which, even though fallen, is the superior finite image of God's own holiness. In fact, man in his very sin is a symbol of the holiness of God from which he has fallen. As Bushnell phrased it in a sermon, "the dignity of human nature is shown from its ruins." Only a being of great dignity could fall so far; only a resplendent temple of God could produce such ruins. The grandeur of man is apparent in his ability to tear himself away from the beauty of God's holiness. The human fall is tragic, and tragic rebellion, even as the hero brings himself to utter grief, is a sign of greatness. Therefore, when physical nature reflects the ruin of man, it also symbolizes what man has fallen from—the glory of God once symbolized so directly and so magnificently by man as the image of God. In this sense, then, the religious imagination has been "fitly insphered" by the beauty of God in the material universe. "This, we say, is indeed the tremendous beauty of God; and the strange, wild jargon of the world, shattered thus by sin, becomes to us a mysterious, transcendent hymn." Nature's hymn to human tragedy is also a hymn to the God against whom humans have rebelled. That, above all, is what Bushnell meant by the "moral use" of a creation that groans and travails for a lost good.[25]

The person whose character has been transformed by the Form of God can also imaginatively discern the majestic power of God in physical nature. Nature becomes symbolic of the powerful weight of God's awesome presence. As nature's mechanical laws are taken as images of God's powerful determination to create cosmos out of chaos, there is a truth in Kepler's cry, "O God, I think thy thoughts after thee!" For to an imagination, including a scientific imagina- tion, inspired by the Spirit of God, the things of the physical world do bespeak the thoughts of God. Not only nature's laws, but also clouds, thunder, the dawn of morning, "every form of beauty and plenty and gladness and power and terror discourses to our hearts' feeling somehow of feelings, dispositions, meanings, thoughts, somewhere, that are consciously not our own."[26] Yet such dis- courses of God are essentially revelations of God's power as creator. They are devoid of testimony about sacrificial love and hence do not bespeak the real beauty of God's mind. Only historical symbols can image forth God's love. "We could almost as soon look for sacrifice in a steam-engine as in nature." The images of God's power in nature must be supplemented by symbols of his love in sacred history. For the true measure of God's greatness is his sacrificial love, not his omnipotence.[27] The symbolic imagination attains its fullness when it reads the symbols of nature and of supernature as they coalesce into one organic whole.

Horace Bushnell developed his interpretation of physical nature as an alternative to that of the didactic Enlightenment. Rather than treating the end of nature as the promotion of human duty and happiness, and the system of nature as a collection of moral teach- ings, Bushnell affirmed with Edwards that the ultimate end of creation is the display of God's glory and that the highest response to nature is an imaginative one that attends to nature's symbolic meanings. He replaced the Enlightenment's mechanical universe with Coleridge's dynamic cosmos in which the freedom of superna- ture interacts with nature's fixities. Rejecting natural theology's arguments from physical design, he pointed to the disorder within nature's order as a symbol of disharmony within the human soul and in the affairs of men. Repulsed by the Enlightenment's correla- tion of the kindly beauties of nature with some soft beauty in the divine life, Bushnell turned to the flaws in nature as emblems of human ruin and, indirectly, as tokens of the divine holiness. Nothing could have been more antithetical to the legalism, mechanism, and perfectionism of the didactic Enlightenment than Bushnell's vision of nature and nature's symbols.

Yet Bushnell's breakthrough was not complete. Father of a modern symbolic view of nature, he was still a son of the Enlightenment. In fact, when it suited his social prejudices, nature could become even more mechanical and rigid than it was for his Enlightenment contemporaries. And when it confirmed his ethic of work, nature could become as didactic in meaning as it was for a Dwight or a Beecher.

Nature revealed no flexibility when Bushnell appealed to its structures in his discussions of race and sex. Bushnell pled for the emancipation of slaves, and he bemoaned slavery's destruction of the family, its abolition of the rights of life and limb, and its exclusion of the opportunity for moral and intellectual development among blacks. But he held that like other "feebler races" black people were limited by nature in what they could achieve and were doomed by the processes of nature to eventual extinction. The problem, he felt, was that blacks, unlike Anglo-Saxons, did not possess a high enough degree of the powers of supernature. "No savage race of the world has ever been raised into civilization," he believed, "least of all, into a state of virtue, by mere natural development." Nature does not lead "savage races" forward; it fixes their doom. The color of their skin is a symbol of blacks' fate: "It is as if their color was the stamp of night on their history, both past and future." Bushnell in effect excluded blacks from the powers of supernature that can overcome the fixities of nature; he thus implied, according to his own definitions, that the black race is not fully human. As Lewis Weeks has said, Bushnell was sensitive to the need to rescue blacks from the institution of slavery—to that extent he recognized their human rights; but he was unable to extricate himself from institutional racism—to that extent he denied blacks their humanness.[28] Bushnell's racism led him to lock the black race in an iron cage of naturalistic determinism.

If Bushnell felt the need to rescue the black man from the horrors of bondage, however, he felt no need to give women the key to their deliverance from social inferiority. Although a proponent of the need for coeducation, Bushnell deemed women's suffrage a "reform against nature." He judged the so-called right of women to vote—and what that would lead to, the right to hold office—contrary to Scripture and good historical precedent, and he feared an inevitable consequence—the destruction of the marriage covenant. He was certain that women would neglect their husbands and children and that their public lives would transform them psychically and physically into man-like creatures. But all such consequences and historical "evidence" were just so many illustrations of what was apparent from nature: women are destined to be subordinate to men; they are naturally the governed rather than the governors. "The man is taller and more muscular, has a larger brain, and a longer stride," which indicate that the male personality "has some attribute of thunder. But there is no look of thunder in the woman." Nature has determined, through its separate gifts to the sexes, that the male will carry "the governmental function," the "forwarding force, the brave-and-dare element," while the female will possess "the indoor faculty, *covert,* as the law would say, and complementary, mistress and dispenser of the enjoyabilities." In complete disregard of the likes of Queen Elizabeth, Bushnell could say that the laws of nature are responsible for our never seeing "the woman who can hold a particle of authority in us by her own positive rule or the emphasis of her own personality." Bushnell insisted that female *subordination* did not mean female *inferiority*. In fact, he claimed, nature has blessed women with superior spiritual qualities. "Their moral nature is more delicately perceptive. Their religious inspirations, or inspirabilities, put them closer to God." According to Bushnell's doctrine of being, in other words, women possess to a greater degree than men one of the principles that differentiates supernature from nature—the capacity for inspiration. But they apparently lack that other differentiating principle—will, or the power to transcend and throw into new combinations the given realities of nature.[29]

Thus within his own cosmic vision of the relation between nature and supernature, Bushnell relegated woman to a status that was less than fully human. Despite his distinction between subordination and inferiority, like so many other men of Victorian America, when Bushnell ascribed qualities of spiritual superiority to women, it was a way of reinforcing their inferior social status. Nature's laws became society's mandates:

> Oh, it is the greatness of woman that she is so much like the great powers of nature, back of the noise and clatter of the world's affairs, tempering all things with her benign influence only the more certainly because of her silence, greatest in her beneficence because most remote from ambition, most forgetful of herself and fame; a better nature in the world that only waits to bless it, and refuses to be known save in the successes of others, whom she makes conspicuous; satisfied most, in the honors that come not to her—that "Her husband is known in the gates, when he sitteth among the elders of the land."[30]

In his pleas for a comprehensive, holistic approach to religious language, Bushnell complained that often "in expelling one error" theologians are "perpetually thrusting themselves into another, as if unwilling or unable to hold more than half the truth at once."[31] The lamentation applies to Bushnell's own views of nature. It was as if, in expelling the mechanistic nature of the Enlightenment, he had thrust himself into a natural mechanism even more rigid in his opinions of blacks and women, unable or unwilling fully to grasp the truth of his own flexible cosmos. His comprehension of that universe was also impeded by a certain New England parochialism and by occasional lapses into didactic moralism.

Bushnell's early life in the vicinity of Litchfield, Connecticut, gave him an undying love for the beauties of western New England. The hills and peaks, lakes and brooks, forests and fields of the area formed lasting impressions of how nature *should* appear. And his family's homestead became the test of all other environments—a realm of dignified simplicity and carefully cultivated comfort.[32] During his adult life, Bushnell took frequent fishing, hunting, and walking tours throughout New England, and according to one traveling companion, the clouds, mountains, and bird songs set him to talking about nature's symbolic meaning.[33] But Bushnell also beheld American nature from the engineer's angle of vision. An accomplished surveyor, he laid out a park in Hartford that still bears his name, forecast the route of the transcontinental railroad, and as president pro tempore of the University of California, surveyed and recommended the site for the campus at Berkeley. As he said in a letter to his daughter, one should aim at a balance of artistic and practical loves.[34]

Precisely because, in his opinion, New England had found a way to maintain that balance, it was superior to other parts of the United States. New England had achieved the harmony of natural beauty and the simple improvements of civilization. Bushnell looked askance at the wild, uncultivated nature of the West. That kind of wilderness symbolized the West's headlong rush into barbarism. During a year in California (1856), Bushnell was admittedly over-whelmed by the beauties of land and sea, and his letters back home went to great lengths in describing whole carpets of wildflowers, the immense redwood forests, the striking colors that played on landscape and seacape. The redwoods moved him to write, "when I was returning, after seeing the Big Trees, I was tempted to call it, without any feeling of irreverence, the Park of the Lord Almighty." And a ride through Stockton Pass led him to exclaim that the scene "was the nearest thing to a garden of Eden actually extant that I ever saw." Yet that parallel carried a double meaning, for California was both a paradise and the very seat of sin, and California's physical nature symbolized both. Bushnell looked upon the lawlessness of San Francisco in particular as the epitome of the social barbarism issuing from man's sinful heart: "California is in a truly wretched state, never so wretched as now. . . . It would be no surprise to me to hear, almost any day, that fire and murder were loose in San Francisco, rank as in the days of Robespierre." Despite his genuine appreciation for the Big Trees, he took the absence of hardwood as a token of California's brittle society and fragile future: "With all the growths of wood, there is no wood, in the whole extent of the State, that can be called hard timber, such as would be fit to make a wagon of." This could only make him ask: "What does it signify as regards the future men? Will there be any better stuff in them?" Little wonder that long before the conclusion of his stay in California, Bushnell longed to return to his native New England with its lawful society and its hardwood symbols of sturdy human stock.[35]

During a year in Minnesota (mid-1859 to mid-1860), Bushnell found fewer symbols of barbarism, but he again revealed his pref-erence for the New England landscape. Impressed by the wilder-ness of northern Minnesota's lake country, assuaged by the state's soft Indian summers ("a good match for Italy"), invigorated by the crystal beauty of the Minnesota winter, Bushnell constantly ex-pressed in his letters his desire to return to New England scenery. In fact, his most enthusiastic letters report his discovery of a transplanted New England family with whom he could stay, a family with "well-filled bookcase" and manners and customs that kept him in touch with the New England to which he yearned to return.[36] What the scenery of California and Minnesota lacked, what New England possessed, was the balance between nature and will. New England had best brought together in America nature and supernature, wilderness and civilization, primary and secondary creation. New England, it seemed, had understood that the highest form of physical beauty is a cultivated garden:

> God creates in the rough—land, sea, rivers, mountains, and wild forests. So far only does he make scenery, but he never creates a proper landscape. The rich fields, and gardens, and green meadows and lawns, the open vistas of ornament, the road-ways, bridges, cottages and cleanly dressed shores of water—all that constitutes the special beauty of the world, is something added, as finish, after the world is made; . . . Not even the flowers, lurking in the woods, could show much beauty till they were transplanted and taught what shape they might take in their kind, and into what colors they might blush.[37]

Nature subdued by the human will, or at least nature improved by deliberate human action, was the height of physical beauty. Symbols of physical nature transformed by man's civilizing actions were the best natural symbols of spiritual truth. That conviction could lead Bushnell to hear in nature a call to a work ethic as demanding as Lyman Beecher's and to salute the same New England virtues that Timothy Dwight had extolled in Greenfield Hill. In an address at the centennial celebration of Litchfield County in 1851, Bushnell looked back with more than nostalgia on the "age of homespun" of his youth. The simple, earnest, industrious life of his forebears in Litchfield had produced a human character suitable to a new America about to march into a technological age. By being kept close to nature and enfolded in the warm community of home life, his forefathers had learned the dignity of labor, had cooperated to defeat the powers of nature, and had despised the "drone of idleness." The lesson of his heritage was clear: "Let no delicate spirit that despises work grow up in your sons and daughters. Make these rocky hills smooth their faces and smile upon your industry."[38] New England, with its sharp but healthful climate and its tradition of taking seriously "life's simple duties," had distinct advantages in building the necessary character. Bushnell therefore sang praises to the virtues of "agriculture at the east" in refrains reminiscent of Dwight's pastoral poetry: "A New England farmer, swinging his scythe under a July sun, and foddering his cattle on a snow-bank, has a body and mind that are tough enough for all weather." In fact "a softer climate makes softer men."[39]

Smoothing rocky hills, making nature to smile upon human industry, cultivating a rugged character were to Bushnell's mind the vocation for more than simply rural New Englanders. It was the responsibility of all Americans to make supernature triumph over nature and to dispel the vice of idleness with constant acts of secondary creation. Improved systems of communication became a chief means of meeting that responsibility. Barbarism, or the "wildness, lawlessness and violence" created by peoples' distance from centers of culture, was the most outstanding danger threatening the developing new nation. The western United States in particular opened the distinct possibility of wrecking the delicate balance between nature and civilization. Thus the road was a symbol of the necessary response to the American wilderness: "The Road is that physical sign, or symbol, by which you will best understand any age or people. If they have no roads, they are savages; for the Road is a creation of man and a type of civilized society."[40] Nature civilized, nature bent to the purposes of (New England) culture—that was supernature's responsibility to nature. And the prosperity, individual and national, that results from meeting that responsibility was not to be discredited. Sounding exactly like those American gospelers of wealth who drew strict correlations between industriousness, virtue, and wealth, Bushnell said, "it is the duty of every man to be a prosperous man, if by any reasonable effort he may. God calls us to industry and tempts us to it by all manner of promises." Though the dangers of prosperity are real—greed, ostentation, lack of public-spiritedness—the prosperity itself that comes from turning nature into city is not an evil. For "it is the fixed law of God that what advances the wealth and happiness of the whole shall stand in final harmony with the good of every part."[41]

Although Bushnell never abandoned his position that God created nature for the sake of its "improvement" by the human agent, he was not a spokesman for indiscriminate use of the land. And although until his dying day he applauded the virtue of hard work, his statements on prosperity through industriousness were not his last word on the meaning and role of work.

In his transformation of nature, each person should be sensitive to how his creative acts contribute to the whole of God's system of nature and supernature. Those acts should be creative rather than destructive in design. Bushnell was quite aware that acts supposedly creative could in fact be destructive:

> For example, it is not absurd to imagine the human race, at some future time, when the population and the works of industry are vastly increased, kindling so many fires, by putting wood and coal in contact with fire, as to burn up or fatally vitiate the world's atmosphere. That the condition of nature will, in fact, be so far changed by human agency, is probably not to be feared. We only say that human agency, in its power over nature, holds, as may well enough be imagined to hold, the sovereignty of the process. . . . the scheme of nature itself is a scheme unstrung and mistuned, to a very great degree, by man's agency in it, so as to be rather unnature, after all, than nature.[42]

Bushnell drew back from the full vision of his prophecy: he admitted only the possibility, not the probability, of the pollution of the world's atmosphere. But his recognition of the possibility was a significant check on any counsel he might be tempted to give regarding the willful exploitation of nature. He never pursued the implications of his prediction with respect to the "day of roads" or the march of technological civilization. But he did recognize the human capacity to reduce nature to a state of unnature as a symbol of the power of human evil.

Bushnell made his most ardent defenses of the work ethic and the necessity of prosperity before his spiritual turning point of 1848. In August of that year he delivered an oration before the Phi Beta Kappa Society at Harvard. The address, "Work and Play," reflected the easy frame of mind created by his spiritual experience, and it moved beyond the anxiety-producing work ethic which sees nature only as an occasion for the industrious exercise of the will. The central claim of the oration was this: "the highest and complete state of man, that which his nature endeavors after and in which only it fulfills its sublime instinct, is the state of play." In fact, the Christian life, as a life of liberty, is "only pure spiritual play." The critical difference between work and play is that work is activity done on behalf of an end, while play is activity as an end. And work entails a deliberate effort of the will, while play is impulsive, springing not so much from conscious choice as from an exuberant fund of vitality. "So that one is something which we require of ourselves, the other something that we must control ourselves not to do. We work because we must, because prudence impels. We play because we have in us a fund of life that wants to expend itself." To be sure, work and play are related. Both are divine gifts to human existence, and one is not to be adopted totally at the expense of the other. And often the discipline of work is required to deliver us to the point where the spontaneity of play takes over. The play of genius, for example, builds upon the difficult exercise of talent. Yet still the two are different, and play, not work, is the more expressive of what life is all about. The activities most representative of distinctively human consciousness—reason, imagination, humor— are acts of spontaneous inspiration which cannot be worked up by efforts of the will. "Inspiration sought is inspiration hindered," and play is essentially inspiration.[43]

Bushnell has here defined the human activity that is characteristic of the imaginative approach to nature. The imaginative, religious detection of symbolic truth in nature is play, the spontaneous response to tokens of God and man in the physical world. And Bushnell has elevated inspirability, or the capacity to receive the inflow of God's Spirit, over nature-transforming acts of the will as the superior principle in supernature. What he judged as the "female characteristic" is made superior to the male, and it is a characteristic possessed by all persons. Finally, he has transcended the overwrought, legalistic attitude bred by a Protestant ethic that encourages the fretful duty always to be working. At the core of the religious life is play, not work, liberty, not duty, the free impulse of thought and love, not the commands of law:

> As childhood begins with play, so the last end of man, the pure ideal in which his being is consummated, is a state of play. And if we look for this perfected state, we shall find it nowhere, save in religion. Here at last man is truly and completely man. Here the dry world of work and the scarcely less dry counterfeits of play are left behind. Partial inspirations no longer suffice. The man ascends into a state of free beauty, where well-doing is its own end and joy, where life is the simple flow of love, and thought, no longer colored in the prismatic hues of prejudice and sin, rejoices ever in the clear white light of truth. Exactly this we mean, when we say that Christianity brings an offer of liberty to man; for the Christian liberty is only pure spiritual play. Delivered

of self-love, fear, contrivance, legal constraints, termagant passions, in a word, of all ulterior ends not found in goodness itself, the man ascends into power, and reveals, for the first time, the real greatness of his nature.[44]

Once again, without totally shedding his immediate religious and cultural heritage, Horace Bushnell had broken free of the most constricting segments of that heritage. He continued to see will as a crucial factor dividing supernature from nature, and he continued to call for the laborious transformation of nature. Yet he had caught a vision of religion that surpassed all exertions of the will and all acts of labor. In that vision religion was fundamentally the spontaneous flow of love and thought, and nature stood less as a call to work than as an invitation to the free play of the imagination. Then nature and nature's laws could be seen through to that "vast, mysterious, incomprehensible power, which best we know, when most we love."

Horace Bushnell's organic perspective led him considerably beyond the mechanistic world view of the Enlightenment. Yet he rejected Darwinism, a theory that stands as a nineteenth-century monument to organic thinking. Bushnell's adamant refusal to adopt Darwin's biological theses led Theodore Munger to complain about a major shortcoming in Bushnell's thought. "Bushnell was as much of an evolutionist as he could be in his day," Munger wrote. He had accepted Louis Agassiz's classification of species and had himself insisted that nature is an ongoing, developmental process. But Bushnell failed to follow the implications of his own theory of organic growth: "nature had not spoken to him its great secret. It is pathetic to think of him as standing on the border-land of evolution, but not entering it."[45] Munger, a late nineteenth-century liberal, had wanted Bushnell to locate God's revelation in the evolutionary patterns of nature and history, something that Bushnell refused to do despite his conviction that, through fits and starts, the world had been moving progressively forward. But Munger was also voicing a criticism of Bushnell's unwillingness to adopt and improve Darwin's theory of nature. And certainly Bushnell's response to Darwin's *Origin of Species* was biased.

Even while advancing the argument that there is no inherent conflict between religion and science because of the "unity and composite wholeness of truth," Bushnell could muster no sympathy for Darwin's theory of the transmutation of species. The theory was both unproved and unprovable, a mere hypothesis "where the proposed point of discovery is not made out, and there is no reason to fear it ever will be." If the theory should turn out to be true, "if that must be the fact, we may well enough agree to live without religion." In one sentence Bushnell abandoned his argument about the essential unity of religious and scientific truth! He reacted to Darwin this way, first of all, because he believed that the new biology was destructive of the very foundation of scientific knowledge. "If species do not keep their places, but go a masking or really becoming one another, in strange transmutations, what is there to know, and where is the possibility of science?"[46] Bushnell shared with most intellectuals of his day the assumption that all natural knowledge is dependent upon a *Scala Naturae* constituted by immutable species. That assumption had long been held by religious, philosophical, and scientific thinkers, and it was the point of departure for many of the assaults on Darwin.[47] But Bushnell was also offended by Darwin's theory for another reason. The clear implication of Darwinian science was that man could no longer be considered a microcosm of the entire organic kingdom. That implication upset Bushnell's scheme of creation in which man gathered up and extended through his supernatural powers the overall intention of life itself.

As indefensible as Bushnell's reponse to Darwin was, it was not nearly as pathetic as Munger made it out to be. For Bushnell took more seriously than Darwin himself the internal factors that account for organic wholeness. Loren Eiseley, an admirer of the boldness of Darwin's theories, observed that Darwin's preoccupation with exterior struggle in the evolutionary process "diverted biologists for decades from the most mysterious aspect of the living organism—how its elaborate interior system is so subtly controlled and regulated." Darwin showed no "deep recognition of the life of the organism as a functioning whole which must be co-ordinated interiorly before it can function exteriorly. He was . . . a separatist, a student of parts and their changes." Much time would have to pass before biologists, with their comprehension of genetic structures, and social scientists, with their deeper appreciation for the subjective human factor, would adopt a more holistic approach to their phenomena.[48] Horace Bushnell certainly cannot be credited with significantly advancing science along this path. But within the confines of his outmoded view of a fixed scale of being, he was devoted to explicating the inner coordination of organic wholes. Nature and supernature constituted for him "one system," a system coordinated by the interior, supernatural principles of will and spirit. Life, especially intelligent life, was a leap forward in the order of being that could not be explained apart from a life-force that evades the categories of parts and their changes. Human language, so closely tied to the physical world, was to be understood only in terms of the inner intention of its user. And nature could open its symbolic meaning only when taken up into the free organic flow of the imagination. Nature had not spoken to Bushnell the whole secret of evolution. But it had spoken to him enough of the secret so that his reflections on language, nature, and the supernatural were thoughts on an organicism which he believed was the axis of the universe.

NOTES

1. "Revelation" (MS in Yale Divinity School Library, 1839), pp. 1–2, 27–28.

2. *Christ in Theology* (Hartford, Conn.: Brown and Parsons, 1851), pp. 145–46; *God in Christ* (Hartford, Conn.: Brown and Parsons, 1849), p. 145.

3. *Nature and the Supernatural* (New York: Charles Scribner's Sons, 1877), pp. 264–65.

4. Ibid., pp. 36–37, 40, 43–48.

5. Ibid., pp. 16, 20–28, 38.

6. Ibid., pp. 85, 90.

7. Ibid., p. 58; "The Finite Demands the Infinite," *The Spirit in Man, Sermons and Selections* (New York: Charles Scribner's Sons, 1903), pp. 200–1.

8. "The Spirit in Man," *Sermons for the New Life* (New York: Scribner, Armstrong & Co., 1873), p. 33.

9. "God Preparing the State of Glory," *Spirit in Man*, pp. 215–16.

10. *Nature and Supernatural*, pp. 72–73; "Life, or the Lives," *Work and Play* (New York: Charles Scribner, 1864), pp. 268, 287–89.

11. *Nature and Supernatural*, pp. 272–73.

12. "Progress," *Hours at Home* (1869), 8:207. Cf. *Nature and Supernatural*, pp. 411–12.

13. *Nature and Supernatural*, p. 83.

14. Ibid., p. 165. Cf. "The Power of an Endless Life," *Sermons for the New Life*, p. 313.

15. *Nature and Supernatural*, p. 167.

16. Ibid., pp. 98, 140, 190–92, 215, 406–8.

17. *Moral Uses of Dark Things* (New York: Charles Scribner & Co., 1869), p. 191.

18. Ibid., p. 48.

19. Ibid., pp. 281–82.

20. Annie Dillard, *Pilgrim at Tinker Creek* (New York: Harper's Magazine Press, 1974), pp. 63, 135, 160.

21. Ibid., p. 65.

22. *Nature and Supernatural*, p. 507.

23. "Religious Nature, and Religious Character," *Sermons on Living Subjects* (New York: Scribner, Armstrong & Co., 1872), p. 141.

24. Ibid., pp. 144–47; "Light on the Cloud," *Sermons for the New Life*, p. 153.

25. *Nature and Supernatural*, pp. 187–89, 193; *Moral Uses of Dark Things*, pp. 222–24, 284–86; "Dignity of Human Nature Shown from its Ruins," *Sermons for the New Life*, pp. 50, 54, 64–65; "Religious Nature, Religious Character," *Sermons on Living Subjects*, p. 134.

26. "God's Thoughts Fit Bread for Children," *Spirit in Man*, p. 75.

27. "The Power of God in Self-Sacrifice," *Sermons for the New Life*, pp. 357, 360.

28. For the development of this point and for considerable evidence of Bushnell's racism, see Lewis Weeks, "Horace Bushnell on Black America," *Religious Education*, 68 (1973): 28–41. See also Bushnell's *A Discourse on the Slavery Question* (Hartford, Conn.: Case, Tiffany, 1839) and "Of Distinctions of Color," *Moral Uses of Dark Things*, pp. 296–318.

29. *Women's Suffrage; The Reform Against Nature* (New York: Charles Scribner & Co., 1869), pp. 49–72.

30. "The Age of Homespun," *Work and Play*, pp. 398–99.

31. "Christian Comprehensiveness," *New Englander*, 6 (1848): 82.

32. Theodore Munger, *Horace Bushnell: Preacher and Theologian* (Boston & New York: Houghton, Mifflin & Co., 1899), p. 6.

33. *Life and Letters of Horace Bushnell*, ed. Mary Bushnell Cheney (New York: Harper & Brothers, 1880), p. 531.

34. Ibid., p. 435.

35. Bushnell's letters regarding California society and nature are contained in ibid., pp. 365–405.

36. Bushnell's letters concerning his stay in Minnesota are in ibid., pp. 423–38.

37. "Our Advantage in Being Finite," *Sermons on Living Subjects*, pp. 340–41.

38. "Age of Homespun," *Work and Play*, p. 402.

39. "Agriculture at the East," ibid., pp. 230–31.

40. "The Day of Roads," ibid., p. 403. For his lengthy discussion of the dangers facing an expanding nation (first "barbarism" and then "Romanism"), and the need for religion and education as well as systems of communication, see Bushnell's *Barbarism the First Danger* (New York: American Home Missionary Society, 1847).

41. "Prosperity Our Duty," *Spirit in Man*, pp. 139, 147.

42. *Nature and Supernatural*, pp. 45–46.

43. "Work and Play," *Work and Play*, pp. 12–18, 29–31.

44. Ibid., p. 38.

45. Munger, *Horace Bushnell*, pp. 212, 344.

46. "Science and Religion," *Putnam's Magazine*, 1 (1868): 265, 271.

47. Loren Eiseley, *Darwin's Century* (Garden City, N.Y.: Doubleday Anchor, 1961), pp. 5–10.

48. Ibid., pp. 199, 342–44.

10

Moral Uses of Nature's Symbols

Horace Bushnell's highest professional aim was to be an imaginative preacher; as a consequence, he was devoted more to cultivating the homiletical art than to developing a well-rounded philosophical or theological point of view. Even after ill health forced him to retire from the Hartford church, Bushnell was happiest when he found opportunities to preach. A sentiment expressed in a letter of 1862 was typical: "As my old pulpit is now vacant, I am trying to put in a sermon a week there. How long I shall stand so much, I don't know. I could go on to the world's end, or to mine, for there is nothing I so much delight in as preaching."[1] All of his other theological labors were done in the service of this chief delight. He worked out his theory of language with an ear tuned to the words he would use in the pulpit. He explored the functions of the religious imagination as a means of communicating imaginatively in his sermons and of evoking an imaginative response from his hearers. He reflected upon the relation between nature and supernature, and upon the symbolic qualities of doctrine and of the material world, in order to found theoretically the symbols he would employ in his sermons. Theology was bent to his practical task as a preacher, and often his theology and his preaching came together in one form: most of his theological essays and treatises were cast embryonically as sermons.

Bushnell was a highly regarded preacher whose sermons were well attended and widely discussed. Yet, as his biographer remarks, he was not popular after the manner of a number of nineteenth-century American preachers. Although he avoided theological abstraction in the pulpit, his imagery sought to make "reason and devotion one," and his sermons demanded sustained attention from the congregation.[2] Someone once said that the language of the popular preacher Henry Ward Beecher moved in shocks rather than sentences. Horace Bushnell's pulpit language progressed in carefully wrought sentences designed to provoke symbolic thinking.

Yet if Bushnell did not attempt to win a cheap popularity with superficial sermons, he was eager to bring his preaching into line with the Age of Eloquence that was producing, in his time, such an attractive alternative to the dry, dull, doctrinal preaching of Protestant orthodoxy. Bushnell believed that if the minister were to communicate effectively, his sermons should be interesting, striking, original, and remembered. Preaching should be an art, a symbolic discourse which, like powerful poetry, fans the flames of the imagination. The minister therefore should not recoil from making his personal presence felt in the pulpit; he should strive to create a "personal atmosphere." He should seek to make his language original rather than borrowed, the content of his sermons concrete and specific rather than abstract and general, the tone of his delivery persuasive rather than authoritative or demanding. And the minister must give himself to the cultivation of certain talents: the ability to use lively images in the place of theological formulas; the capacity for letting his style flow naturally from powerful thoughts and wide reading; the knack for speaking directly to persons.[3]

In defending such pulpit talents Bushnell joined the chorus of numerous orators at America's lyceums and lecture halls.[4] He also agreed with the Unitarian intention of making preaching an art of persuasion. Bushnell had special words of praise for William Ellery Channing because the greatest of the Unitarian preachers understood that a key to effective communication is the creation of a personal atmosphere:

> Where then was [Channing's] power? For there certainly was a most grandly impressive power in his pulpit efforts. It consisted, I conceive, to a very great extent, in his personal atmosphere. No one could argue with him, because every one was obliged to feel him. The subdued manner, the keen-edged, quivering delicacy of his moral perceptions, the unqualified honesty of the man, sanctified by his profoundly tender, always delicate reverence toward God, made the atmosphere of the place sensational, and no one was permitted to choose whether he would be impressed or not.[5]

Bushnell's praise of Channing's preaching was not unqualified, however. For finally Channing's sermons did not really seem to preach at all; they were gentle ethical lessons, not clarion calls to faith.[6] With that criticism Bushnell indicated what he believed preaching should be essentially—an invitation to salvation through faith. If all formal pulpit talents were not aimed at the substance of the Christian message, they were not the talents of preaching at all but of ethical oratory. Such aim could be taken only when the minister himself possessed "faith-talent," or the redeemed imagination which opened as a "high window" on the supernatural, when he remained keenly aware of the tragedies and conflicts of human history, and when he became a symbol "charactered" by God's Word and Spirit.[7] Then the preacher might deal with the Christian message in a manner lacking in ethical oratory—in a manner that "gets us out of ourselves." The imaginative proclamation of redemption must take the human being off his own center; it must direct him beyond concern for his own perfection and even beyond the vicious circle of concern over his own sin. "Any strictly subjective style of religion is vicious. It is moral self-culture, in fact, and not religion. We think of ourselves abundantly in the selfishness of our sins. What we need, above all, is to be taken off the self-center and centered in God."[8] The "altar forms" of Scripture best direct the self away from its own center, but if properly understood and handled by the preacher, the symbols of nature may achieve the same end.

In some respects Bushnell's homiletical aims and achievements were those of Jonathan Edwards. Despite his self-conscious efforts to attain eloquence, Bushnell, like his eighteenth-century predecessor, was chiefly concerned to discover those images which, when directed to the whole life of the person, would move him to respond in faith. And despite his preoccupation with method and style, Bushnell was wary of a style that called attention to itself rather than to the substance of what was being said. He criticized his dear friend Cyrus Bartol, Unitarian minister in Boston, for failing to preach the human need for the "supernatural lift" of faith and for constructing such beautiful, polished, delicate sermons that only beautiful, polished, delicate persons could respond to them.[9] Under the pressures of a busy week, Bushnell sometimes preached extemporaneously, but usually he carefully wrote out his sermons and then read them from the pulpit. He was a solemn, earnest, vital presence in the pulpit, with none of the rhetorical embellishments of the fiery orator. Early in his preaching career, he had a "nervous swing of the right arm, which set an exclamation point to an important sentence," but his mature style was largely gestureless. "His voice was a naturally good and strong one, but he never learned to manage it well, straining it sometimes, not by loudness but by emphasis." And there were reports that, although he avoided histrionic emotionalism, he sometimes had his hearers weeping quietly.[10]

Nonetheless, the preaching of Horace Bushnell was quite different from that of Jonathan Edwards. With few exceptions, Bushnell's sermons lacked the great sense of urgency that characterized Edwards's revivalist exhortations. Although he recognized revivals as legitimate means of occasionally renewing religious commitment, Bushnell made clear in his *Christian Nurture* that to his mind too much emphasis was being given to revivalism in nineteenth-century American religion. Revivalism left the impression that the whole of Christianity could be collapsed into a conversion that occurs at a specific time and place, whereas Christianity is in fact a life into which one grows. Revivalism placed the entire burden of the Christian life on the shoulders of the converted individual, ignoring the need for organic structures of family, church, and society which nurture one into the religious life. Even in his most ardent sermons, therefore, Bushnell avoided both the New Haven theologians' fearful sanctions and Edwards's dire portraits of the precariousness of life's poise. To be sure, Bushnell invoked images of the "dark things" of nature and history to give his hearers a present experience of the power of sin. But his images were tempered by gentleness and patience. And certainly, like Edwards, he chose to reach human hearts through the indirect path winding through intermingled ideas, feelings, and images. But he took that path less in order to awaken earthshaking decisions than to foreshadow a course of life that one might pursue. Organic growth rather than immediate decision was the end that Bushnell kept in constant view. Like the preaching of Channing, that of Bushnell was an art of gentle persuasion. His images were more striking than those of his Unitarian counterpart, and they were reflections of the majesty of God and the fall of man rather than tokens of innate, perfect human virtues. Still, his images were more persuasive than pressing; they were gentle rather than compelling, patient rather than urgent.

Bushnell provided the clue to the purpose of his preaching in his view of the gentle, indirect action of God in the redemption of men. God does not redeem humans by force; he patiently loves them into salvation. "Force and crude absolutism are thus put by; the irritations of a jealous littleness have no place; and the great God and Father, intent on making his children great, follows them and plies them with the gracious indirections of a faithful and patient love."[11] Force and absolutism were also put by in Bushnell's relations with his family and his congregation. For all of his stress on will as the critical principle of supernature, for all of his paeans to manly industriousness, Bushnell was the gentlest of souls. His children found him warm, playful, and spontaneous. And when he talked religion with them, his daughter recalled that "it was always the winning, never compelling side of religious experience, which he presented to us."[12] In his preaching he sought to win his hearers with gracious indirections. That aim had perhaps its most memorable realization in a sermon which he delivered at Yale College, "The Dissolving of Doubts." He told the students that they should never be afraid to doubt the very foundations of their religious beliefs, for that fear would lead to a sacrifice of the intellect. Further, they should "have it as a law never to put force on the mind, or try to make it believe; because it spoils the mind's integrity, and when that is gone, what power of advance in the truth is left?" Religious conviction is a matter of growth, struggling growth, and one should "never be in a hurry to believe, never try to conquer doubts against time."[13] Bushnell's counsel of patience was not always without its immediate effects, however. One of the Yale students who heard the sermon on doubt reported that he walked out of the chapel "into a new, an unfearing, a believing life."[14]

Bushnell searched for those images which vividly, but gently and over time, would win sinners to a sense of their predicament and open to them the path of faith. He was no keeper of private notebooks in which he experimented with his images before making them public. He experimented in print and from the pulpit. Yet in doing so, Bushnell produced a book of essays and sermons which revealed remarkable parallels with Jonathan Edwards's "Images or

Shadows of Divine Things." Bushnell's book, *Moral Uses of Dark Things*, was a series of meditations on the religious meaning of the dark, grotesque, disharmonious aspects of the world. Features both of human history (bad government, dead history, insanity) and of physical nature (winter, venomous animals, the sea) served as occasions for Bushnell's reflections, reflections dominated by considerations of how nature impinges upon the life of the person. *Moral Uses* briefly sketched Bushnell's theory of symbolic imagination and brought that theory to bear upon actual symbols. And like Edwards's private workbook, Bushnell's published volume comprised exercises in didactic moralism and symbolic interpretations that moved beyond moral lessons.

Bushnell's purpose in writing the pieces in *Moral Uses* was to elaborate his alternative to Paleyism. Having rejected Paley's argument that all things have their "physical uses," Bushnell now proposed to illustrate the way in which those things have their "moral uses" instead. That is to say, the universe, including nature's disorders, could be shown to serve "the last ends of God"—both the ultimate end of God's holiness and the penultimate end of human intelligence. Yet, without himself introducing and developing the distinction, Bushnell in fact understood "moral uses" in two different ways in the book. The moral uses of nature were those lessons that man can learn in his ongoing struggle to survive in an unfriendly world and in his attempt to attain some measure of virtue in this life. And they were the symbolic meanings relevant to our understanding of God and man, meanings available to an imagination "contempered" to God's Spirit. The dark things of nature were morally useful both in what they taught about religion and in how they conveyed religious truth symbolically.

The didactic import of nature appears in those facets of the material world which breed a tough character, stimulate the will, and generally promote human efforts to do good. Hard winters, for example, though serving no apparent physical ends, remind us that "our God is not a summer God only" but a God of grand prerogatives who demands of us in the cold months of the year the moderation of passion, the dulling of the senses on behalf of principled thinking, and the cultivation of the habits of industry and a disciplined will. Winter both teaches and enforces these moral lessons. "If there be any people on earth who have reason to accuse their climate, it is they who enjoy a perennial season of growth and verdure, and a soft and sunny sky throughout the year. There it is that mind also is soft, enervated by ease and luxury." Nature's most devastating plagues and pestilences awaken us to the debilities and degradations of sin and prompt acts of charity toward the afflicted. Even Bushnell's dreaded insects assume didactic meaning: they teach us ever to be on guard against lethargy; in fact, "a part of their value is that they annoy us enough to keep us awake." All the unsightly things of nature, the ugly bog and the carrion bird, are tokens of God's retribution on a sinful world and invitations to "fall to work in ways of culture and amendment, to improve what the Creator's hand has left us." Nature teaches about the truths of God, and it stimulates energetic acts of the human will.[15]

Such interpretations of the moral uses of dark things conformed to Bushnell's Protestant work ethic, his designation of the will as the principle of supernature, his preference for the New England environment, and his fondness for a nature transformed by culture. Bushnell heard in nature's disharmonies God's demands upon the human will, the groans of human sin, and a call to constant dutifulness and action. And nature spoke these things effectively: she prompted the living of her own moral lessons. Although Bushnell was more attuned to nature's disharmonies than Paley and his American imitators, in giving nature this moralistic interpretation he was an heir of the didactic Enlightenment. Yet in *Moral Uses* Bushnell also assigned a symbolic meaning to nature's dark side. The disorderly features of nature were also moral in their use because they conveyed symbolic truths to be appropriated by the character-transformed imagination. Like Coleridge from whom he learned so much, Bushnell was convinced that Christianity delivers human awareness into a stage beyond mere knowledge "about," into a state of consciousness in which the finite becomes transparent to the infinite. At that latter level, nature is a symbol, not a lesson.

In *Moral Uses* Bushnell sets the stage for a symbolic interpretation of nature when he alludes to theories he has developed at length elsewhere: the meaning of language, the functions of the imagination, the links between material world and Divine Mind, the symbolic intentions of doctrine. Human language, he says, is bedded in the types or images of the physical world; those natural images themselves constitute a language. The types in nature presuppose a being who can speak through them: "what we all see with our eyes I think I have some right to assume, namely, that this whole frame of being is bedded in Mind." Images of nature have both an objective and a subjective dimension: they are objective facts containing subjective meaning for the Infinite Subject who speaks through them and for the human imagination which grasps them. The supreme end of creation as a collection of symbols is God, their author and speaker; the secondary end is man, for whom and to whom the images bespeak the mind of God. Nature's coming to be through a scheme of cause and effect symbolizes God's power and grandeur. Nature's disorders are symbolic of the chaos of human sin, the glory of God from which man has fallen, and the need for God's redeeming love.[16]

With those theoretical principles announced and briefly sketched, Bushnell turns to the reading of nature's events and appearances as symbols laden with religious meaning. Thus winter not only teaches the need for industry and a disciplined will. It is also a symbol of the divine power. The winter storm, in particular, becomes a series of foreign notes played off against nature's harmony; in its majesty the chromatic storm resonates with the human imagination's own depths. When we listen to the winter storm's symbols we may perceive "that under this same winter-piece, performed by God's aërial orchestra, we have had our soul in vibration, as never under any combinations of art, and instrument, and voice, that have won the greatest applause. It had no rhythm, it was not a movement of time and harmony, but it was a grand chromatic of the creation, that we felt all through, heaving out our soul in tremulous commotion before God."[17] The waste in nature also is symbolic of the power of the Creator. When we recognize that the whole of nature is not economically designed, we may catch within nature's very profligacy a glimpse of the unboundedness of God's being, a vision of a resourceful God who transcends all categories of physical use or utility.[18] And the ocean—through its great depths, the power of its waves, the far reaches of its horizon—becomes a "liquid symbol" of God's infinity. After drawing numerous moralistic lessons from the sea—its raw being calling the human will to master it, its trials and storms building a resilient human character, its very existence acting as a blessing on communication and commerce—Bushnell ponders the sea's symbolic meaning:

> It is of the greatest consequence . . . that such a being as God should have images prepared to express him, and set him before the mind of man in all the grandeur of his attributes. These he has provided in the heavens and the sea, which are the two great images of his vastness and power; the one, remote, addressing itself to cultivated reason and science; the other nigh, to mere sense, and physically efficient, a liquid symbol of the infinitude of God. . . . Every kind of vastness— immensity, infinity, eternity, mystery, omnipotence—has its type in the sea.[19]

What the immensity of the sea, the power of the winter storm, the wastefulness of nature cannot symbolize in and of themselves, however, is the true greatness of God's character—his power of sacrificial love. Symbolism of that divine greatness must be drawn from the dramas of human history. Nature alone provides emblems of God's secondary greatness—his omnipotence and infinity. Nature reflects, more directly than the character of God, the character of man. Nature is a mirror held before us; in it we may see a reflection of our own souls, and within that reflection another image—the God from whom we have fallen. Nature's disharmonies thus offer something in addition to moral teachings; they are symbols of the human condition.

Now stinging insects and other venomous creatures do not simply warn of the dangers of moral indolence; they are "a representation of man to himself," symbols that "reflect, express, and continually raise in us the idea of what we are." And they give us, in their indiscriminate use of their poison, a lively image of our own pursuit of evil for evil's sake. "Evil for evil's sake, disinterested evil, is the fearful possibility and fact that must have signs and a language provided. In this office all the venomous animals do service, and more especially such as do not use their functions for self-defense, or the conquest of supplies, but distill their poison *gratis* or without reason."[20] The grand mutation or organic change in nature, the dynamism that breaks through the fixities of cause and effect, is a "soul-history correspondent"; it reflects both the transitoriness of human existence and the finite's yearning for a return to harmony with the infinite.[21] And plagues and pestilences not only declare the divine retribution on sin or issue a call for Christian charity; they embody as symbols the fallen human condition, the human soul in ruins.[22]

Many of the chapters in *Moral Uses of Dark Things* were originally sermons, and in sermons published in other volumes Bushnell proved that nature continued to speak to him in moralistic tones. He instructed his congregation in how God builds strong wills through the wild forces of nature, how the change of seasons impresses upon us the lesson that everything must be done at its appropriate time, how unexercised limbs and organs signify the withering of unused moral and spiritual powers.[23] But in his other sermons Bushnell also pursued the symbolic qualities of the material world. Although he remained persuaded that nature alone could not directly symbolize God's character as loving redeemer, his sermons drew upon natural metaphors of God's redemptive activity. Scripture had set the precedent for such symboling, and when joined with the "altar forms" of history and with a redeemed imagination, nature's images could provide hints of God's mysterious power to redeem. Those who had eyes to see and ears to hear, those, in other words, whose imaginations had been sanctified by the paradigmatic Logos, could detect in nature images of God's true character.

Nature in its wide variety thus takes on symbolic import in Bushnell's preaching. The rush of a powerful river toward its unseen end is a token of the known's reaching after the mystery of the divine unknown; a blue sky symbolizes the purity of God; clear waters and white snow betoken the purity from which men have fallen.[24] In Edwardean fashion Bushnell focuses upon the eventfulness of nature and insists that the laws behind the visible events are of great imaginative power. Modern science has proved, to the advantage of religious faith, that unseen laws and forces, not sensed phenomena, are the enduring qualities of the material world:

> All which is most permanent and solid in what we call nature is what is invisible in it, just that which no man ever saw with the eyes or knew through any one of his five senses. . . . In short, we discover, whenever we glance at the world of things around us, that what is visible is least

real, and that behind the visible, discoverable only to faith and reason, are hidden the vast changeless laws and forces, which give to the works of God, as set forth by science, whatever appearance of eternity and stability they exhibit.[25]

The unseen laws and forces of nature are therefore symbolic of the stable orderliness of God's creative mind.[26]

That part of nature, in both its visible appearance and its invisible laws, to which Bushnell gives considerable attention is light. Bushnell's preaching invokes images of light almost as much as Edwards's, the scriptural conventions leading him to expand upon their meaning. He invites his Hartford congregation to reflect upon the implications of the Christian being "a child of the sun, not of the earth."[27] He asks them to consider that life in sin is existence "under heavy storm clouds," and that the only light which sinners see is the "lightening flash" of God's anger. The gaining of faith is the kindly dawning of the morning sun which illuminates a new world. God is both an illuminating light who gives us a true vision of ourselves and our world, and a warming light who nourishes our growth into a redeemed life.[28] In a sermon that is a continuous metaphor of light, Bushnell traces the transitions from spiritual ignorance to the knowledge of faith to the world's becoming a vast symbol to the eyes of faith. In outline and development, the sermon is in substantial agreement with Edwards's "A Divine and Supernatural Light."[29] But the sermon possesses a distinctively Bushnellian tone. The imagery of light serves as a way of advising spiritual patience rather than urging repentance and conversion:

There is nothing in what has befallen, or befalls you, my friends, which justifies impatience or peevishness. God is inscrutable, but not wrong. Remember, if the cloud is over you, that there is a bright light always on the other side; also, that the time is coming, either in this world or the next, when that cloud will be swept away and the fullness of God's light and wisdom poured around you.[30]

Finally, however, it was not the imagery of light that Bushnell found most "morally useful" in gently conveying the consequences of sin, the nature of faith, or the divine act of redemption. More serviceable were organic symbols. Since Bushnell held that life in sin and life in redemption are organic, it is not surprising that the organic realm, the realm of growth, mutation, and interconnectedness, was the source of most of his natural symbolism. Organic existence also best expressed Bushnell's overall aim in preaching—patiently to nurture people into the struggling life of religious growth that is Christianity. Bushnell did occasionally warn his hearers of the limitations inherent in organic metaphors. Those metaphors do not adequately convey the fact of human freedom and can mislead one into thinking of human existence as a mere "vegetable process" unfolding toward fixed ends. Neither sin nor redemption is a fixed process of development. Borrowing images from the realm of things, even organic things, can, without sufficient qualification, obscure the powers of persons. "Things all serve their uses, and never break out of their place. They have no power to do it. Not so with us." Therefore, the growth and connectedness apparent in organic things at best hint at a vital power of soul that transcends their fixity. Yet of all the things of nature, those that are organic are most symbolic of human life. Organic things symbolize the dynamic, vital process of spiritual growth, make clearer than mechanical nature the fact that human existence is aimed at future ends, and signify man's rapid transit through the seasons of his existence.[31]

In a sermon apparently directed against the Unitarian notion of man's ability to unfold naturally his own innate perfections, Bushnell turns to an organic metaphor, convinced that a proper understanding of the organic kingdom uncovers an important truth: the key to all growth is nourishment, nourishment from outside the self. In a comparison of the growth of plants and animals with growth in the Christian life, Bushnell points to an organic principle which "gets us out of ourselves":

> I only mean to universalize the great truth that pertains to all vital creatures and organs; viz., that they differ from all dead substances, stones for example, in the fact that they subsist in a healthy state of vital energy and development, by receiving, appropriating, or feeding upon something out of themselves. . . . all these vital creatures, vegetable and animal, are only so many types of the soul, which is the highest, purest form of vital being we know; and that, as they all subsist by feeding on something not in themselves, and die for hunger without that food, just so the soul is a creature wanting food, and fevering itself in bitter hunger when that food is denied.[32]

Bushnell frequently appeals to the image of external nourishment in his portrayals of sin and redemption. Sin is a withering of the self, a thwarting of the vital principle, and it renders human life abortive because sustenance is not drawn from the source of all being. The possibility of sin resides in man's own transnatural power of freedom, but lower forms of life symbolize the fearful consequences of that freedom:

> God wanted possibly, in the creation of men, free beings like himself, and capable of common virtues with himself—not stones, or trees, or animals—and that, being free and therefore not to be controlled by force, they must of necessity be free to evil. . . . This being true, creatures may be made, that perish, or fall into lost conditions. Besides the world is full of analogies. The blossoms of the spring cover the trees and the fields, all alike beautiful and fragrant; but they shortly strew the ground as dead failures, even the greater part of them, having set no beginning of fruit. And then of the fruits that are set how many die as abortive growths, strewing the ground again. How many harvests also are blasted, yielding only straw. In the immense propagations of the sea, what myriads die in the first week of life. Thus we find nature everywhere struggling in abortive growths, fainting, as it were, in the perfecting of what her prolific intentions initiate. And all these abortions are so many tokens in the lower forms of life, of the possibility that there also may be blasted growths in the higher.[33]

Bushnell also invokes the analogy between sin and the overgrowth of parts to the detriment of the whole. Just as trees growing rapidly in a dense forest, unless thinned out, lose vital juices to their lower branches and become spindly of trunk, so persons who grow over-active in their inferior, unspiritual pursuits fail to draw sustenance from their religious source and lack breadth of spiritual being.[34]

Sin as a loss of vital soul force through inadequate nourishment intimates the natural metaphors which Bushnell employs in his preaching on redemption. When Christ is made the form of the soul, when the sinner is symboled by God's Spirit, a regenerative power is inserted into the life of the person. Now he so partakes of the divine life that God "is somehow able to come into the very germ principle of our life, and be a central, regulating, new-creating force in our disordered growth itself."[35] The ritual of the Lord's Supper is set within this organic interpretation of redemption. Bushnell tells his Hartford congregation that the Supper is a symbol through which the spiritual nourishment of redemption is made sensibly available. The supper is neither an evocation of thinking about a past event nor a mystical blending of our bodies with the body of Christ. Its meaning, rather, is its symboling palpably the insertion of a new principle of growth into human life. Christ's transforming power "comes into our deep sympathies back of all our mere thinking, to be assimilated in us secretly as food is assimilated in our bodies."[36] And the organic imagery of redemption is Bushnell's way of describing Christianity as a way of life. One is to "live to God in small things" and not expect Christianity to be one jolting conversion experience after another. God himself is observant of small, seemingly insignificant matters. "He descends to an infinite detail, and builds a little universe in the smallest things. He carries on a process of growth in every tree, and flower, and living thing."[37] By the same token, the life of redemption involves attention to small details, a growth within ordinary matters toward a great end of which an earthshaking conversion is merely proleptic:

> The importance of living to God, in ordinary and small things, is seen, in the fact that character, which is the end of religion, is in its very nature a growth. Conversion is a great change; old things are passed away, behold all things are become new. This however is the language of a hope or confidence, somehow prophetic, exulting, at the beginning, in the realization of future victory. The young disciple, certainly, is far enough from a consciousness of complete deliverance from sin. In that respect, his work is but just begun. He is now in the blade; we shall see him next in the ear; and after that, he will ripen to the full corn in the ear. His character, as a man and a Christian, is to accomplish its stature by growing. And all the offices of life, domestic, social, civil, useful, are contrived of God to be the soil, as Christ is the sun, of such a growth.[38]

Bushnell never tired of warning in his sermons that religious growth does not reach perfection in this life, that progress in character is no vegetable process, and that the power of spiritual growth comes from a source not our own. Still he maintained that the Christian life is organic, even as life itself is organic, and no revivalistic experience should obscure the truth that religion is patient maturation. That symbolic truth, quite as much as images of man in his ruin and God in his majesty, was a moral use of physical nature.

Horace Bushnell was preeminently a preacher. That fact has led even his friendly interpreters to complain about the style of much of his theology. A theology that serves the practical purposes of preaching produces strengths that are also weaknesses, so the criticism runs. Bushnell's theology possesses flashes of intuitive insight, quick discernment of fundamental issues, provocative figurative language, a personal tone, and hints of genuine originality. All of these qualities are appropriate and admirable in the preacher, but they lead to objectionable characteristics in the discursive theologian. Logical contradictions are ignored or dismissed; key words and ideas are not carefully defined; judgments are made before intensive investigation of a subject and before ideas are allowed to mature; and intellectual opponents are not engaged with sustained rational argument.[39]

The criticism accurately indicates both the flaws in Bushnell's theology and their likely source. Bushnell was guilty of all the charges, a consequence of his impatience with academic theology. Yet if made without reference to historical context, the criticism obscures significant achievements of Horace Bushnell, preacher *and* theologian. Bushnell had set about to do nothing less than restore to theology the imaginative wonder that has always characterized that humanistic enterprise at its best. In an age and in an environment when sterile propositions and revivalist rhetoric were offered as the essence of the theological task—and, as a consequence, men of poetic sensitivity revolted against the entire undertaking—Bushnell's symbolic theology, as vague as it often was, invited religious thinkers to return their language to the complex, tangible world that is the human spirit. If, in issuing the invitation, Bushnell himself was unable totally to throw off the influence of New England's theological moralism, he nonetheless went a considerable distance in making preaching and theology activities of the symbolic imagination. Furthermore, not since Jonathan Edwards had an American theologian so preoccupied himself with a theory of nature and nature's symbols. If Bushnell lacked the systematic mind of Edwards, he nevertheless probed as deeply as his forebear the grounds and issue of man's religious, symbolic response to the material world. Bushnell certainly shared with his teacher Nathaniel Taylor and with the didactic Enlightenment as a whole an aversion to speculative metaphysics, but he did engage in extensive reflection on the creation and its author in a manner which he deemed appropriate to the tangible realities of the imagination. Once again, in the theology and the preaching of Horace Bushnell, physical nature contained more than moral teachings; it housed religious symbols.

NOTES

1. *Life and Letters of Horace Bushnell*, ed. Mary Bushnell Cheney (New York: Harper & Brothers, 1880), p. 478.

2. Theodore Munger, *Horace Bushnell: Preacher and Theologian* (Boston & New York: Houghton, Mifflin & Co., 1899), pp. 278–79.

3. "Pulpit Talent," *Building Eras in Religion* (New York: Charles Scribner's Sons, 1881), pp. 186–90, 192, 196–97.

4. Bushnell as a representative of the new eloquent oratory is discussed by Barbara M. Cross, *Horace Bushnell: Minister to a Changing America* (Chicago: University of Chicago Press, 1958), pp. 75–85, and Donald A. Crosby, *Horace Bushnell's Theory of Language* (The Hague: Mouton, 1975), pp. 135–42.

5. "Pulpit Talent," *Building Eras*, p. 212.

6. Ibid.

7. Ibid., pp. 202–3; "Training for the Pulpit Manward," *Building Eras*, pp. 233–34, 242–45.

8. *The Vicarious Sacrifice* (New York: Charles Scribner & Co., 1866), p. 542.

9. *Life and Letters*, pp. 230–31.

10. Ibid., pp. 412, 458–59; Munger, *Horace Bushnell*, pp. 276–78, 288–92.

11. "The Gentleness of God," *Christ and His Salvation* (New York: Charles Scribner, 1864), p. 30.

12. *Life and Letters*, p. 465.

13. "The Dissolving of Doubts," *Sermons on Living Subjects* (New York: Scribner, Armstrong & Co., 1872), pp. 181–82.

14. David N. Beach cited in Munger, *Horace Bushnell*, p. 292.

15. *Moral Uses of Dark Things* (New York: Charles Scribner & Co., 1869), pp. 189, 192–99, 206, 212, 219–20, 224, 237–38.

16. Ibid., pp. 7–9, 222–23, 228–29, 295.

17. Ibid., p. 203.

18. Ibid., pp. 50–51.

19. Ibid., pp. 359–60.

20. Ibid., pp. 284, 291.

21. Ibid., pp. 320–22.

22. Ibid., p. 240.

23. "The Gentleness of God," *Christ and His Salvation*, pp. 41–42; "The Great Time-Keeper," *The Spirit in Man, Sermons and Selections* (New York: Charles Scribner's Sons, 1903), pp. 304–5; "The Capacity of Religion Extirpated by Disuse," *Sermons for the New Life* (New York: Scribner, Armstrong & Co., 1873), p. 174.

24. See, for example, "The Preparations of Eternity," *Spirit in Man*, pp. 334–35; "Our Advantage in Being Finite," *Sermons on Living Subjects*, p. 339; "The Lost Purity Restored," *Sermons for the New Life*, p. 264.

25. "Spiritual Things the Only Solid," *Spirit in Man*, p. 326.

26. "In and By Things Temporal Are Given Things Eternal," *Sermons on Living Subjects*, pp. 274–75.

27. "Feet and Wings," ibid., p. 71.

28. "Heaven Opened," *Christ and His Salvation*, p. 439; "Spirit in Man,"

Sermons for the New Life, pp. 44, 49; "Our Advantage in Being Finite," *Sermons on Living Subjects*, p. 338.

29. "Light on the Cloud," *Sermons for the New Life*, pp. 143–64.

30. Ibid., p. 162.

31. "Every Man's Life a Plan of God" and "The Power of an Endless Life," ibid., pp. 13–14, 306–7; "The Great Time-Keeper," *Spirit in Man*, p. 307.

32. "The Hunger of the Soul," *Sermons for the New Life*, pp. 73–74.

33. "Salvation for the Lost Condition," *Christ and His Salvation*, pp. 75–76.

34. "The Capacity of Religion Extirpated by Disuse," *Sermons for the New Life*, pp. 175–77.

35. "Salvation by Man," *Christ and His Salvation*, p. 272; "The Power of an Endless Life," *Sermons for the New Life*, p. 321.

36. "The Meaning of the Supper," *Spirit in Man*, p. 279.

37. "Living to God in Small Things," *Sermons for the New Life*, p. 286.

38. Ibid., pp. 292–93.

39. See Frank Hugh Foster, "Horace Bushnell as a Theologian," *Bibliotheca Sacra*, 59 (1902): 601–7; Munger, *Horace Bushnell*, pp. 275–76; Crosby, *Bushnell's Theory of Language*, pp. 142–43; Cross, *Horace Bushnell*, pp. 87, 157.

Epilogue

The American cultural heritage has been tied inextricably to the American physical environment. As fact and fiction, as matter and idea, as datum and symbol, nature has figured as a cardinal component in American styles of painting, literature, politics, science, and economics. It is as if the American wilderness and its resources destined us as a people to become, in Perry Miller's phrase, "nature's nation." Images both of what our nature *is* and of what it *should be* have inspired detailed reports from foreign observers and energetic activities from utopian settlers, hymns of praise from romantic poets and mandates to action from builders of cities and railroads, urgent pleas by environmentalists and exploitative acts by wielders of power. The endless processes of national self-recognition and self-realization have been bound up with the realities of our physical environment. "Nature," a key word for Western culture as a whole, became a crucial part of the axial language of Americans determined to arrive at some understanding of who they were and who they might become.

From the very beginning of the settlement of New England, religion shaped the imaginative reponse to nature. The land yielded the facts, but the Bible provided the ideas and images for the interpretation of the facts. Leaders of the Massachusetts Bay Colony construed the Puritan removal to the New World as an exile and an exodus, and their howling wilderness as both a place fraught with dangers and a sanctuary where "God's true ordinances" might be safely maintained.[1] Puritan poets, theologians, and preachers were fascinated by the specific events and appearances of their natural world, and they detected in those things "remarkable providences" that instructed them in their daily lives and in the ways of

231

God, as well as spiritual types that symbolized Christian truths. The origins of a tension between religious didacticism and religious symbolism appeared in seventeenth-century Puritan responses to the physical world. That tension was not lacking in the mind of America's most redoubtable Puritan theologian, Jonathan Edwards.

In comparison with most New England theologians who succeeded him, however, Edwards was decidedly symbolic in his approach to physical nature. He did meditate upon the moral lessons of his environment, he did preach didactic sermons, and he did portray God as a Moral Governor whose laws were embodied in nature. Yet, as he indicated in his notebook on nature, he believed that the best form of the natural type was one that represented spiritual truth through itself, rather than one that merely illustrated a religious meaning. His sensational revival sermons employed images that would lead his hearers to partake of the horrors of hell and the pleasures of heaven by participating in the pains and joys of their everyday experiences of nature. He insisted that firsthand knowledge of God was to be gained through the spiritual perception of faith which takes the things of this world as symbols of God's holy beauty; such perception, he felt, was far superior to an "imagination" which invents things absent in space and time. Perhaps Edwards's symbolic understanding of physical nature was nowhere more apparent than in his thoughts on the being and beauty of the cosmos. The world was to him an image of an image, a reflection of the intelligent creature's reflection of God's glory. And the harmony of the physical world was but an image of the beauty of essential man's "true virtue," which in turn symbolized the beauty of the Greatest and the Best of Beings.

The theology in New England which immediately followed Edwards was marked by the dominance of nature's didactic meaning. Nature consisted of a collection of signs which taught about religious truths. The religious awareness appropriate to nature's lessons was a legal consciousness.

Edwards's own followers did not totally abandon their master's scheme of thought, but they did shift the focus from nature's symbols to nature's precepts. While hailing God as the end of creation, true virtue as a beauty higher than natural harmony, and faith as a relishing of divine truth, Samuel Hopkins portrayed God as essentially a lawmaker and governor, God's creation as a system of laws, and faith as a matter of duty. As American theology increasingly came under the influence of the didactic Enlightenment, nature was valued even more for what it could teach about the laws and duties of religion. Butler, Paley, and the Scottish philosophers inspired theologians in New England to assume that the world of fact and the world of value are so intimately joined in God's creation that to know the "is" is to know the "ought," and to presuppose that the facts of nature testify to God's altogether beneficent provision for man's physical well-being. Enlightenment thought also encouraged American theologians to believe that the study of the "fixed and steady course of nature" could be the model for understanding the laws of the human psyche, the character of God, and the facts of religious duty. Both the rigorous moralism of the New Haven Theology and the gentle didacticism of Unitarianism were founded upon those Enlightenment convictions. Taking moral government as their major theological theme, Timothy Dwight, Nathaniel Taylor, and Lyman Beecher interpreted nature as a code of moral laws and moral facts binding on both God and man, and as a series of calls to the duties of religion. In order to replace the ontological and aesthetic speculations of Edwards with a study that sticks to empirical facts, they developed a psychology designed to unpack the fixed laws of the mind and to provide a "scientific" means of converting the individual and the nation. Exciting and urgent revivalist preachers, the New Haven men substantially altered Edwards's revivalist homiletics. The natural images of their sermons, like the facts of their moral universe, were teachings and warnings, not symbols. William Ellery Channing, though certainly no New Haven man, was equally concerned to explain nature as a code of moral laws and religious consciousness as an awareness of duty. In Channing the didactic moralism of New England reached its humanistic issue: nature expressed virtuous sentiments innate to the individual and gently called every man to the duty of attaining perfection through the cultivation of moral reason.

Horace Bushnell was convinced that Protestantism in New England had become excessively legalistic and anthropocentric in its views of nature, and unacceptably literalistic in its description of religious consciousness. He believed, as well, that the tangible world, the very stuff of theology and religion, had been obscured by grand "moral facts," which, for all of their literalness, were abstract and lifeless. Bushnell, therefore, set out to restore to theology and religion their poetic sensitivity to the physical world. He argued that the religious consciousness attains its heights in a symbolic awareness of formless religious truth within the outward forms of an image and that the task of the theologian is to promote the concrete metaphorical meanings in religious language. He held that nature, the realm of the law of cause and effect, is suffused with supernature or with the free principles of will and spirit. And he affirmed that the system of nature-supernature is rich with organic metaphors of the spiritual life and, because of its disharmonies, is most directly symbolic of human sin. In his preaching Bushnell preferred those natural images that reflect God's dynamic activity in his creation, the dignity of man in his ruin, and the life of the religious person in his growth. Thus Bushnell threw over much of the literalism, didacticism, and legalism of his background in order to bring into significant correlation natural symbols and religious imagination. But he was still a product of his background. In his subjection of God to the general moral principle of suffering love, in his interpretation of nature as a challenge to the human will, and in his placing of blacks and women within a rigidly mechanical set of natural laws, Bushnell revealed how dependent he was upon the categories of the didactic Enlightenment and New England moralism. If in Channing there culminated the perfectionist tendencies of New England moralism, in Bushnell the tension between natural moralism and natural symbolism reached its tautest strain.

In avoiding the conflict between moralism and symbolism, American Protestantism has most frequently moved to the extreme of moralism. As an ethic of absolutes, moralism proposes that all momentous human decisions are made between what is manifestly right and what is manifestly wrong. Religious moralism is a religion of absolutes, with religious law unambiguously indicating moral choices and religion consisting essentially in obedience to law. The twentieth-century ethicist Reinhold Niebuhr discerned how moralism has exerted a formative influence on American culture in general and American politics in particular. Much to the detriment of prudent wisdom, Americans have been prone to overlook the manner in which moral decisions inevitably must often move to the lesser of two evils and may at best approximate the highest good. The American penchant for moralism has led us to two extremes: sentimentality on the one hand, or the conviction that to know the good is to do it; and self-righteousness on the other, or the belief that to know and be on the side of the right is to sanctify all our actions.[2] The didactic legalism in American Protestantism contributed its share to the moralism which Niebuhr scored. That same Protestantism was also partly responsible for advancing the Enlightenment notion, so eagerly defended by many modern psychologists, that the fixed laws of physical nature are the model for the laws of the mind, and for the suspicion, so prevalent in our society, that all "metaphysical speculation" is worthless in comparison with the "clear facts of science." In late eighteenth- and early nineteenth-century American theology, didactic moralism had already been linked with a psychology insensitive to the mysterious freedom of the human self and to the ontological and symbolic import of nature's outward forms.

Quite apart from the larger cultural and intellectual consequences of New England moralism, it severely restricted religious thought and practice. Its preachers were content to discover in nature specific sanctions, moral lessons, and images of virtuous sentiment. In the process, they gave little or no attention to natural images of God's glory or to emblems of human evil—symbols which do not teach discrete moral truths but convey a religious meaning. In those preachers one may detect the origins of what so much American preaching would soon become—unimaginative exhortation, hollow moralizing, sentimental storytelling. And the New England theologians' adopting of Paley's universe represented a retreat from the hard realities of nature and the depths of human suffering. For, within that universe, God, despite his heavy legal demands, seldom showed an angry face, and he harmoniously arranged everything to promote human happiness. It would require little time and few theological adjustments for the God of Americans to become, in the words of Sidney Mead, "like Alice's Cheshire Cat, a disembodied and sentimental smile."[3]

New England moralism was also an inadvertent departure from the fundamental principles of its own Protestant Christian heritage. Historic Christianity announced that the law of love, revealed in Christ, is both the fulfillment of law and a norm which renders relative all other moral absolutes. Reformation Protestantism reaffirmed the Pauline understanding of the relation between love and lawful duty: by virtue of the disclosure of God's love, life under the law is not abrogated, but it is to be abandoned as the avenue to salvation. Faith, man's heartfelt trust in God's love (itself a gift of that love) is the only means of salvation. A moralism which makes faith a duty, and revelation a system of mandates, loses sight of the trans-moral and trans-legal dimension of Christianity which grants a person freedom. And a moralism which reduces religion to instructions in duty entails a rejection of Christianity's central symbol, the Incarnation. As Coleridge understood, the Incarnation illuminates the manner in which God reveals himself in metaphor. The metaphor of God assuming flesh does more than teach *about* a truth; God presents himself in his wholeness through the transparency of the metaphor. The Incarnation is thus a paradigm for understanding how our finite world opens on the infinite in such a way that its beholder may transcend attention to discrete moral truths and discern the presence and power of the divine life. The degree to which American religious thinkers like Edwards and Bushnell were able to find in nature "images or shadows of divine things" is a measure of their preservation of a religious heritage against the onslaughts of moralism.

To admit the deleterious consequences of a moralism that has pervaded American culture and religion, however, is not to deny a danger inherent in a Christianity which makes symbolism its hallmark. A preoccupation with nature's symbols easily becomes an ignorance of society's most pressing problems, attention to the trans-moral meaning of religion a loss of precise ethical purpose. For all of the acuity of Edwards's metaphysic of symbol, the beauty of his ethic, and the artistry of his preaching, his conscience was not nearly as afflicted by specific social injustices as was that of his moralistic disciple Samuel Hopkins. And Channing's sense of duty eventually led him to a more perceptive and courageous position on the plight of the black man than Bushnell's less didactic reading of nature's laws and symbols. Neither Edwards nor Bushnell can be accused of producing a religious perspective devoid of ethical implications for given social problems. But within their own theologies there is missing a passion for justice directed toward specific social evils—something that is not lacking in the outlook of their more moralistic counterparts. If the risk inherent in religious moralism is a rigid legalism that breeds self-righteousness and thwarts the imagination, the risk implicit in religious symbolism is an aestheticism that produces an otherworldy fideism and weakens the social conscience. Something of the latter is discernible in the desperate counsel, often heard today, that "religion should stick to its business and not meddle in politics or social problems." At best, that is advice that religion should withdraw from the realities of its setting; at worst, it is a thinly disguised endorsement of the status quo.

If a Christianity centered on symbols is, in its trans-legal freedom, to avoid a religious consciousness emptied of social content, it must connect a transcendent symbolic awareness with moral resolve. It was that connection which Martin Luther had in mind when he wrote that the Christian person freed by faith from salvation through the law gives the freest charitable service to his neighbor.[4] And it was that type of linkage that Reinhold Niebuhr found in the faith of Abraham Lincoln and believed was so applicable to the twentieth-century situation:

> This combination of moral resoluteness about the immediate issues with a religious awareness of another dimension of meaning and judgment must be regarded as almost a perfect model of the difficult but not impossible task of remaining loyal and responsible toward the moral treasures of a free civilization on the one hand while yet having some religious vantage point over the struggle. Surely it was this double attitude which made the spirit of Lincoln's "with malice toward none; with charity for all" possible. There can be no other basis for true charity; for charity cannot be induced by lessons from copybook texts. It can proceed only from a "broken spirit and a contrite heart."[5]

In the terms of this book, the religious person who has had his awareness awakened by nature's symbols to a divine truth transcendent of law is obligated to bring that awareness to bear responsibly on his social world. That has never been an easy task for Americans caught in the conflict between symbolism and moralism. But, as Niebuhr insisted, it is not an impossible task.

Much has occurred to change our thinking about nature and religious imagination since the passing of the New England Theology. Contemporary science and technology have radically altered our views of—indeed, the very shape of—nature and cosmos. Modern theories of language and symbol have expanded and refined our comprehension of the acts of the imagination. Yet, the thoughts and words of theologians from Edwards to Bushnell have contributed to our living heritage. And in their struggle to decide the relation between nature and imagination, those theologians raised issues which continue to clamor for our attention.

NOTES

1. See George H. Williams, *Wilderness and Paradise in Christian Thought* (New York: Harper & Row, 1962), pp. 99, 107–8.

2. Reinhold Niebuhr, *The Irony of American History* (New York: Charles Scribner's Sons, 1952), p. 40; *Love and Justice* (Philadelphia: Westminster Press, 1957), p. 294.

3. Sidney E. Mead, *The Lively Experiment: The Shaping of Christianity in America* (New York: Harper & Row, 1963), p. 152.

4. Martin Luther, "Treatise on Christian Liberty," *Martin Luther, Selections from His Writings*, ed. J. Dillenberger (Garden City, N.Y.: Doubleday Anchor, 1961), p. 74.

5. Niebuhr, *Irony of American History*, p. 172.

Index